Commodity Prices
and the New Inflation

Commodity Prices and the New Inflation

BARRY P. BOSWORTH
ROBERT Z. LAWRENCE

THE BROOKINGS INSTITUTION
Washington, D.C.

Soc
HB
221
B593

Robert Manning Strozier Library

OCT 6 1982

Tallahassee, Florida

Copyright © 1982 by
THE BROOKINGS INSTITUTION
1775 Massachusetts Avenue, N.W., Washington, D.C. 20036

Library of Congress Cataloging in Publication data:
Bosworth, Barry, 1942–
  Commodity prices and the new inflation.
  Includes bibliographical references and index.
  1. Prices. 2. Raw materials—Prices. 3. Commodity control. 4. Inflation (Finance) I. Lawrence, Robert Z., 1949– . II. Title.
HB221.B593   338.5'2   81-70467
ISBN 0-8157-1034-8   AACR2
ISBN 0-8157-1033-X (pbk.)

9 8 7 6 5 4 3 2 1

Board of Trustees
Robert V. Roosa
Chairman
Andrew Heiskell
Vice Chairman;
Chairman, Executive Committee
Louis W. Cabot
Vice Chairman
Vincent M. Barnett, Jr.
Barton M. Biggs
Frank T. Cary
A. W. Clausen
William T. Coleman, Jr.
Lloyd N. Cutler
Bruce B. Dayton
George M. Elsey
Hanna H. Gray
Huntington Harris
Roger W. Heyns
Bruce K. MacLaury
Robert S. McNamara
Arjay Miller
Herbert P. Patterson
Donald S. Perkins
J. Woodward Redmond
Charles W. Robinson
James D. Robinson III
Henry B. Schacht
Roger D. Semerad
Gerard C. Smith
Phyllis A. Wallace

Honorary Trustees
Eugene R. Black
Robert D. Calkins
Edward W. Carter
Douglas Dillon
John E. Lockwood
William McC. Martin, Jr.
H. Chapman Rose
Robert Brookings Smith
Sydney Stein, Jr.

THE BROOKINGS INSTITUTION is an independent organization devoted to nonpartisan research, education, and publication in economics, government, foreign policy, and the social sciences generally. Its principal purposes are to aid in the development of sound public policies and to promote public understanding of issues of national importance.

The Institution was founded on December 8, 1927, to merge the activities of the Institute for Government Research, founded in 1916, the Institute of Economics, founded in 1922, and the Robert Brookings Graduate School of Economics and Government, founded in 1924.

The Board of Trustees is responsible for the general administration of the Institution, while the immediate direction of the policies, program, and staff is vested in the President, assisted by an advisory committee of the officers and staff. The by-laws of the Institution state: "It is the function of the Trustees to make possible the conduct of scientific research, and publication, under the most favorable conditions, and to safeguard the independence of the research staff in the pursuit of their studies and in the publication of the results of such studies. It is not a part of their function to determine, control, or influence the conduct of particular investigations or the conclusions reached."

The President bears final responsibility for the decision to publish a manuscript as a Brookings book. In reaching his judgment on the competence, accuracy, and objectivity of each study, the President is advised by the director of the appropriate research program and weighs the views of a panel of expert outside readers who report to him in confidence on the quality of the work. Publication of a work signifies that it is deemed a competent treatment worthy of public consideration but does not imply endorsement of conclusions or recommendations.

The Institution maintains its position of neutrality on issues of public policy in order to safeguard the intellectual freedom of the staff. Hence interpretations or conclusions in Brookings publications should be understood to be solely those of the authors and should not be attributed to the Institution, to its trustees, officers, or other staff members, or to the organizations that support its research.

For our parents

Foreword

EXTRAORDINARY changes in world supplies and prices of primary commodities dominated economic events in the 1970s. Greatly increased prices for petroleum and food products disrupted the world economy and confronted policymakers with problems for which they were unprepared. Higher prices for these commodities contributed to the surge of worldwide inflation in 1973–74 and a widespread contraction of economic activity in 1975. Again in 1979, a doubling of petroleum prices in world markets strained the international economic system and interrupted economic growth.

Both the causes and consequences of rapid changes in commodity prices continue to be sharply debated by economists and economic policymakers. In this study, Barry P. Bosworth and Robert Z. Lawrence identify and quantify a variety of factors they believe to be responsible. These include a business cycle that was synchronized worldwide, disruptions of supply in individual markets resulting from climatic and political events, capacity constraints, exchange-rate changes, and increased speculative activity. In many situations, the evidence is strong that government action made the problems worse.

The authors focus on inflation and macroeconomic policy in three major industrial countries: the United States, Japan, and Germany. They conclude that domestic inflation was considerably accelerated by increases in basic commodity prices—primarily those of grain and petroleum—though differences in economic structure and policy led to varying results in the three countries.

Bosworth and Lawrence also find that macroeconomic policy alone cannot resolve the conflict between inflation and unemployment. Hence they advocate government policies aimed at specific markets. Public intervention to stabilize prices in individual markets can be justified, they argue, by the potential that market disruptions pose for generating inflation and by the inadequacy of nongovernmental stabilization efforts.

They develop specific proposals to stabilize prices in the grain and petroleum markets.

The research on which this book is based was financed by a grant from the Sloan Foundation. For helpful comments and suggestions, the authors are grateful to Henry J. Aaron, Alan S. Blinder, Hendrik S. Houthakker, Milton Russell, Walter S. Salant, Charles L. Schultze, and Douglas M. Woodham. They are also grateful to Jeffrey A. Goldstein, Lesley R. Kalmin, Michael K. Kuehlwein, Arthur C. Kupferman, Lorin D. Kusmin, and Andrea V. Mills for research assistance, and to Kathleen Elliott-Yinug, Lisa F. Saunders, and Evelyn M. E. Taylor for secretarial assistance. Caroline Lalire edited the manuscript, Ellen Smith assisted in checking it for accuracy, and Florence Robinson prepared the index.

The views expressed here are those of the authors and should not be ascribed to the Sloan Foundation or to the trustees, officers, or other staff members of the Brookings Institution.

BRUCE K. MACLAURY
President

January 1982
Washington, D.C.

Contents

1. Introduction   1
   Modeling Inflation *4*
   Summary of the Book *17*

2. The Role of Primary Commodities in Industrial Economies   24
   Definition and Categories of Primary Commodities *24*
   Commodity Prices *27*

3. The Contribution of Primary Commodity Price Increases to Inflation   38
   An Aggregate Analysis *42*
   A Disaggregated View *48*
   Conclusions *60*

4. Sources of Commodity Price Fluctuations   62
   Demand *63*
   Supply *70*
   Quantitative Evaluation *73*
   Monetary Factors and the Demand for Commodities as Assets *77*

5. Grains and Petroleum: The Role of Institutional Changes   88
   Grains *88*
   Petroleum Prices in the 1970s *107*
   How Are Petroleum Prices Set? *121*

6. The Policy Choices: Some General Considerations   132
   Demand-Management Policy and Inflation Shocks *134*
   Rationale for Government Intervention *141*
   Alternative Means of Intervention *150*

7. Commodity Stabilization Policies: Some Specific Proposals   160
   Grain Price Stabilization *161*
   Energy Policy *169*
   Other Commodities *186*
   Concluding Remarks *192*

Appendixes

A. Calculation of the Impact of Raw Material Price Increases on Inflation *194*
B. Sources of the Data Used in the Statistical Analysis of Chapter 4 *197*
C. Statistical Tables for Chapter 5 *199*
D. The Incidence of a Sales Tax on a Depletable Natural Resource *201*

Index 211

Text Tables

2-1. Major Basic Commodities Traded Internationally	26
3-1. Average Annual Percentage Change in Prices for the Ten Most Important OECD Countries, 1960–79	39
3-2. Reduced-Form Price Equations for the Ten Most Important OECD Countries, 1961–79	46
3-3. Percentage Share of Raw Materials in Final Demand, United States, Japan, and West Germany, 1970	49
3-4. Contribution of Primary Commodity Prices to Inflation, by Major Component, United States, 1971–79	51
3-5. Contribution of Primary Commodity Prices to Inflation, by Major Component, Japan, 1971–79	53
3-6. Contribution of Primary Commodity Prices to Inflation, by Major Component, West Germany, 1971–79	55
4-1. Change in Capacity for Processing Nonferrous Metals within Western Economies, Selected Periods, 1955–79	72
4-2. Results of Equations for the Relative Price of Agricultural Commodities	74
4-3. Results of Equations for the Relative Price of Nonferrous Metals	76
4-4. Turnover of Futures Contracts in Selected Commodities, U.S. and U.K. Markets, as Percent of World Consumption, 1972–80	84
4-5. Correlation Coefficients for Commodity Prices, Equities, and Inflation, 1952–79	85
4-6. Variance and Covariance in Real Returns for Alternative Assets, 1960–79	87
5-1. World Cereal Production, Reserves, and Prices: Deviations from Trend, 1960–61 through 1979–80	90
5-2. USSR Grain Balance: Deviations from Trend, 1961–62 through 1979–80	96
5-3. World Grain Consumption, by Selected Countries and Regions, 1970–71 through 1979–80	101
5-4. Main Factors in U.S. Corn Price Increases, 1972–73 Marketing Year	105
5-5. World Growth of Supply, Demand, and Reserves of Crude Oil, Selected Periods, 1955–79	116
5-6. Contract and Spot Market Prices for Crude Oil, 1977–80	119
5-7. OPEC Crude Oil Production and Supply Coordination: Deviations from Trend, 1974–78 and 1974–79	127

CONTENTS xiii

7-1. Macroeconomic Indicators during a Full Year of Oil Supply Interruption in the United States, 1984   180

Appendix Tables

C-1. U.S. Supply and Demand Balance for Grains: Deviations from Trend, 1961–62 through 1979–80   199
C-2. Rest-of-World Supply and Demand Balance for Grains: Deviations from Trend, 1961–62 through 1979–80   200

Text Figures

1-1. The Unemployment Response to Inflation Shocks   16
2-1. Long-Run Relative Price Trends for Primary Commodities   30
2-2. Relative Price of Primary Commodities, by Major Component, 1954–80   32
2-3. Nominal and Relative Prices of Primary Commodities, 1950–79   36
4-1. Indexes of Industrial Production in the Market Economies, 1953–79   66
5-1. Price Trends under the International Wheat Agreement, 1950–79   94
5-2. Rest-of-World Supply and Demand Balance for Grains: Deviations from Trend, 1961–62 through 1979–80   98
5-3. U.S. Supply and Demand Balance for Grains: Deviations from Trend, 1961–62 through 1979–80   100
5-4. Indexes of Feed Concentrate Consumption and Consuming Animal Units in the United States, 1955–79   103
5-5. Petroleum Prices, 1950–79   109
5-6. U.S. Consumption, Imports, and Domestic Supply of Petroleum, 1950–77   111
5-7. World Crude Oil Production, 1973–79   120
5-8. Price Paths in a Market for a Depletable Natural Resource   122
5-9. Growth in Free-World Production and Price of Crude Oil, 1970–79   126
6-1. The Impact of Price Shocks on the Inflation Rate and Price Level   136

Appendix Figures

D-1. Demand Curve: The Special Case   204
D-2. Price Paths: The Special Case   204
D-3. Price Paths: The Competitive Case   204
D-4. Demand Curve: The Monopolist   206
D-5. Price Paths: The Monopolist   206
D-6. Price Paths: The Monopolist with a Competitive Fringe   206

CHAPTER ONE

Introduction

IN THE YEARS 1972–74 the world economy experienced an unprecedented increase in primary commodity prices.[1] The period began with a disruption of the world grain market in 1972 and culminated in a fourfold increase in petroleum prices in late 1973 and early 1974. Within this three-year period the prices of raw materials rose by 150 percent in world markets and touched off the worst inflation of the postwar period in the industrial nations. These events had far-reaching ramifications as domestic policy efforts to curtail the inflationary repercussions led to severe economic recession and sharply higher unemployment in nearly all the developed economies. Within the member nations of the Organization for Economic Cooperation and Development (OECD) the average inflation rate soared from 5 percent in 1972 to 12 percent in 1974. In 1975 alone the decline of production from the 1960–74 growth trend was 8 percent of total output,[2] and the number of people unemployed rose approximately 6 million above the 1973 figure.

After 1974 many primary commodity prices fell as dramatically as they had previously risen, but again in 1979 world oil prices doubled and prices of other basic commodities rose rapidly. These events continue to exert a strong influence on the world economy. Significant and lasting changes have occurred in the marketing structure of some basic commodities like petroleum and bauxite, and the efforts of producers of other primary commodities to achieve greater control over their prices have been stimulated. Since the production of raw materials is relatively more important to the less-developed countries than to the industrial ones, the former have made these commodities the focal point for discussions about changes in the international economic order. The sharp rise of primary commodity prices has also been interpreted by some observers

---

1. The term *primary commodities* refers herein to products grown on or extracted from the land that have been subject only to the first stage of processing.
2. The growth trend from 1960 through 1974 was 4.8 percent annually.

as evidence of increasing strain on the world's reserve of nonreproducible resources, and thus indicative of the need to redirect or slow the pace of overall economic growth.

In addition, the size of the primary commodity price fluctuations has profoundly affected the usual interpretation of the causes of and cures for inflation in modern industrial economies. For a few economists, a rise in primary commodity prices merely represents a shift in relative prices—a shift that can be accommodated without general inflation by a decline of prices in other markets. The rise in prices increases the proportion of income spent on primary commodities and thus reduces demand for others. It follows that, in a competitive economy where prices are determined by supply and demand, other prices would decline if the monetary authorities prevented an overall rise in the money supply. Other economists view a rise in primary commodity prices as a cyclical indicator of excess aggregate demand, and therefore indicative of the need for restrictive policies to slow the expansion of demand within the world economy as a whole. From both perspectives, the general prescription for policy is the same: the monetary authorities of individual countries should refrain from validating the inflation through accommodating the increased demand for money balances.

Still a third group of economists have argued for a different interpretation of the inflation implications of such abrupt prices changes within a relatively narrow category of commodities, and thus implicitly for an accommodative monetary policy that accepts some general inflation as a necessary consequence of the surge in the prices of raw materials. They believe that because of the inflexibility of prices and wages within the industrial sector, substantial slack and unemployment would have to occur before those prices would decline enough to offset the rise of primary commodity prices.

As the macroeconomists debated the consequences of the commodity market disruptions and the appropriate policy responses to them, microeconomists were similarly divided over their causes. One school, pointing to the pervasiveness of price increases across a wide range of commodity markets, emphasized general factors, such as a synchronized international business cycle during the first half of the 1970s. Another school emphasized the unusual number of special events that occurred in the 1972–74 period: natural disasters, the end of an extended era of excess capacity and depressed prices, and a series of government actions to reduce production and reserves. A somewhat more aggregative

INTRODUCTION 3

supply-side interpretation was put forward by those who saw the rise in relative prices as evidence of a long-term trend toward exhaustion of natural resources.

But few of the serious microeconomic studies have been able to explain fully the behavior of primary commodity prices during this period. Although part of the explanation of individual commodity prices is found within the conventional determinants of price, such as the level of demand, inventories, production, and capacity utilization, much remains unexplained by these factors. Moreover, there seems to be a strong positive correlation among the prediction errors from individual commodity market models. The models tend to underpredict the increase of prices in 1973 and 1974 and to miss the extent of the price decline in 1975. This strongly suggests that a common variable has been omitted. Although these residuals can be ascribed to a surge of speculative fever, the precise nature of the speculative process has not been adequately modeled.

Some economists have attributed the prediction errors to the effects of the dramatic explosion in international liquidity that occurred in the early 1970s. But this explanation has been received with skepticism by proponents of traditional theory, who place little emphasis on the role of commodities as investment assets. Keynesian macroeconomists believe that monetary disturbances can affect commodity markets only indirectly, through the influence of interest rates on the level of aggregate demand. Likewise, conventional microeconomists, entrenched in the classical dichotomy between monetary and price theory, ignore the changes in output and relative prices that a monetary disturbance might bring about.

This study addresses both the consequences and the causes of commodity market disturbances. Throughout it recognizes that modern industrial economies have a wide range of market structures. Some markets closely approximate the traditional Walrasian behavior, in which flexible prices speedily bring supply and demand into balance—Arthur Okun has called these auction markets. Other markets, however, have more sluggish price responses, and temporary imbalances between supply and demand are met by variations in production, inventory levels, and backlogs of orders—Okun refers to these as customer markets.[3] Our

---

3. Arthur M. Okun, "Upward Mobility in a High-pressure Economy," *Brookings Papers on Economic Activity*, 1:1973, pp. 207–52 (hereafter *BPEA*).

central thesis is that the causes and consequences of commodity market behavior can be fully appreciated only within the context of a general equilibrium model of an economy that has both auction and customer markets.

Both auction and customer market prices will behave differently when these markets coexist. If all prices are either flexible or rigid, nominal disturbances may have no effect on relative prices; but when markets differ in the rate at which prices adjust, nominal disturbances will affect total output and relative prices, and real disturbances, such as crop failures, will affect the overall price level. Similarly, the appropriate policies in such an economy may be very different from those that are optimal when only auction or only customer markets exist. When all prices are flexible, aggregate demand policies will be sufficient; when all prices are resistant to changes in demand or supply, incomes policies might be called for. But in the mixed economy the solutions are less obvious: aggregate demand policies may be confounded by the inertia in the wage-price process, while incomes policies are vulnerable to the autonomous disturbances that affect auction markets.

In the next section we examine the current status of some issues in inflation theory that are critical in assessing the role of primary commodity price fluctuations. And we end the chapter with a brief summary of the study's conclusions.

Modeling Inflation

Inflation was the dominant economic issue of the 1970s. It occupied the attention of policymakers, who sought to control it, and economists, who sought to explain it. The emergence of "stagflation," or the simultaneous existence of high levels of unemployment and continuing inflation, conflicted with the traditional explanation of inflation as simply the product of excessive aggregate demand. In addition, the obvious inflationary consequences of disruptions in world commodity markets forced analysts to consider a wider range of possible causes.

The traditional view of inflation, and thus of the appropriate remedies, interprets the economy as an aggregation of competitive flexible-price markets, in which prices reflect the interaction of demand and supply. Shifts in resource use are readily achieved through price increases in those markets where more resources are required and price declines in

INTRODUCTION

markets with reduced demand. In such an economy inflation can be constrained by aggregate demand policy alone. The adjustment of relative prices can occur within a constant overall price level so long as the growth of money balances (adjusted for secular trends in velocity) does not exceed the growth in real output. In fact, inflation can be viewed as strictly a monetary phenomenon. Any tendency of the average price level to rise can be offset by a refusal of the monetary authorities to accommodate the resulting increase of demand for money balances. This brings about a reduction in total demand, decreased utilization of capital and labor, and downward pressure on prices and wages. Most important, it is assumed that a significant reduction in inflation can be achieved at the cost of a relatively small increase in unemployment. According to this flexible-price view, the observed momentum or stickiness in wages and prices is not fundamental but results from a long history of monetary accommodation to inflationary pressures. And such actions were based on the mistaken belief that the costs of nonaccommodation would be high.

We believe that this interpretation of inflation as reflecting excess demand alone, reinforced by expectations of accommodation policy, does not fit well with the complexities of modern economic systems. The adjustment of prices is far more sluggish than that theory would suggest. This sluggishness reflects fundamental market characteristics as well as expectations. To a large extent declines in nominal demand are absorbed by reducing output and employment rather than prices and wages. While, theoretically, nonaccommodation will eventually lower inflation, the costs will be high. Hence inflation has resulted from a series of initiating shocks and an understandable failure to hold to purely nonaccommodation policies.

Recent explanations of inflation have focused not on the role of excess aggregate demand but on the process of adjustment to change in individual markets and the ways in which these markets interact. Within modern economies there are wide differences in market structures. Some resemble the flexible-price model described above: homogeneous products are sold in a close approximation to an auction-type market and prices are affected quickly by alterations of demand or supply. Such markets dominate in the sale of agricultural commodities and financial assets. Most labor markets and markets for industrial products and services, however, display more fixed-price characteristics—that is, much of the adjustment to changing demand is reflected in quantity rather than price. Many of the issues of controversy are fundamental to assessing the role of primary commodity price fluctuations.

This study incorporates an interpretation of the inflation process that in a simplified form can be characterized as (1) an underlying momentum of inflation that builds up through repetitive cycles of wage and price increases in the industrial sector of the economy and (2) a set of initiating forces or shocks, superimposed on the momentum process, that shifts the inflation rate from one level to another.

The momentum arises from the tendency of wage and price increases within the industrial sector to feed on one another and persist during sustained periods of economic slack. Wage increases are fueled by a desire to match past price increases and the wages of others and by expectations that the process will continue. Similarly, on the price side, business firms see their own actions as reflecting a pass-through of past cost increases. This continual cycle of wage and price increases is only loosely related to overall demand; it is largely the result of a long history of past inflation and of expectations that it will continue. It also reflects an underlying market structure quite different from the competitive, flexible-price model that dominates textbook discussions.

The shocks or disturbances that exacerbate the inflation momentum come from a variety of sources. Certainly, excess aggregate demand continues to be an important potential initiating force for inflation. It was the dominant factor throughout the last half of the 1960s in the United States, and in 1972–73 a worldwide economic expansion created strong demand pressures in many markets. But in the last decade inflation has also been severely aggravated by sharp price changes in a few major commodity markets like food and energy. Finally, government has become much more involved in individual markets, and its actions sometimes initiate upward pressure on prices or wages. These disruptions in large individual markets can have a dramatic direct effect on the average inflation rate. But they also have a secondary and longer lasting effect, since the surge of inflation that originates with sharp price increases in a few markets rapidly spreads throughout the economy as other participants accelerate their own wage and price increases in an effort to catch up. The result is an upward ratchetting of the underlying inflation rate in the industrial sector and a carry-over of inflation into future periods.

This brief outline skips several basic questions. First, why does the inflation of prices and wage rates within industrial markets persist so

INTRODUCTION

long after a reversal of the initiating forces and in the face of substantial unemployment? It is this inertia that is responsible for the high unemployment costs implicit in a monetary policy of nonaccommodation.

Second, what is the role of prices in the determination of wages? If wage-rate changes respond directly to prices—that is, when the focus is on real wages—price shocks have both a direct and secondary effect on inflation, because workers in the industrial and service sectors will try to recover any real income loss. Alternatively, if the focus in wage decisions is on relative wage rates (a wage-wage linkage), the inflation effect of commodity price changes will be limited to their direct effect on the price level, because there is no mechanism by which they affect money wage rates. Thus the role of prices in wage determination is critical in judging whether fluctuations in primary commodity prices are a major cause of sustained inflation.

Third, does inflation respond asymmetrically to primary commodity price changes? Even though these price fluctuations may in part explain variations in the inflation rate, it is uncertain whether they affect the apparent secular rise in inflation within the industrial economies. An upward ratchetting of inflation would seem to require a continual rise in the relative price of primary commodities—increasing scarcity—or a differential response of the rest of the economy to increases and decreases in primary commodity prices.

Finally, are primary commodity prices an independent source of inflation or do they simply reflect the general pressure of excess demand? Many commodity markets exhibit flexible-price behavior, with great sensitivity to variations in supply and demand. In addition, their demand can be expected to be closely related to overall levels of income and production. Thus a surge of price increases in these markets may be a simple counterpart of the backlogging of orders in the industrial sector and rising levels of job vacancies in labor markets that occur during peaks of economic activity. This is largely an empirical issue that will be examined in later chapters.

Sources of Inertia

The concept of rigid nominal wages or prices has long been recognized as a critical element of Keynesian economics, as the way to explain a sustained period of underemployment equilibrium. But the explanation of why some wages and prices fail to decline in the face of insufficient demand has been a problem for economists who expect economic phenomena to reflect rational decisionmaking in efficient markets. Too often the argument was reduced to the intellectually unsatisfying assertion that the participants suffered from money illusion—a persistent desire for a specific money wage despite wide variations in the price of goods they could buy.

In the last decade considerable progress has been made in clarifying the alternative concept of fixed-price markets. The term *fixed price* means a price that fails to adjust quickly to demand and supply when one of them changes, not a rigid or unchanging price.[4] The essential characteristics of these markets, in contrast to the competitive norm, are the lack of an auctioneer, the fact that the quality of the product is often highly variable and difficult to evaluate before purchase, and the fact that the parties must act on limited and frequently erroneous information. These factors introduce an element of bilateral monopoly into markets: the buyer and the seller attempt to form an ongoing relationship, so that concern for the current period's balance of supply and demand is only one element in the determination of prices and wage rates.

WAGE RATES. The role of structural factors in limiting the response of wage rates to variations in unemployment is most evident in collective bargaining. Whereas the individual in an idealized competitive economy is pictured as choosing between the offered wage and other available alternatives, collective bargaining is similar to the dealings of a bilateral monopoly, since it is a group decision and the decision to reject the wage offer can also include the denial of the job to others. These tendencies are reinforced by the practice of multi-year bargaining by which the current year's wage increase may reflect economic conditions of previous years or is indexed to current rates of price inflation. In a typical year fewer than half of union pay increases are the result of contracts negotiated during that year. At the empirical level wage agreements in the large union establishments show little or no sensitivity to cyclical changes in labor market conditions.[5]

Even in the absence of collective bargaining wage rates cannot be

4. A market-clearing price implies that the producer would not supply an additional unit without a rise in price. Yet clearly many producers would be all too willing to sell more units at the going price.

5. See, for example, Daniel J. B. Mitchell, "Union Wage Determination," *BPEA*, 3:1978, pp. 537–82, and the earlier studies cited there. Collective bargaining agreements cover about 35 percent of the private nonfarm wage bill (p. 540). In addition, pay practices in nonunion establishments are affected by the union agreements.

INTRODUCTION   9

expected to adjust quickly to cyclical fluctuations. The heterogeneity of the work force, when combined with costly and imperfect means of evaluating workers before employment, leads firms that are concerned about labor quality to adopt practices that minimize long-run employment costs rather than to adjust wage rates fully to cyclical changes in the labor market. Employment practices in such situations are like an implicit contract between the employer and the employees as the employer seeks to adopt policies that achieve long attachments and low quit rates. During periods of temporary or cyclical declines in demand, these firms will maintain some on-the-job underemployment and temporarily lay off workers rather than reduce wage rates. Such policies substitute for additional new-hire costs in the future expansion.[6]

In reality labor markets vary enormously, ranging from close approximations to an auction market to tenured-type arrangements. Arthur Okun has labeled the two extremes "casual" and "career" jobs. In casual job markets employees can be used as though they were homogeneous, and the job requirements can be tailored to the lowest common denominator. Wage-rate changes will then be an active part of the adjustment of short-run supply and demand, since the employer does not value experience and expects considerable job turnover; he has few alternatives to wage-rate increases in strong markets and few inhibitions to cutting wage rates in slack markets. In career job markets, however, the focus of employment practices will shift from maximization of short-run advantage to a concern for longer-term stability of the employer-employee relationship (which may be thought of as maximizing long-run advantages).

PRICES. A limited response to cyclical variations in demand is also evident in the behavior of industrial prices. Many empirical studies find little cyclical sensitivity in the average level of industrial prices beyond the pass-through of changes in input costs. Again this stability is in many respects the logical result of important institutional distinctions between

6. There is extensive discussion of the rigidity of pay practices in Arthur M. Okun, *Prices and Quantities: A Macroeconomic Analysis* (Brookings Institution, 1981). That book also includes an annotated bibliography of research on search theory, implicit contracting, and other characteristics of fixed-price markets. A summary of recent research work can be found in Robert J. Gordon, "Recent Developments in the Theory of Inflation and Unemployment," *Journal of Monetary Economics*, vol. 2 (April 1976), pp. 285–319. And an interpretation of some of these practices as reflecting rational behavior is provided by Robert E. Hall, "Employment Fluctuations and Wage Rigidity," *BPEA, 1:1980*, pp. 91–123.

industrial markets and the auction-type market of the competitive model.[7] In auction markets the individual firm cannot influence the price and concentrates on the quantity to offer for sale.

In most markets, however, the firm sells a differentiated product for which it sets a price and stands ready to supply the quantity demanded by the market. The firm establishes a price as a markup over "standard unit costs." In many industrial processes standard unit costs—which play the same role as the marginal cost concept of economists—are relatively constant over wide variations in capacity utilization and are therefore not significantly altered by small variations in demand. Similarly, competitive conditions (as measured by the price elasticity of demand for the firm's products), which determine the size of the optimal markup, are not necessarily changed by cyclical shifts in the level of demand. The entry or exit of firms into or from the market does represent a change in competitive conditions, but because of large fixed costs these are long-term decisions that are not drastically altered by cyclical factors.

In addition, as with labor markets, the search costs associated with gathering information on prices make it advantageous to both the buyer and the seller to establish a continuing relationship. The buyer economizes on the cost of search, and the seller gains a higher level of sales through repeat business if he can discourage his customers from shopping elsewhere. In effect, the costs of shopping introduce a bilateral monopoly surplus that can be shared between the buyer and the seller. The concern with maintaining a continuing relationship introduces an intertemporal connection between today's prices and tomorrow's sales. Today's customer has a value beyond his current purchases because of the potential for repeat business. In effect, the customer is as much an asset of the firm as its plant and equipment, and similarly needs to be conserved. Therefore, a firm will not fully adjust prices to transitory changes in today's market conditions as it looks forward to the impact on future sales. The result will be a dampening of variations in pricing markups over the business cycle.

In addition to the institutional factors, the sensitivity of inflation to demand fluctuations is reinforced by expectations about government stabilization policies. Firms and workers fail to respond to slack market

---

7. An alternative dichotomy of markets can be made between those where the producer focuses on the quantity to sell and the market determines the price (price-taker, quantity-setter) and those where the producer establishes a price and the market determines the quantity sold (price-setter, quantity-taker).

conditions and unemployment because they expect the government to move rapidly to reflate the economy. They also expect monetary policy to accommodate continuing inflation because of concern for the unemployment costs of more restrictive policies.

The Role of Prices in Wage-Rate Decisions

Commodity price changes have an obvious direct effect on the inflation rate in the period in which they occur. In addition, the resulting increases in living costs may initiate catch-up efforts by workers to restore real wages through larger nominal wage increases and thus escalate the underlying wage-price cycle. There are, however, two competing explanations for the momentum of wage inflation with sharply different implications for the role of price shocks. A focus on real wages (a price-wage transmission) and thus a direct role for past or expected future prices in wage determination implies that the individual worker is constantly reevaluating the work-leisure decision. (In the face of rising prices the worker threatens to quit working unless he receives a compensatory wage increase.) Yet empirical studies have repeatedly found that, on average, the labor force participation rate is insensitive to variations in real wages. The second interpretation emphasizes the choice between alternative jobs and thus a relative wage link (a wage-wage transmission) between markets.[8] (The worker is prepared to quit in order to take on an alternative job unless he receives a wage comparable to that available elsewhere.) In this case, prices have no direct effect on wage decisions. In the early 1970s most empirical studies emphasized the price-wage linkage, but in the last half of the decade a shift toward a wage-wage interpretation of wage inflation became apparent in many studies.[9] The change of emphasis was motivated primarily by evidence

---

8. The emphasis on real wages, or a price-wage link, was stressed by Milton Friedman in his presidential address before the American Economic Association, "The Role of Monetary Policy," *American Economic Review,* vol. 58 (March 1968), pp. 1–17. The emphasis on relative wages is evident in Edmund S. Phelps's article, "Money Wage Dynamics and Labor Market Equilibrium," in Edmund S. Phelps and others, *Microeconomic Foundations of Employment and Inflation Theory* (Norton, 1970), pp. 124–66.

9. This evolution of views is well represented by three studies published in the *Brookings Papers on Economic Activity* by Robert J. Gordon from 1972 to 1980: "Wage-Price Controls and the Shifting Phillips Curve," *BPEA, 2:1972,* pp. 385–421, where price changes have a unitary impact on wages; "Can the Inflation of the 1970s Be Explained?" *BPEA, 1:1977,* pp. 253–79, where there is no cost-of-living price effect on wage rates; and "Comments," *BPEA, 1:1980,* pp. 249–57, where a coefficient of 0.25 is found.

that a good part of the energy price shocks of the 1970s was quickly absorbed in the United States by a reduction in real wages rather than by a full pass-through of the high prices.

At the empirical level the relative importance of the price-wage and wage-wage explanations has been difficult to determine. The close historical correlation between price and wage inflation does not imply that the first causes the second: there is after all a strong causal link in the opposite direction as wage increases raise prices. In the presence of strong serial correlation, an examination of lag structures (to determine which changed first) does not eliminate the potential bias of this two-way causation. In addition, many factors affect both prices and wages directly without implying that the influence on wages operates through prices. Variations in aggregate demand, for example, build in a common cyclical pattern. Moreover, the sharp price increases of the mid-1970s did not appear to be fully reflected in nominal wage rates, and real wages declined in the United States. The emphasis on real wages and on the full reflection of prices in wage determination seems too extreme a view.

An intermediate view, consistent with the emphasis on durable employee-employer relationships stressed in the previous section, allows prices to play a limited role as an issue of great concern to the employee and as something the employer should consider when trying to arrive at a fair wage that limits job dissatisfaction and employee turnover. Price increases may be part of the process by which workers form expectations of an acceptable rate of wage increase. A historical record of improvements in productivity and a general advance of wage rates in excess of prices would contribute to expectations that such a trend would continue. In effect, a general dissatisfaction with one's economic situation during a period of declining real wages may trigger more job searching. In this case, employers in "career" job markets would find it advantageous to consider price changes in setting wage rates, to hold down quit rates. But they would need to be cautious with such a policy to ensure that their relative wage rates, and thus their costs, are not driven out of line with those of their competitors.

Collective bargaining is one important means by which prices can have a direct effect on wage rates. Cost-of-living adjustment clauses provide an obvious example of a formal price-wage linkage, although the provisions of these contract clauses seldom provide full compensation for price increases. The average wage increase for workers covered by such agreements in the United States is estimated at 0.6 percentage point

INTRODUCTION

for each 1 percentage point of price increase. About 40 percent of union workers within the private nonfarm sector of the U.S. economy are covered by cost-of-living clauses, and the union wage bill is about 35 percent of the total.[10] On this basis alone, the provisions of these clauses would suggest a minimum total wage response for the economy as a whole of about one-tenth of the rise in prices.

The impact of prices on union wage rates, however, is not limited to the formal contract provisions. Cost-of-living clauses are more significant as evidence that price inflation affects the wage decision under collective bargaining and thus may affect other agreements that do not resort to formal indexing. Once elements of bilateral monopoly are introduced into the wage determination process, such factors as price inflation, which are not directly relevant to the balancing of demand and supply in the individual market, can play an important role. In addition, if a significant part of the wage bill is directly indexed to prices, a wage-wage linkage for the remainder can provide much of the dynamic process of adjustments.

The empirical studies now seem to agree that in the United States price changes have a direct effect on average wage rates within a year of about 25 percent (a 1 percent rise in consumer prices raises nominal wage rates by 0.25 percent). When the analysis is extended to other countries, however, the uncertainty about the effect is greater. In general, studies of wage determination in Western Europe and Japan find a stronger direct role for prices. A recent study by Jeffrey Sachs, for example, argues that wage setting in Europe and Japan is dominated by real wages (a coefficient on consumer prices near unity), in contrast to a relative wage interpretation for the United States.[11]

Asymmetric Responses to Inflation Shocks

Much of the recent discussion of primary commodity price fluctuations and their contribution to inflation has concentrated on their ratchet effect; that is, price increases are passed through into final product

---

10. The 35 percent estimate is the weight of union wages in the employment cost index of the Bureau of Labor Statistics. The various forms of escalator provisions are discussed in Victor J. Sheifer, "Cost-of-Living Adjustments: Keeping Up With Inflation?" *Monthly Labor Review*, vol. 65 (June 1979), pp. 14–17.

11. Jeffrey D. Sachs, "Wages, Profits, and Macroeconomic Adjustment: A Comparative Study," *BPEA, 2:1979*, pp. 269–319.

prices, but no symmetric deflationary response occurs when prices decline. Thus, it is argued, fluctuations in primary commodity prices are a source of the ever-rising general inflation rate. This is a particularly common argument in comparing agricultural prices at the farm and retail level. Whether such asymmetries exist has become a major debating point between proponents and opponents of commodity stabilization programs. We believe there is little theoretical or empirical basis for a ratchet effect, but the argument is largely irrelevant to the issue of the inflation costs of primary commodity price fluctuations.

For a profit-maximizing firm an increase in the cost of materials will lead to a shift in the cost curve and higher prices. But when material costs decline, the cost curve will return to its initial level and so will the profit-maximizing price. If the firm possesses some market power, it will use that power to raise its price-cost margin without regard for the timing of cost changes. This symmetry of pricing in response to costs also seems to be confirmed empirically. In a review of recent studies James Tobin concluded that costs are passed forward into prices in both directions—down as well as up.[12] Apparently, much of the confusion results from ignoring the lags in the response of prices to cost changes as firms seek to smooth the response of prices over time. The asymmetry issue was examined specifically for the margin between farm and retail food prices in the United States in a study by Dale Heien for the Council on Wage and Price Stability.[13] He concluded that retail food prices were equally responsive to farm price increases and decreases after allowance for lags in price adjustments and the fact that other costs had changed.

An alternative argument focuses on the alleged downward rigidity of nominal wage rates; that is, increases in prices pull up wage rates, but price declines do not bring them down proportionately. This argument may have some validity at low rates of inflation but is of limited importance when all wage rates are rising rapidly. The issue is whether

---

12. James Tobin, "The Wage-Price Mechanism: Overview of the Conference," in Otto Eckstein, ed., *The Econometrics of Price Determination: Conference*, Washington, D.C., October 30–31, 1970 (Board of Governors of the Federal Reserve System and Social Science Research Council, 1972), p. 7.

13. The main points were summarized in Executive Office of the President, Council on Wage and Price Stability, *The Responsiveness of Wholesale and Retail Food Prices to Changes in the Costs of Food Production and Distribution,* Staff Report (COWPS, 1976). The underlying report by Heien was "A Study of the Relationship between Farm-Level Prices and Retail Food Prices," report prepared for the Council on Wage and Price Stability, 1976.

or not wage-rate increases moderate when the rate of price rise slows. Again the empirical evidence does not support an asymmetric response of wage-rate changes to changes in prices.[14]

The behavior of policymakers may, however, create a situation where inflation responds asymmetrically to price shocks. At least in the short run, a trade-off exists between inflation and unemployment. Thus a demand-management policy that refuses to accommodate the impact on the average price level of higher commodity prices must cause some loss of output and increase in unemployment. At the same time there are reasons for believing that this inflation-unemployment trade-off is not a simple linear relationship; that is, an incremental reduction in unemployment will have a greater effect on inflation at low than at high levels of unemployment. A larger unemployment change will therefore be required to maintain a constant inflation rate in responding to positive exogenous price shocks than in responding to deflationary shocks. Such a situation is depicted in figure 1-1. An upward shift of the inflation-unemployment relationship requires a rise in unemployment from U_0 to U_1 to maintain an unchanged inflation rate, whereas an equal magnitude of a deflationary shock requires a smaller offsetting reduction in unemployment from U_0 to U_2. There are social costs attached to both unemployment and inflation. A balancing of the two concerns would result in a demand-management policy that is more accommodative to inflationary than deflationary price shocks. If commodity prices fluctuate both up and down with no secular trend, the overall price level will still tend to have an inflationary bias. The empirical importance of this phenomenon may be limited, however, because several studies have found only scant evidence of nonlinearity in the inflation-unemployment trade-off within the limited range that the unemployment rate has fluctuated in the postwar years.

On the other hand, the concern for both inflation and unemployment means that an inflationary price shock will be accommodated to some extent by the monetary authorities through an expansion of the money supply. Yet the same confluence of pressures will not occur under a deflationary price shock. Those who argue for an unvarying monetary policy will hold to the same position on both the upside and downside. But it is unlikely that those concerned with unemployment will pursue

14. Morris Goldstein, "Downward Price Inflexibility, Ratchet Effects, and the Inflationary Impact of Import Price Changes: Some Empirical Evidence," *International Monetary Fund Staff Papers*, vol. 24 (November 1977), pp. 569–612.

Figure 1-1. *The Unemployment Response to Inflation Shocks*

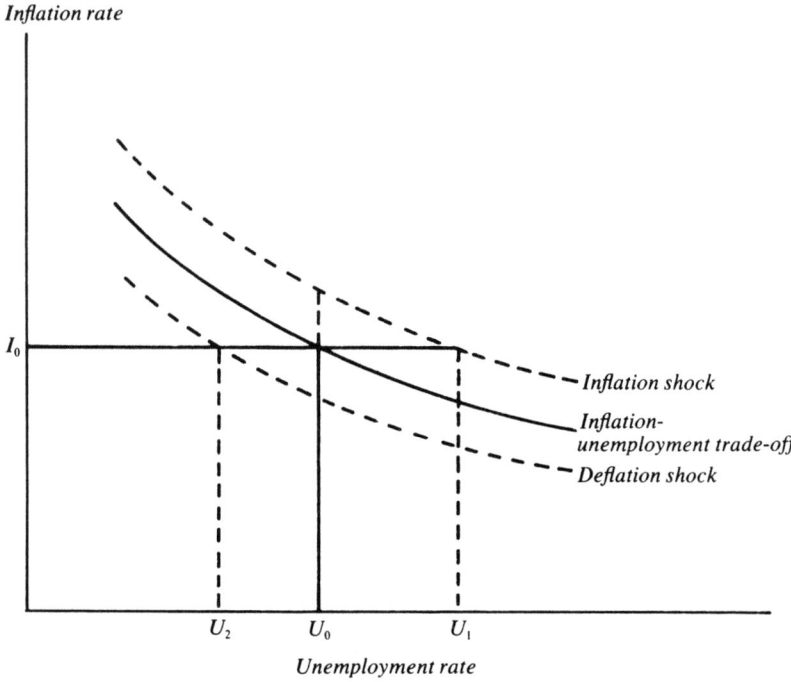

the argument for accommodation with the same vigor when it means an offsetting reduction of the monetary growth rate in response to a deflationary price shock. They are more likely to see such a shock as an opportunity to pursue a more expansionary employment policy.

The primary purpose of this study, however, is not to argue that commodity price fluctuations impart an inflationary bias to the economy. Instead, we argue that the main social cost of inflation is associated with the variability of the inflation rate and departures of the actual rate from that which the participants in the economy had expected. The sluggish response of industrial wages and prices to variations in demand and supply implies that demand-management policies cannot offset the effect of these price shocks on the aggregate price level without the cost of lower output and higher unemployment. This argument does not rest on any notion of a ratchet effect in the inflation process; rather, it depends on the extent to which the economy is dominated by flexible-price or by

INTRODUCTION   17

fixed-price markets and on the importance of price inflation in determining wages.

Primary commodity price fluctuations indeed played a major role in the worsening of inflation during the 1970s. The 1950s and 1960s were marked by rapid technological progress in the agriculture, energy, and extractive industries that contributed to strong downward pressure on relative prices in these markets. The price trends were important sources of restraint on the general inflation in that period. As discussed more fully later, opposite forces were to work on these markets in the 1970s. On average, the relative price of primary commodities rose, but, more important, the sharply increased magnitude and frequency of the price fluctuations became major sources of instability for the economy as a whole.[15]

Summary of the Book

After some prefatory remarks on primary commodity markets, we address three important issues associated with the commodity price fluctuations of the 1970s: the consequence for overall inflation in the industrial nations, the causes of the fluctuations, and the range of policies that could be adopted to dampen their influence on inflation in the future.

Contribution to Inflation

For the OECD economies, the rise of primary commodity prices (including secondary effects on domestic wages and prices) represented on average about one-third of the general inflation and over two-thirds of the acceleration of inflation between 1970–71 and 1974. This average, however, disguises the wide variation in the experience of individual countries. Inflation had varying effects on countries because of (1) differences in the mix of their raw material requirements, (2) divergent patterns of change between domestic and international markets because of government policies of intervention in some markets, (3) offsetting movements in exchange rates, (4) variations in the responsiveness of

15. This same point has been made by many others. See, for example, *Economic Report of the President, January 1978*, pp. 138–41; and Alan S. Blinder, *Economic Policy and the Great Stagflation* (Academic Press, 1979).

domestic wages and prices to these largely external price shocks, and (5) differences in the macroeconomic policies pursued during the period.

In chapter 3 these differences are explored in detail for three major economies: the United States, Japan, and West Germany. The impact over the 1970s as a whole was most pronounced for the United States because of its practice of keeping domestic food prices in line with those of the world market, a gradual movement toward world market prices in energy, a high level of energy use relative to gross national product, and, most important, an adverse movement in exchange rates. For the United States the contributions to the overall inflation of agricultural prices in 1973 and energy prices in 1974 were of about equal magnitude.

Before 1973 both West Germany and Japan followed agricultural policies that maintained a domestic level of agricultural prices that was substantially above world market prices. They were therefore able to absorb the rise in world grain prices by simply reducing their import tariffs. But they were affected more than the United States by the rise in energy prices in 1974. Again the impact on Germany was limited somewhat by its heavy reliance on coal and on its earlier policy of taxing oil imports to protect the domestic coal industry. So its overall rise of energy prices was less than in Japan. The impact within the United States was similarly held down by price controls on domestically produced petroleum and other energy sources, particularly natural gas.

The United States was the most sharply affected by the rise of oil prices in 1979 because the crisis precipitated a breakdown of the system for domestic petroleum price control. Still, for all the countries examined, the rise of oil prices in 1979 had a smaller effect on the domestic price of other goods and services than in 1974. This might indicate that workers and firms had learned to respond differently to such external price shocks.

The magnitude of the difference in price movements for a similar commodity group among countries (adjusted for exchange-rate changes) is one of the more surprising conclusions of our study. This difference was the result of extensive government intervention in the major agricultural and energy markets. Despite the attention that has been directed to price changes in other primary commodity markets, like nonferrous metals, these markets have not been an important source of inflation because of their relatively small size. As far as inflation is concerned, the troublesome sectors have been food and energy.

Causes of Price Fluctuations

Most of chapter 4 is devoted to examining the extent to which the commodity price fluctuations resulted from the interaction of supply and demand. This knowledge is important in determining the extent to which the price behavior of 1973–74 was the result of an unusually highly synchronized expansion of industrial production in the major economies together with many supply disruptions in the major markets. We find strong statistical support for a model that emphasizes such factors, but at the same time the size of the price increases in 1973–74 cannot be fully explained.

The rest of the chapter deals with the implications of treating commodities as an investment asset. This means analyzing the motives for holding stocks in addition to the determinants of the flows of production and consumption, which the demand-supply model emphasizes. We are unable to find strong confirmation for Hendrik Houthakker's hypothesis that the 1972–74 surge of commodity prices can be traced to a monetary imbalance that developed after the shift to a flexible exchange-rate system.[16] But the growth of futures markets during the 1970s and some evidence of commodity hoarding indicate that asset behavior, with its emphasis on speculative activities and risk, helped to increase the variability of commodity prices.

An analysis that examines demand and supply within the context of a global market also cannot adequately explain changes in the price of grains. Before the 1970s the world market price was essentially controlled by the U.S. government. Production controls and a domestic price-support program provided a price floor, and a large grain reserve prevented significant price increases. In the late 1960s and early 1970s the United States moved to eliminate the reserve because farmers believed that its overhang on the market depressed prices and because policymakers viewed the program as too costly to taxpayers. This reduction of reserves coincided with an important shift in agricultural policy by the Soviet Union, which began to use increased imports rather than reductions in domestic consumption to adjust to production shortfalls.

---

16. Hendrik S. Houthakker, "Comments and Discussion," *BPEA, 3:1975*, pp. 718–20.

In addition, Japan and the European Community's policy of divorcing their domestic economies from events in the world agricultural market (by variable import levies) concentrated the burden of adjusting to world crop failures on consumers in the United States and the less-developed countries.

The analysis of chapter 5 suggests that it was the reduction in world grain consumption after 1973 rather than a higher level of production that provided room for Soviet imports to increase and for grain prices to decline to more normal levels. But because so much of the adjustment was achieved by reducing cattle herds, there is a risk that rebuilding these herds in the 1980s will cause a return to a tight world market with no reserve to smooth out the inevitable fluctuations in production.

The international petroleum market also experienced important institutional changes that dominated the behavior of prices during the 1970s. The principal change has been the shift in power from a consortium of international oil companies, which managed for decades to play off one producer government against another, to a loose confederation of oil-producing countries. As outlined in the latter part of chapter 5, this shift of power, which culminated in the large price increases of 1973, can be traced to the gradual change in the relationship between the companies and the producing countries in the years before 1973.

The effort to arrive at a consensus on the appropriate market model within which oil prices should be interpreted is central to the discussion of the appropriate policy actions that should be taken. But though the different models of oil-market behavior (competitive, dominant firm, monopolist, cartel, and so on) can suggest the qualitative implications of such factors as market structure, alternative technologies, and aggregate supply conditions, the small historical sample of price behavior makes it difficult to formulate an empirical model in which one can have confidence. And even if the correct model could be established, it would not allow the accurate prediction of short-run price movements in a market where the equilibrating forces that push the market toward its long-run path work slowly and poorly.

Two conclusions seem relevant to policies that focus on the short-term effects of oil supply interruptions: first, the disruptive conditions of 1974 and 1979 were largely the result of panic buying on the demand side, which drove spot market prices up; and second, the fluctuations in spot market prices appear to have an asymmetric effect on contract prices, since increasing spot prices raise contract prices whereas declines are often met by efforts to curtail production.

Policy Options

Some general issues for economic policy in the face of primary commodity market instability are taken up in chapter 6. First, once it is admitted that some relatively fixed-price markets exist, it becomes clear that commodity price changes are not simply changes in relative prices. Instead, macroeconomic policy confronts a dilemma: a monetary policy that tries to accommodate the pressure of inflation and maintain real output will impose the costs of a more variable rate of inflation; on the other hand, a policy of nonaccommodation will impose the costs of a more variable level of real output and employment. We find that neither of the two extremes of pure accommodation or nonaccommodation is likely to be the best solution, and within that range the choice of a specific policy hinges on several disputed empirical issues and on subjective views about the relative costs of inflation and unemployment. We reach the important conclusion that no good option for macroeconomic policy exists. Hence the rest of the chapter focuses on microeconomic policies of intervention to stabilize prices in specific markets.

Price stabilization offers benefits to both consumers and producers (though the determination of how the benefits are allocated between the two is complex), but private markets embody strong incentives for private agents to provide the optimal amount of such activity. A role for government intervention must rest on a perception of "market failure" or on external benefits that do not accrue to private parties. In this regard we find two main arguments for intervention. First, the substantive existing role of government in these markets, its perceived propensity to change the rules of the game, and the lack of credibility of any pledge to renounce intervention in the future limit the range of future prices at which speculators expect to be allowed to trade. Thus their activities will not be adequate to cover the extremes of potential price movements. To some extent, in other words, intervention calls for more intervention. Second, the inflationary impact of price fluctuations in major commodity markets in an economy with many fixed-price markets creates an external cost that cannot be offset by macroeconomic policies alone.

The practical difficulties of stabilization policies caution us, however, that limiting the activity to price stabilization alone may be difficult. This difficulty stems primarily from the divergent interests of the parties involved and the tendency to attempt to maintain artificial long-run prices in the name of short-run stabilization. For price stabilization, buffer stocks are the preferred method of intervention in markets for storable commodities. Yet there are no examples of a pure buffer stock program; producers have insisted on combining a buffer stock with supply restrictions. Also, many technical issues must be considered in establishing a buffer stock (for example, avoiding interference with the long-run price, minimizing the offsetting reduction in private stocks, and determining the optimal degree of stabilization).

More specific stabilization proposals are the subject of chapter 7. These must be drafted to recognize institutional differences among markets. In the case of grains we conclude that efforts to negotiate an international agreement, along the lines pursued by the United States during the 1970s, are unlikely to be successful. An international agreement necessarily embodies a degree of international intervention in domestic agricultural policies that is intolerable to most countries. The current pronouncement of the United States, however, that it will pursue an open-door policy on future grain exports, regardless of the magnitude of future crises, is not believable. Consequently, other nations tend to emphasize self-dependence and to isolate their domestic economies from the vagaries of the international market. These barriers to trade place the burden of adjusting to future world-market disruptions on an ever-shrinking number of nations, are a major cause of the extreme volatility of market prices, and are detrimental to the long-run objective of increasing U.S. grain exports. Yet efforts to build a more adequate U.S. grain reserve are limited by arguments that American consumers would bear an unfair share of the costs.

We conclude that the most feasible policy option is a series of bilateral agreements under which foreign governments purchase a guaranteed, but prespecified, magnitude of access to the U.S. market, expressed in terms of a minimum and maximum level of annual sales. Such agreements would define the extent of the U.S. commitment, reduce the "free-rider" problem, and free the United States to pursue a national grain reserve policy to meet its commitments to producers, domestic consumers, and foreign customers. At the same time, such agreements would minimize the interference with the domestic policies of other countries. The

INTRODUCTION 23

development of a substantial grain reserve in the United States is critical, however, if such a program is not to intensify instability in the world market.

We are led to be equally pessimistic about the possibility of multinational producer-consumer agreements leading to increased stability in world energy markets. In this case, moreover, because the producer countries do not have the internal balancing pressure of domestic consumers, as does the United States in grain, they are less interested in price stability, and bilateral agreements are likely to worsen the problem. Instead, the most beneficial international agreements would seem to be cooperative efforts by consuming nations to limit imports in order to prevent surges of prices in the spot market for oil. Such import limitations would leave each nation free to choose its own program to balance domestic demand with supply.

A petroleum reserve is clearly the most effective domestic policy response to potential supply interruptions. And, for the United States, it is relatively easy to justify a reserve of at least one billion barrels. The United States, however, has repeatedly delayed building such a stock; for the near future it will be forced to rely on a choice between an excise tax with a rebate or a rationing program with marketable coupons or similar demand-rationing devices. From an economic perspective these two proposals are similar in that most of the problems involved in handing out coupons apply equally to the rebate of the tax. The two proposals differ primarily in their approach to the equity or distributional issue. Proponents of the excise tax, who focus on efficiency, advocate a rather simple resolution of the equity issue and thus a simple program of rebates. The proponents of coupon rationing advocate a more complex treatment of the equity issue, with widespread requests for exemption. In any case, neither of these proposals is at a stage where it could be implemented in a crisis. Thus the United States would be forced to rely on a combination of market price increases and gas lines. The chapter concludes with a brief review of stabilization proposals for other commodities.

CHAPTER TWO

The Role of Primary Commodities in Industrial Economies

BEFORE we turn to a detailed analysis of the reasons behind the commodity price developments of the 1970s, some general prefatory remarks are in order.

Definition and Categories of Primary Commodities

Primary commodities are normally defined as products grown on land (like crops), extracted from land (like minerals), or raised on land (like cattle) that have been subject to only the first stage of processing. Because the "first stage of processing" is an ambiguous concept, it is difficult to devise a foolproof method of applying this definition to specific situations.[1]

In this study the definition of primary commodities is that of the United Nations and is based on the standard international trade classification (SITC).[2] The term *basic commodities* is used when basic nonferrous metals are included with primary commodities. Nonferrous base metals, comprising SITC code 68, are the products of more than a rudimentary degree of processing. But they are the least fabricated form

---

1. For a discussion of some of the practical difficulties, see C. P. Brown, *Primary Commodity Control* (Kuala Lumpur: Oxford University Press, 1975), pp. 2–3.
2. "The term 'primary commodities' comprises goods listed in Sections 0 to 4 of the SITC, Revised, with the exception of manufactured foods and tobacco (from Sections 0 and 1), synthetic fibres, synthetic rubber, and waste and scrap of primary commodities (from Section 2), and petroleum products (from Section 3). . . . The metals included in the index for non-ferrous base metals are: copper, nickel, aluminum, lead, zinc, and tin." See Department of International Economic and Social Affairs, *Methods Used in Compiling the United Nations Price Indexes for Basic Commodities in International Trade*, UN Doc. ST/STAT/SER.M/29/Rev. 2, p. 3.

THE ROLE OF PRIMARY COMMODITIES 25

in which these metals enter international trade, and are therefore frequently analyzed together with primary commodities.

Primary commodities can be grouped by use—for example, foods and feeds, industrial raw materials, and fuels—or by sector of origin—for example, agriculture and mining. Both groupings are helpful for economic analysis. Grouping by use highlights the difference between the demand for fuels and raw materials that are inputs into the industrial sector, and the demand for foods and feeds, which is less sensitive to cyclical changes. Grouping by sector of origin emphasizes the greater dependence of agricultural supply on climatic variability.[3]

Here we use four main commodity categories: food (which accounted for 27 percent of the value of basic commodity trade in 1977), other agricultural raw materials (15 percent of 1977 trade value), minerals (52 percent of trade), and nonferrous metals (6 percent of trade). Although there are many primary commodities, a small number account for a large percentage of the total value of world trade. In 1977 the meat, fish, and grain trade constituted about 40 percent of the food trade, while 79 percent of the agricultural raw materials trade was accounted for by vegetable oils and oilseeds, wood products, and fibers. Crude petroleum, iron ore, and coal were the most important minerals, and aluminum and copper constituted 64 percent of the value of nonferrous metals traded. Table 2-1 provides a more detailed listing of the most important commodities and reports their role in world trade in 1970 and 1977. Although crude petroleum has increased its share of total trade values from 17 percent in 1970 to 42 percent in 1977, values in the remaining categories have grown at fairly uniform rates.[4]

---

3. The sensitivity of various primary commodity prices to the international business cycle can be illustrated by the following correlations for the period 1956–71 for percentage changes in UN commodity price indexes with percentage change in the UN index of industrial production:

Commodity	Correlation
Agricultural raw materials	0.61
Food	−0.05
Ores	0.51
Base metals	0.64
Petroleum	−0.36

4. Primary commodities in turn accounted for 33 percent of the total value of world trade in 1970. Under the impetus of higher prices, the share of primary commodities rose to 44 percent in 1974 and 37 percent in 1978. For a more detailed discussion of primary commodities in international trade, see General Agreement on Tariffs and Trade, *International Trade, 1978/79* (Geneva: GATT, 1979), p. 4, and earlier issues.

Table 2-1. *Major Basic Commodities Traded Internationally*
Billions of dollars

Commodity	Standard international trade classification	Value of exports 1970	Value of exports 1977
Food			
Live animals and meat	001,011,012	5.19	13.10
Dairy products	022,023,024,025	2.39	7.45
Fish	031	1.59	5.96
Cereals	041–047	7.26	20.94
Fruits, nuts, and vegetables	051,052,054	4.19	11.44
Sugar and honey	061	2.70	7.61
Coffee, cocoa, tea, and spices	071,072,074,075	5.15	19.65
Animal feed	081	2.12	7.07
Total	. . .	30.59	93.22
Other agriculture			
Tobacco, unmanufactured	121	1.18	2.84
Hides, furs and skins	211,212	1.19	3.16
Oilseeds	221	2.12	7.28
Rubber	231	2.16	5.23
Wood	241–243	4.34	12.71
Pulp	251	2.61	5.63
Fibers	261–265	4.58	9.03
Animal and vegetable oils	411,421,422	1.95	6.46
Total	. . .	20.13	52.34
Minerals			
Crude minerals	271–276	2.19	5.32
Ores (iron, nonferrous base metals, uranium, and thorium)	281,283,286	5.86	11.12
Coal	321	3.25	10.91
Petroleum	331	15.60	145.16
Natural gas	341	0.70	9.29
Total	. . .	27.60	181.80
Nonferrous base metals			
Silver, platinum, copper, nickel, aluminium, lead, zinc, tin, uranium, thorium, and miscellaneous nonferrous base metals	681–689	12.14	21.56
Total	. . .	**90.46**	**348.92**
Total excluding petroleum	. . .	**74.86**	**203.76**

Source: United Nations Conference on Trade and Development, *Handbook of International Trade and Development Statistics, Supplement 1980*, UN Doc. TD/STAT. 9, pp. 152–205.

Commodity Prices

While the object of this book is to analyze the impact of commodity price movement on the price level for which absolute commodity prices are relevant, our explanation of the prices of particular commodity groups focuses on relative prices, since we are concerned with only a small sector of the economy and rely for the most part on the standard microeconomic formulation that explains relative price movements. We therefore deflate our commodity price series by a price index of manufactured goods (the UN manufactured export price index), which we use as a crude indicator of changes in the long-run nominal supply price (at constant or trend real cost) of commodities. The use of a relative price formulation also has the advantage of minimizing the problem of exchange rates, since both the numerator and the denominator are expressed in the same currency and movements in the exchange rate cancel out.

Trends and Cycles

Primary commodities are a heterogeneous group. Making generalizations about them is hazardous, for they are produced with techniques ranging from primitive and rudimentary to sophisticated and capital-intensive, and are sold in markets that range from highly concentrated to almost perfectly competitive. Nonetheless, a large proportion of most primary commodity trade occurs in markets where prices are responsive to shifts in supply and demand.

In analyzing primary commodity prices, one should distinguish three time horizons: the long run of at least twenty years, in which "fundamental" forces (such as income and population growth), resource discoveries, and technological change are the most important determinants of price trends; the medium run of between three and twenty years, in which more volatile factors like business cycle fluctuations and what can be loosely referred to as changes in production capacity induce price cycles;[5] and the short run, in which a wide range of transitory develop-

---

5. The term *capacity* is used in a broad sense here to denote processing plant, herds, forests, and fields under cultivation.

ments like crop failures, strikes, speculative booms, and inventory changes can produce very volatile fluctuations.

THE LONG RUN. The debate over the secular trends in primary commodity prices has a long history. On one side stand the pessimists, who predict that commodities will become increasingly expensive. They argue that the exponential growth in world incomes and population raises demand growth, while supply growth slows because nonrenewable resources are depleted more rapidly than they can be discovered and the yields from renewable resource production shrink as the margin of cultivation is extended to less fertile land.

On the other side are the optimists, who argue that technological change outpaces the growing need for primary commodities and ensures a declining price trend. They emphasize improvements in methods of exploration, production, and utilization; increased recycling; and the development of substitutes that use resources less intensively.[6] The optimists also point out that in physical terms the share of primary commodities in total production has declined secularly.

As income rises above subsistence levels, there is a decline in the proportion of income devoted to goods that have a high primary commodity content, such as food, textiles, and furniture, and an increase in the proportion devoted to goods that have a lower primary commodity content, such as engineering products, electronics, and chemicals. This change in the commodity composition of demand away from primary commodities is reinforced by the expansion of the tertiary and government sectors, which have a high service component. Technological change also has contributed to this secular trend. Innovation often occurs in sophisticated, highly fabricated products, which are intensive in the use of skilled labor and the application of scientific knowledge. Their manufacture further reduces the ratio of primary commodities to

6. See Harold J. Barnett and Chandler Morse, *Scarcity and Growth: The Economics of Natural Resource Availability* (Johns Hopkins Press for Resources for the Future, 1963), pp. 164–201. The authors found that from 1870 to 1957 the unit cost of extractive resources (agriculture, minerals, forestry, and commercial fishing) in the United States had a declining trend. Similar conclusions in a study that updated Barnett and Morse for the period 1958–72 are found in Manuel H. Johnson and James T. Bennett, "Increasing Resource Scarcity: Further Evidence," *Quarterly Review of Economics and Business*, vol. 20 (Spring 1980), pp. 42–48. An additional statistical analysis is provided by V. Kerry Smith, "Natural Resource Scarcity: A Statistical Analysis," *Review of Economics and Statistics*, vol. 61 (August 1979), pp. 423–27. The diversity of views is well represented in V. Kerry Smith, ed., *Scarcity and Growth Reconsidered* (Johns Hopkins University Press for Resources for the Future, 1979).

income. The development of synthetic materials like fibers, rubber, and plastic has also eroded the role of many natural industrial raw materials.[7]

Theoretical reasoning and empirical evidence suggest however, that neither the pessimists nor the optimists are correct. The movements toward scarcity or abundance produce economic reactions that prevent the trends from persisting forever. Continuously rising prices encourage technological change, the invention of substitutes, and economy in use. Falling prices do the opposite. In fact, although significant trends in overall commodity prices have been evident for periods of about twenty years, an even longer perspective suggests that periods of commodity scarcity (when factors like population and income growth outweigh those like technological change and increases in the resource base for commodity production) are followed by periods of relative abundance. The index compiled in figure 2-1 strongly supports this view, indicating periods, such as 1870–90, 1921–35 and 1951–70, in which commodity prices declined and were followed by periods (usually associated with wars) in which rising commodity prices prevailed.[8]

An alternative physical approach to the scarcity issue attempts to focus on a comparison of known reserves with the level of current

---

7. This pattern is evident in data on global aggregates. Manufacturing production has consistently increased more rapidly than any major component of world primary commodity production including fuel. The UN world primary commodity production index increased an average of 2.7 percent over the period 1948–75, whereas the UN manufactured goods production index increased 5.6 percent over the same period.

A declining share of primary commodities is also evident in national data. Spencer estimated U.S. consumption of primary commodities in the twentieth century. Vivian Eberle Spencer, *Raw Materials in the United States Economy: 1909–1969*, U.S. Bureau of the Census and Department of the Interior, Bureau of Mines, Bureau of the Census Working Paper 35 (Government Printing Office, 1972). Measured in 1967 dollars, total commodity consumption declined as a percentage of U.S. gross national product from 16.9 in 1910 to 8.3 in 1969. Rates of consumption differ by category, with mineral fuels increasing far more rapidly than foods, but over the entire period even fuels failed to sustain a rate of growth as fast as that of overall income, with the share in GNP declining from 2.9 in 1910 to 2.5 in 1969. Other countries have had a similar experience. The ratio of the average value of 1959 and 1960 primary commodity consumption to 1960 gross domestic product in Japan was 0.25, in the United Kingdom 0.16, and in the European Community 0.17. The corresponding ratios for 1969–70 were 0.15, 0.12, and 0.12. United Nations Conference on Trade and Development, *Handbook of International Trade and Development Statistics, 1972*, UN Doc. TD/STAT. 4, pp. 286–94; and Organization for Economic Cooperation and Development, *National Accounts Statistics* (Paris: OECD, various issues). In part these figures overstate the real decline because of differences in inflation rates between overall GDP and primary commodities.

8. For a more complete discussion of these long-run cycles, see Walter W. Rostow, *The World Economy: History and Prospect* (University of Texas Press, 1978).

Figure 2-1. *Long-Run Relative Price Trends for Primary Commodities*[a]

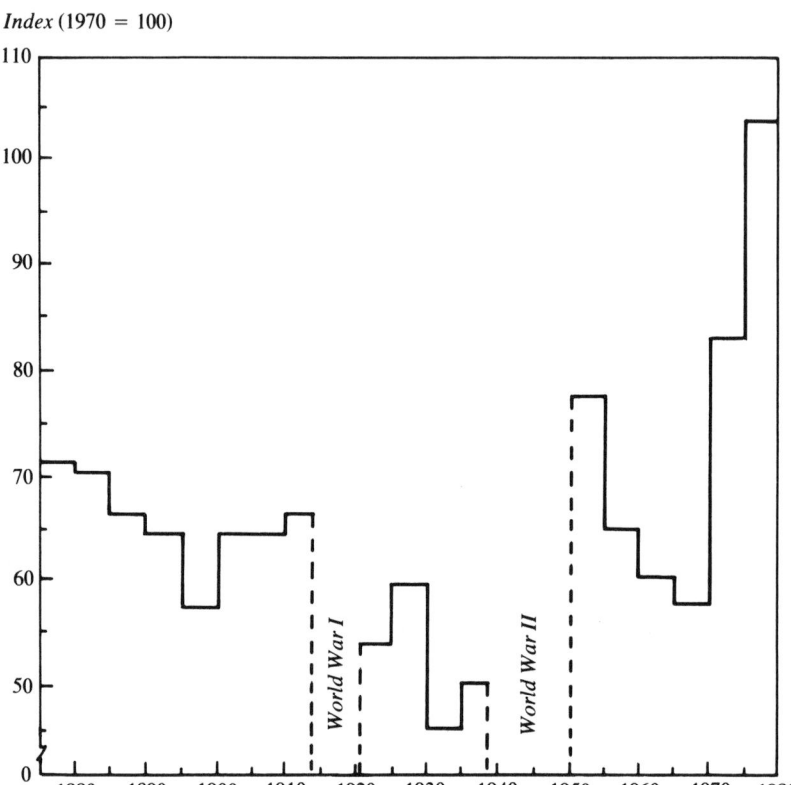

Sources: For 1876–1938: League of Nations, *Industrialization and Foreign Trade* (Geneva: League of Nations, 1945), p. 157; for 1938–48: United Nations, *Statistical Yearbook, 1975*, UN Doc. ST/ESA/STAT/SER. S/3, p. 55; for 1948–50 United Nations, *Statistical Yearbook 1955* (New York: UN, 1955), p. 394; for 1950–76 United Nations, Department of International Economic and Social Affairs, *Methods Used in Compiling the United Nations Price Indexes for Basic Commodities in International Trade*, UN Doc. ST/STAT/SER. M/29/Rev. 2; for 1977–79 United Nations, *Monthly Bulletin of Statistics*, UN Doc. ST/ESA/STAT/Ser. Q, various issues.

a. The relative price for primary commodities equals the UN primary commodity price index divided by the UN price index for manufactured exports.

consumption in order to compute the number of years required to exhaust the resource. Such measures are inherently unreliable, however. Reserves are defined as resources that have been measured or estimated as to their current extent and that can be extracted profitably at current prices and technology. Not all reserves of a known quality have been discovered, and the degree of exploratory effort is a function of the expected prices. In addition, changes in technology and prices increase the feasibility of recovering resources of varying quality. Furthermore, the demand for the materials is influenced by technology, prices, the availability of substitutes, and the contribution of recycling.

It is still too early to tell if the boom of the 1970s marked the beginning of a new phase in these long-run cycles in which the pessimists' view of commodity prices is proved correct. Given the level to which fuel prices have boosted the overall commodity index, the evidence certainly seems to support that view. Yet the behavior of prices for other materials provides counter evidence.

THE MEDIUM RUN. Although primary commodity prices do not have regular periodicity or constant amplitudes, as is illustrated in figure 2-2, they display fairly distinctive cyclical movements around their long-run trends. This cyclical pattern results from the rigidities that prevent these markets from adjusting instantaneously to changed conditions, with the duration of the cycle being related to both the nature of the shocks that set it in motion and the specific features of the particular market affected.

When prices rise, various technological and biological factors constrain the expansion of supply. It requires up to a decade to develop new mineral deposits for production and about three years to build plants for mineral processing. It takes several decades to grow trees for lumber, pulp, and rubber, and from five to ten years for coffee, tea, and cocoa plants to mature. From the time a cattle producer makes the decision to expand his herds, about five years must pass before a sustained increase in slaughter will result. Even annual crops can be grown only in particular seasons.

Conversely, when prices fall, economic considerations limit reductions in supply. Since producers are committed in the short run to pay certain fixed costs, it makes sense for them to continue producing, provided they can cover their variable costs. Thus production continues even when the market price falls below long-run average costs. The degree to which prices can fall without having much effect on supply is directly related to the ratio of fixed to variable factors of production as well as to the alternative uses to which the fixed productive factors can be put. Most primary commodities use fixed factors of production, namely land and capital, relatively intensively; and the uses to which these factors can be put is fairly specific. Economic considerations also limit demand responses. Raw materials used as inputs often dictate the type of machinery. While the choice of new equipment will be influenced by current (and expected) prices, older vintages make the demand response sluggish in the short run.

Figure 2-2. *Relative Price of Primary Commodities, by Major Component, 1954–80*[a]

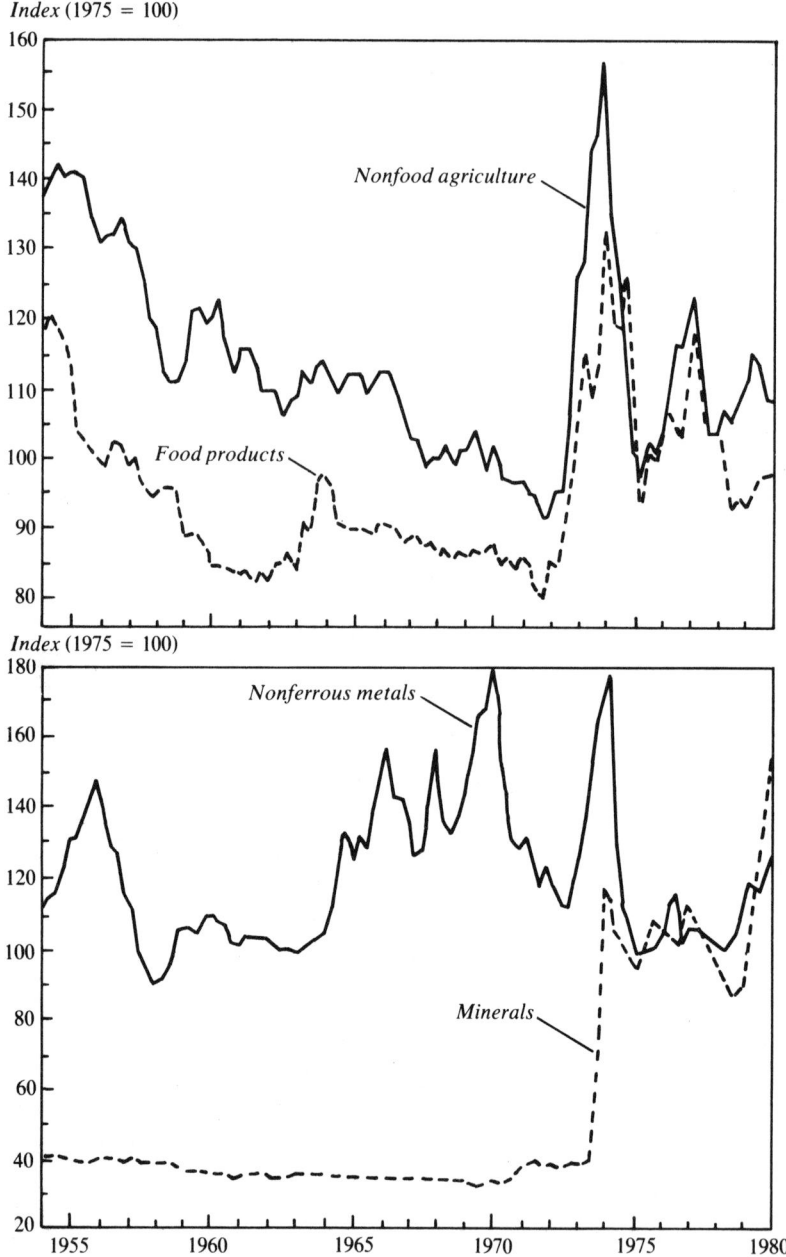

Sources: UN Department of International Economics and Social Affairs, *Methods Used in Compiling the United Nations Price Indexes for Basic Commodities in International Trade;* and United Nations, *Monthly Bulletin of Statistics,* various issues.

a. See note a, figure 2-1.

THE ROLE OF PRIMARY COMMODITIES

THE SHORT RUN. Explanations of the extremely volatile fluctuations in commodity prices have differed in the extent to which such movement is seen to reflect destabilizing speculation by the participants.

According to one view, commodity markets are dominated by speculators who are highly susceptible to volatile shifts in expectations. In his discussion of the workings of the stock exchange, Keynes put forward such a view.[9] He argued that markets, particularly asset markets, may be unstable. In a market dominated by speculators, it might be profitable for each participant to concentrate on forecasting what others will do, rather than on estimating the future path of underlying supply and demand factors. "We have reached the third degree," Keynes wrote, "where we devote our intelligences to anticipating what average opinion expects average opinion to be".[10] He also felt that speculators will always give the current situation a disproportionate weight in forming their opinions. Since long-run considerations are usually ignored, small changes in present conditions spark off inordinately large and cumulative price changes.

History provides many instances of obvious speculative excesses. One of the earliest recorded bubbles of commodity speculation was the Dutch tulip mania of the 1630s. The speculative craze pervaded society, with "intellectuals, the middle classes and the laborer" all taking part. Posthumus told of bulbs that were bought for $8 to $9 a pound and traded at $430 a month later.[11] Few who bought were interested in the bulbs. Like participants in the perennial chain letter, they cared simply that others would follow them.

But though it is plausible that on some occasions markets reflect such myopic behavior, it is intellectually unsatisfying to attribute the regular day-to-day volatility in commodity prices to that behavior. If, for example, the current expectations about future prices are unrealistically high, farsighted speculators can earn a profit by selling commodities

---

9. John Maynard Keynes, *The General Theory of Employment, Interest and Money* (London: Macmillan, 1936), chap. 12.

10. Ibid., p. 156.

11. Nicholas W. Posthumus, "The Tulip Mania in Holland in the Years 1636 and 1637," *Journal of Economic and Business History*, vol. 1 (May 1929), p. 439. There is evidence that a single "Viceroy" tulip was exchanged for "2 loads of wheat, 4 loads of rye, 4 fat oxen, 8 fat pigs, 12 fat sheep, 2 hogshead of wine, 4 barrels of beer, 2 barrels of butter, 1000 pounds of cheese, 1 complete bed, 1 suit of clothes, and 1 silver beaker," which totaled 2,500 florins in value. A "Semper Augustus" was sold for 4,600 florins plus "a new and well made carriage and two dapple grey horses and all assesories." See Harold T. Davis, *The Analysis of Economic Time Series*, Cowles Commission for Research in Economics Monograph 6 (Bloomington, Ind.: Principia Press, 1941), pp. 10–11.

forward today and buying at the lower prices in the future. Such behavior would, of course, drive the forward price down toward a more appropriate level; conversely, unrealistically low prices provide an opportunity for buying today and selling at higher prices tomorrow. Thus the profit motive ought to induce some agents to take advantage of the profitable opportunities implied by the irrational market behavior emphasized by Keynes. There is a reward for taking the long view.

An alternative view emphasizes the consistency of commodity price volatility with a long-run price that is determined by fundamental factors, like the costs of production. In the short run the spot price is determined by the need to equilibrate simultaneously the desired and actual stocks of inventories as well as the flows of current production and consumption.[12]

At any given time, inventory holders have an implicit view of the future path the price is expected to follow. The less responsive current supply and demand are to price changes and the longer it takes for excess (inadequate) stocks to be absorbed (replenished), the larger will be the average deviation of the current price from its "normal" level. Any new information about current or future demands and supplies will change the expected price path and thus the expected yield from holding inventories. The spot price will move rapidly to incorporate this new information and reestablish asset market equilibrium. Thus the volatility in commodity prices does not stem from irrational destabilizing behavior, but rather reflects the objective fact that many volatile determinants of expected future prices will influence current inventory demands.[13]

Besides the speculative return from holding commodities, users derive a "convenience yield" from having stocks on hand. Commodity users

---

12. This view can also be found in Keynes's "rationally" grounded explanation of commodity price volatility. For a discussion of inventory demand, see John Maynard Keynes, *A Treatise on Money* (Harcourt Brace, 1930), chap. 29; and Nicholas Kaldor, "Speculation and Economic Stability," in his *Essays on Economic Stability and Growth*, 2d ed. (Holmes and Meier, 1980), pp. 19–58. See also Hendrik S. Houthakker, "Systematic and Random Elements in Short-Term Price Movements," *American Economic Review*, vol. 51 (May 1961, *Papers and Proceedings, 1960*), pp. 169–72.

13. Just as the inelastic supply and demand responses in the commodity markets induce volatile price fluctuations, so other types of "stickiness," like the slowness of the current account to adjust or the slowness of the price level to respond to a monetary disturbance, help to explain exchange-rate volatility. See, for example, Rudiger Dornbusch, "Expectations and Exchange Rate Dynamics," *Journal of Political Economy*, vol. 84 (December 1976), pp. 1161–76; and Niehans Jurg, "Exchange Rate Dynamics with Stock/Flow Interaction," *Journal of Political Economy*, vol. 85 (December 1977), pp. 1245–57.

THE ROLE OF PRIMARY COMMODITIES 35

keep inventories just as householders keep groceries in the pantry to save on shopping trips and to be prepared for unexpected guests. When the probability of supply shortfalls increases, the precautionary demand for inventories will increase. Supply and demand interact to make prices extremely volatile. For example, when the supply of oil is reduced because of an embargo, the ex ante demand for oil inventories will rise. Thus the short-run effect of the inward shift in the supply curve may well be an outward shift in the demand curve—both of which drive prices upward. Conversely, inventory demand will decline when the probability of interruptions in supplies is lowered. The response of users to supply changes in managing their inventories thus contributes to the short-run instability of commodity market prices. Hoarding by users may be as important as speculation by investors. That supply may affect inventory demand also makes it difficult to distinguish demand and supply schedules.

Prices in the 1970s

The behavior of commodity prices in the 1970s awakened interest in the issues surrounding commodity price cycles. Between 1970 and its peak in the fourth quarter of 1974, the UN primary commodity price index rose by 140 percent. Prices declined sharply during the global recession of 1975; but the recovery from that recession set in motion a second, smaller cycle that saw commodity prices rising through mid-1977 and then declining to about 4 percent below their 1975 levels by the end of 1978. In 1979, however, the index rose by 29 percent in a boom that, though considerably smaller than that of 1972–74, nonetheless exceeded the increase of the 1950–51 Korean War period (see figure 2-3).

Much of the price rise over the decade as a whole can be attributed to the general inflationary environment; export prices of manufactured goods rose by 82 percent in the first half of the decade and 43 percent between 1975 and 1979. But even the relative prices of primary commodities (compared with manufactured goods) rose by 91 percent between 1970 and 1979, and the cyclical variability remains.

While differing somewhat in timing and size, changes in each of the four main commodity categories contributed to the profile of the total index (see figure 2-2). In 1971 the prices of fuels and several agricultural commodities began to increase. By the end of 1972 the boom in prices

Figure 2-3. *Nominal and Relative Prices of Primary Commodities, 1950–79*

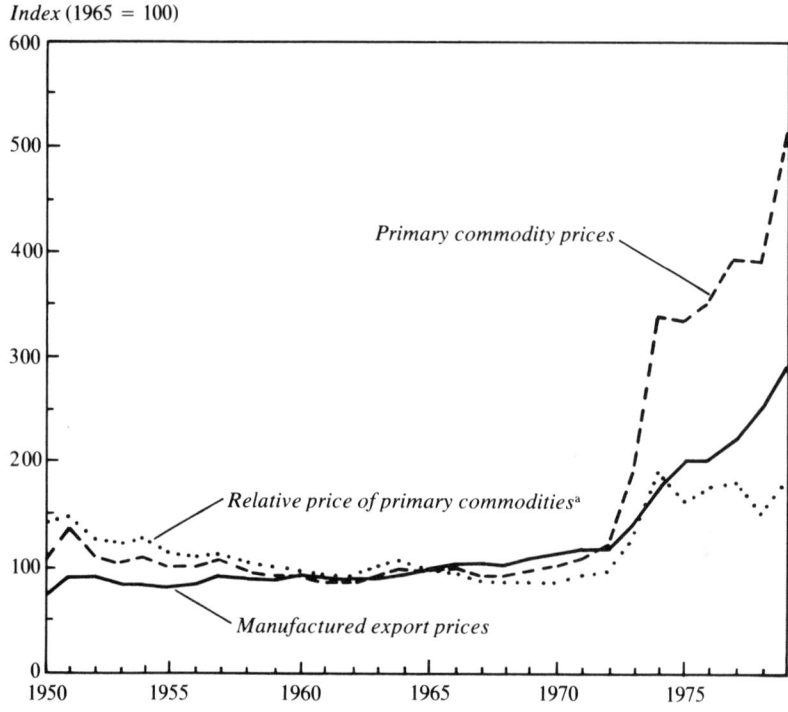

Sources: Same as figure 2-2.
a. See note a, figure 2-1.

was evident for almost all commodities except nonferrous metals, which took off only in 1973. The peak in the prices for agricultural materials and food came in the first quarter of 1974. Metals followed early in the second quarter. A second peak in food prices (due to sugar, fat, and grain prices) occurred in late 1974. By the first quarter of 1975, relative prices for all four categories were considerably below their 1974 highs.

In most commodity markets the second cycle (from 1975 to 1978) was more normal. Beverage prices were an exception, however, since they more than trebled from 1975 to 1977 because of the damage inflicted on Brazilian coffee production by the 1975 frost. Overall, primary commodity prices fell somewhat behind in 1978, but they rebounded sharply in 1979. The boom from the third quarter of 1978 to the end of 1979 was centered in minerals (up 74 percent) and nonferrous metals markets (up

38 percent). At the end of the second half of the decade, nominal primary commodity prices were 80 percent higher than in 1975. By contrast, manufactured goods prices were up about 50 percent.

On the average, the level of relative commodity prices in the second half of the 1970s was higher than it had been for a century. This reinforced the view that a new era of materials scarcity and high prices had begun in which the balance of economic power had shifted from consumers to producers. Although such a shift has clearly occurred in the markets for fuels, it is more difficult to judge whether similar changes occurred in other commodity markets. At a disaggregated level the picture is mixed. For each of the component indexes the movement in the 1970s changed sharply from its postwar trend. Relative agricultural and mineral prices had declined fairly steadily since the Korean War boom, and since the early 1960s nonferrous metal prices had a slight upward trend. In the 1970s, however, food and agricultural materials were trendless. Metal prices, on the other hand, were particularly depressed in the latter part of the decade while coal and fuel prices soared to historic highs.[14] When fuel prices are excluded, the relative price of primary commodities during the 1975–79 period is almost identical to that of a century earlier.

14. We used the UN export price index for manufactured goods as our measure of international inflation. Because this index rose less rapidly before 1969 than broader measures like the OECD's GDP deflator, and more rapidly than that deflator in the 1970s, this deflation procedure tends to understate the increases in the relative price of primary commodities during the 1970s.

CHAPTER THREE

The Contribution of Primary Commodity Price Increases to Inflation

NO MAJOR industrial nation was spared the experience of high and accelerating inflation during the first half of the nineteen seventies. The rate of inflation, as measured by the rate of change in the weighted gross domestic product (GDP) deflators of countries belonging to the Organization of Economic Cooperation and Development, doubled from an annual average of 4.3 percent between 1965 and 1970 to 9.9 percent in the 1972–74 period (see table 3-1), and in 1974, for the first time in the postwar era, reached a double-digit figure, 12.1 percent.

Although all the major OECD countries experienced a worsening of inflation during the decade, there were significant differences among them. In this chapter we pay particular attention to three countries: the United States, Japan, and West Germany. The United States, which had consistently had a low rate of inflation in earlier decades, experienced, as did most countries, a sharp acceleration of inflation in 1973–74 and achieved a limited slowing of inflation after that. Japan and West Germany, on the other hand, made considerable progress toward moderating inflation in the last half of the decade. West Germany is particularly atypical in that its inflation rate surged in 1970–71 but rose only slightly during the 1973–74 period.

The pervasiveness, magnitude, and timing of the inflation startled those economists who had previously explained inflation by the degree of excess domestic aggregate demand supplemented with some measure of price expectations. In the United States, for example, the 1974 inflation rate was a particular surprise.[1] The reactions of economists

---

1. Gordon notes that the Livingston panel, a group of economists who forecast the U.S. consumer price index six months ahead, anticipated an inflation of about half (6.0 percent) the actual 11.6 increase in 1974. Robert J. Gordon, "Can the Inflation of the 1970s Be Explained?" *Brookings Papers on Economic Activity*, 1:1977, pp. 253–54 (hereafter *BPEA*).

Table 3-1. *Average Annual Percentage Change in Prices for the Ten Most Important OECD Countries, 1960–79*

Country	1960–65	1965–70	1970–72	1972–74	1974–76	1976–78	1979
Australia	2.2	3.6	7.5	14.0	14.5	8.6	8.8
Canada	1.9	4.1	4.1	12.4	10.1	6.8	10.6
France	4.3	4.5	6.0	9.4	11.6	9.3	10.4
Italy	5.5	3.5	6.7	15.1	17.4	16.7	15.2
Japan	5.1	5.1	4.7	15.4	7.0	4.3	2.6
Netherlands	4.8	5.2	9.0	8.8	10.0	5.8	3.7
Sweden	4.0	4.5	7.0	7.9	12.8	10.4	6.7
United Kingdom	3.6	4.9	8.9	10.9	20.4	12.3	14.6
United States	1.6	4.2	4.6	7.2	7.2	6.6	8.5
West Germany	3.6	3.5	6.7	6.5	5.0	3.9	3.8
OECD total	3.0	4.3	5.7	9.9	9.5	8.1	8.2

Sources: Price changes are measured by the GDP deflator from Organization for Economic Cooperation and Development, *National Accounts of OECD Countries, 1950–78*, vol. 1: *Main Aggregates* (Paris: OECD, 1980); OECD, *Main Economic Indicators* (December 1980); and OECD, *Economic Outlook*, 28 (December 1980).

were diverse. Some argued that the 1974 rise was simply a snapback to underlying inflation levels, which had been temporarily stifled by the 1971–73 wage and price controls. Some regarded the price explosion as the inevitable culmination of aggregate demand policies that had tried to reconcile claims beyond the economy's productive capacities. To others, the attempt to capture the inflationary process with stable structural coefficients had been a misguided exercise in the first place.[2] It was apparent to all that the price increases had been unusually concentrated in one relatively small sector of the international economy—primary commodity markets. The prices of most of these commodities had soared to historic highs and had changed by unprecedented amounts.[3]

2. The interpretation of the inflation surge as a snapback from controls is illustrated in Richard T. Selden, "Monetary Growth and the Long-Run Rate of Inflation," *American Economic Review*, vol. 65 (May 1975, *Papers and Proceedings, 1974*), pp. 125–28; and Robert J. Gordon, "The Impact of Aggregate Demand on Prices," *BPEA, 3:1975*, pp. 613–62. The second perspective is argued in William Fellner, "Lessons from the Failure of Demand-Management Policies: A Look at the Theoretical Foundations," *Journal of Economic Literature*, vol. 14 (March 1976), pp. 34–53. The argument against stable structural coefficients is put forth in Robert E. Lucas, Jr., "Econometric Policy Evaluation: A Critique," in Karl Brunner and Allan H. Meltzer, eds., *The Phillips Curve and Labor Markets*, Carnegie-Rochester Conference Series on Public Policy, vol. 1 (Amsterdam: North-Holland, 1976), pp. 19–46; and Michael L. Wachter, "The Changing Cyclical Responsiveness of Wage Inflation," *BPEA, 1:1976*, pp. 115–59.

3. The *Economist* index of primary commodities has been compiled for 115 years, and in no three-year period has it risen as rapidly (159 percent) as in 1971–74. See Richard N. Cooper and Robert Z. Lawrence, "The 1972–75 Commodity Boom," *BPEA, 3:1975*, p. 673.

In later chapters we consider the causes of these commodity price increases. But first it seems useful to place their consequences in an economy-wide perspective by asking how much of the acceleration in international inflation during the 1970s can be directly attributed to the commodity boom. The discussion in this chapter is relevant irrespective of what lay behind the price rise, and it can be subject to two distinct interpretations. If the rise of primary commodity prices was simply a reflection of excessive government demand-management policies and the breakdown of the international monetary system, then one can view this chapter as documenting the particular channel through which these inflationary pressures worked their way through the economy—or, to use a favorite monetarist image, as detailing the specific areas that flooded when the monetary dam broke. If, on the other hand, the rise of primary commodity prices was caused by external events, one can view the chapter as documenting the effects of those factors on the average price level.

Although some doubts have been expressed about the inflationary contribution of primary commodity prices,[4] most studies that have looked at this question within the United States have found substantial effects. Popkin, using a stage-of-process model, concluded that of the 8.2 percent increase in U.S. consumer prices from 1973 to 1974, 3.7 percentage points were due to increases in commodity prices over and above their trend rates of growth. Shoven and Nordhaus, using an input-output model, concluded that about 53 percent of the 25 percent increase in the net output–weighted wholesale price index over the period of July 1972 to July 1974 could be accounted for by increases in prices of primary commodities and imports.[5]

---

4. Harry Johnson, for example, is quoted as having said that appeals to the details of microeconomic or sectoral developments might provide satisfactory explanations for inflation of about 1 percent a year, but that the rate of the 1973–75 inflation cannot be explained by such details. "General Comments," in Lawrence B. Krause and Walter S. Salant, eds., *Worldwide Inflation: Theory and Recent Experience* (Brookings Institution, 1977), p. 60. Similarly, Gottfried Haberler concludes that "only a small part of the actual [U.S.] price rise of over 10 percent from 1973 to 1974 can be attributed to the 'special' factors, probably not more than one and a half or two percentage points." "Some Currently Suggested Explanations and Cures for Inflation," in Karl Brunner and Allan H. Meltzer, eds., *Institutional Arrangements and the Inflation Problem*, Carnegie-Rochester Conference Series on Public Policy, vol. 3 (Amsterdam: North-Holland, 1976), p. 154.

5. Joel Popkin, "Commodity Prices and the U.S. Price Level," *BPEA, 1:1974*, p. 256; and William D. Nordhaus and John B. Shoven, "A Technique for Analyzing and

This chapter extends the investigation to several countries. Price changes in international markets can be expected to have different effects on individual economies for a variety of reasons. First, while the quotations of commodity price changes are usually expressed in U.S. dollars, many countries have experienced significant changes in their exchange rates over the past decade. Thus the effect varies among countries when expressed in their own currencies. Second, differences in industrial structures among countries imply different primary commodity requirements per unit of production. The U.S. economy, for example, ranks high in its use of energy per unit of output. Third, countries vary in the extent of their reliance on foreign sources of supply, and prices in world and domestic markets may not move in unison because of quotas, transportation costs, controls, and so forth. Similarly, the international market quotations of prices are normally for spot sales, whereas often a high percentage of trade is based on long-term contracts. Fourth, the magnitude and timing of the response of domestic wage rates to changes in the cost of living differ among countries. Thus the secondary repercussions of these price shocks can vary considerably.

Finally, the actual rate of price inflation that a country experiences depends on both the magnitude of the inflationary pressures and the policies taken to combat them. Some countries followed a policy of accommodation in the mid-1970s because they judged the costs of unemployment and other domestic economic disruptions to be too great. Other countries were more willing to pursue restrictive fiscal and monetary policies to offset the inflationary pressures. Still other countries sought to minimize the net inflation impact by reducing domestic value-added taxes or changing import tariffs.

In the first section of the chapter we use the UN primary commodity price index as an indicator of commodity inflation. In the second section we use commodity price indexes of the countries themselves to provide a more accurate measure and to allow us to investigate the assumption that primary commodities trade at uniform prices worldwide.

Decomposing Inflation," in Joel Popkin, ed., *Analysis of Inflation: 1965–1974,* National Bureau of Economic Research Studies in Income and Wealth 42 (Ballinger for NBER, 1977), p. 349. Neither of these two studies included an estimate of the secondary feedback effect on domestic wage rates and other prices. The Nordhaus-Shoven study also used a broad concept of exogenous prices but excluded the prices of services from the basic measure of inflation.

An Aggregate Analysis

Most primary commodities are traded internationally. One way to measure the international effects of the commodity boom is to assume that the markets for these commodities are competitive and internationally integrated, that arbitrage assures that the dollar price of each commodity is the same worldwide, and that transactions, transportation costs, and trade barriers are insignificant.[6] Although evidence is growing that the law of one price does not hold closely for manufactured goods,[7] the law is still widely accepted as a suitable assumption for homogeneous, internationally traded, primary commodities.[8]

If we assume that the UN index of primary commodity prices in international markets accurately reflects price movements within individual economies, it can be used in a statistical regression to evaluate the role of primary commodity prices in the inflation process. Such a study was undertaken for the United Nations Conference on Trade and Development (UNCTAD).[9] The basic statistical model, which the authors of the study describe as heuristic, relates the rate of price change to changes in aggregate demand conditions, the previous year's rate of price change, and a two-year weighted average of changes in the UN primary commodity price index $(\overline{PC})$.[10] Traditional models of inflation have estimated separate equations for prices and wages: the price

---

6. Ad valorem tariffs are of course compatible with uniform percentage price changes in both domestic and foreign markets.

7. See, for example, Irving B. Kravis and Robert E. Lipsey, "Export Prices and the Transmission of Inflation," *American Economic Review*, vol. 67 (February 1977, *Papers and Proceedings, 1976*), pp. 155–63; Peter Isard, "How Far Can We Push the Law of One Price?" *American Economic Review*, vol. 67 (December 1977), pp. 942–48; and John Williamson and Geoffrey E. Wood, "The British Inflation: Indigenous or Imported?" *American Economic Review*, vol. 66 (September 1976), pp. 520–31. For evidence in favor of the law of one price, see Hans Genberg, *World Inflation and the Small Open Economy*, Economic Research Reports 17 (Stockholm: Swedish Industrial Publications, 1975), especially pp. 21–48.

8. Williamson and Wood, "British Inflation," p. 520; and Rudiger Dornbusch and Paul Krugman, "Flexible Exchange Rates in the Short Run," *BPEA, 3:1976*, p. 559.

9. United Nations Conference on Trade and Development, "Inflationary Processes in the International Economy and Their Impact on Developing Countries," Report by the Secretariat, UN Doc. TD/B/AC.18/2 (June 12, 1975), p. 22.

10. The formula used for weighting is

$$\overline{PC} = [1/(1 + 0.05\, APC)]\, PC + [1 - 1/(1 + 0.05\, APC_{-1})]\, PC_{-1},$$

where *APC* is the absolute value of the annual percent price change, *PC*. This implies that the full change in commodity prices appears within two years, but the larger the increase, the smaller the proportion of the change passed through in the first year.

equation is interpreted as a markup over unit labor and material costs that varies with demand conditions in product markets; the wage equation is assumed to be a function of unemployment and price changes.

In contrast, the UNCTAD analysis is based on a single reduced-form equation in which the wage equation is embedded in the price equation. It therefore avoids some of the statistical problems of simultaneous changes in wages and prices and errors in measuring wage rates. Annual percentage changes in prices (*POECD*) are measured by the price deflator for gross domestic product of the OECD countries. Variations in demand conditions are measured by the percent deviation between an estimated high-employment growth path for GDP and gross domestic product within the OECD economy (*D*) and annual changes in the deviation (ΔD). A dummy variable (*DUM*) was included to adjust for the effects of the Korean War and its aftermath (1952–54). The UNCTAD regression equation result was

$$POECD = -0.21D + 0.16\Delta D + 0.70POECD_{-1}$$
$$(3.8) (2.2) (6.4)$$
$$-0.56DUM + 0.11\overline{PC} + 1.89.$$
$$(6.6) (3.4) (5.2)$$
$$\overline{R}^2 = 0.81; \quad \text{Durbin-Watson} = 1.6$$

(The numbers in parentheses are *t*-statistics.)

In terms of the discussion of inflation in the previous chapter, the actual inflation rate is viewed as a combination of momentum and shocks. The momentum is embedded in the inflation rate inherited from the prior period ($POECD_{-1}$), and the shocks are measured by changes in capacity utilization and commodity prices.[11]

Although this is an extremely aggregative equation, the results are interesting. Apparently the combination of commodity price increases and the traditional excess demand variables is enough to account for the acceleration of inflation in the 1970s. The equation was fitted from data from 1952 through 1969; it was then used to simulate the period 1970–75, with the actual changes in excess demand and commodity prices.

---

11. The change in the capacity variable can be interpreted as reflecting the tendency for strong productivity growth in the early stages of a recovery to reduce costs. Alternatively, in combination with the current level of the capacity variable, it can be interpreted as simply reflecting a lagged effect of capacity utilization. That is, the term $-b_1 D + b_2 \Delta D$ is equivalent to $(b_2 - b_1)D - b_2 D_{-1}$. Note that the deviation (D) is a large positive number when unused capacity is high.

By almost all criteria the equation performs well. The coefficients are significant, have the correct signs, and have plausible orders of magnitude. The 0.11 coefficient on commodity price changes includes both the direct effect on the domestic value-added price and the secondary repercussions on domestic wage rates and other prices.[12] The coefficient on the GDP gap, which implies that a 1 percent decline in output will lower the GDP deflator by 0.16 percent, is well in line with such estimates for individual countries, and the coefficient on lagged prices, which implies that changes in the independent variables have about half their long-run effects within two years, accords with estimates of similar magnitude in the equations of other macroeconomic models.[13] The coefficients remained stable when the equation was fitted over the full 1952–75 period. Although, as might have been expected, the coefficient on the commodity term rose, it did so only by 0.015 percentage point.

The out-of-sample simulations were also impressive. The mean absolute error for 1970–75 is only 0.56 percent. Although inflation in 1972 is underpredicted (a result ascribed in the UNCTAD study to the widespread use of wage-price controls within the OECD), the inflation rates for 1973 and 1974 are predicted with errors of only 0.4 and 0.2 percentage point, respectively.

The estimated equation can be used to obtain a quantitative measure of the impact of commodity price changes. If the forecast values are computed under the assumption of no change in the index of primary commodity prices, the inflation rate within the OECD averages 4.9 percent in 1970–74 rather than 7.9 percent, the actual prediction for the period. The inflation is sustained by the effects of aggregate demand and lagged inflation rates. This period would still have been the most inflationary since 1950 without the commodity boom (assuming the same level of aggregate demand), but there would have been no acceleration of inflation within the period. A more realistic simulation allows for a continued rise in commodity prices after 1971 of 6 percent annually,

12. Data from UNCTAD indicate that the value of primary commodity consumption in the United States, the six European Community countries, the United Kingdom, and Japan was about 10 to 12 percent of those countries' GNP in the early 1970s. See UNCTAD, *Handbook on International Trade and Development Statistics, 1976,* UN Doc. TD/STAT. 6, p. 432. Insofar as these products are imported, they would not have a direct effect on the GDP deflator, which is a measure of domestic value added. Thus the large size of the commodity price coefficient must imply a substantial amount of feedback effects of prices raising wage rates that in turn increase prices.

13. The coefficient of 0.70 on the lagged price change implies that 30 percent of the full impact is felt within a year. At the end of two years, 49 percent (0.7×0.7) would remain.

which implies a constant relative price for commodities at the 1969–71 rate of overall inflation. The extraordinary surge in commodity prices above the 6 percent trend accounts for 20 percent of a predicted 7.9 percent inflation rate in 1973, and 45 percent of the 12 percent rise of prices in 1974. Thus the increase in the relative price of commodity prices is estimated to account for 80 percent of the acceleration of the general inflation between 1970–71 and 1974.

This model must be viewed warily. It involves several difficulties. First, it ignores the substantial changes in exchange rates that occurred during the period. The independent variable, the primary commodity index, is measured in dollars, but the dependent variables, the weighted GDP deflators of the OECD countries, are measured in domestic currencies. Percentage changes in an index denominated in dollars will have different effects on countries in years when they change their exchange rates. In 1973, for example, the UN index, which increased 50 percent in dollars, rose by 53.0 percent in sterling but only 25.7 percent in marks. Apparently these exchange rate effects cancel one another out upon aggregation. Second, the model assumes that the UN index accurately reflects actual commodity price changes within individual countries. The accuracy of that assumption is examined in the next section. A third and smaller point is that, insofar as the OECD countries as a whole import primary commodities from outside the area, these will not show up in the GDP deflators, which measure only domestic value added. Both the second and third problems suggest that the large primary commodity price coefficient embodies a substantial secondary effect on wage rates.[14]

We applied a similar equation formulation to more recent data for the ten most important OECD countries individually (see table 3-2). In these equations the UN price index was multiplied by each country's dollar exchange rate to express the prices in domestic currency equivalents. Again there is strong evidence that primary commodity price changes played an important role, but the differences among countries are interesting. Japan is the only country for which the coefficient on the

14. If an allowance is made for the fact that the consumer prices rose more rapidly than the value-added concept of a deflator embedded in this study, the results seem quite consistent with those reported for the United States by Popkin and Nordhaus-Shoven in their studies (see note 5). Our study also attempts to allow for secondary feedback on wage rates—a linkage excluded from the other two studies. In addition, the equation has some significant problems of estimation bias because primary commodity prices are themselves affected by demand conditions and inflation in the rest of the economy.

Table 3-2. Reduced-Form Price Equations for the Ten Most Important OECD Countries, 1961–79

Country	Independent variable						Summary statistic		
	Lagged price change	Aggregate demand ratio	Change in demand ratio	Primary commodity price change	Lagged primary commodity price change	Constant	R^2	Standard error of estimate	Durbin-Watson
Australia	0.54	37.79	2.23	0.09	0.05	2.06	0.97	1.0	2.3
	(6.6)	(2.6)	(0.2)	(5.6)	(2.7)	(4.3)			
Canada	0.65	8.60	6.25	0.10	**	1.09	0.93	1.2	2.1
	(5.8)	(0.3)	(0.2)	(5.7)		(1.7)			
France	0.67	−16.41	23.98	0.04	0.05	1.63	0.86	1.4	1.5
	(5.4)	(0.5)	(0.5)	(2.0)	(2.2)	(2.2)			
Italy	0.84	66.44	1.77	0.05	0.02	1.06	0.96	1.5	2.6
	(10.2)	(2.7)	(0.1)	(2.7)	(1.0)	(1.6)			
Japan	−0.16	13.69	−3.41	0.12	0.09	5.66	0.81	2.0	1.6
	(0.5)	(0.9)	(0.2)	(5.0)	(1.6)	(2.9)			
Netherlands	0.42	9.68	34.84	**	0.08	3.37	0.74	1.5	2.0
	(2.5)	(0.4)	(1.3)		(2.7)	(3.2)			
Sweden	0.66	58.94	−58.56	0.01	0.07	1.73	0.93	1.0	1.9
	(8.5)	(2.4)	(3.1)	(0.8)	(5.7)	(3.3)			
United Kingdom	0.60	72.60	−89.73	−0.02	0.14	2.38	0.89	2.5	1.7
	(4.6)	(0.7)	(1.4)	(0.4)	(4.3)	(2.5)			
United States	0.74	43.87	−14.82	0.02	0.04	0.94	0.93	0.8	1.9
	(8.0)	(3.9)	(1.3)	(1.5)	(3.2)	(2.3)			
West Germany	0.29	58.64	−9.14	−0.002	0.05	2.94	0.81	0.9	1.4
	(2.0)	(4.5)	(0.6)	(0.2)	(3.2)	(4.5)			
OECD total	0.73	59.68	−41.64	0.03	0.02	1.24	0.97	0.6	2.2
	(9.4)	(2.8)	(2.2)	(2.7)	(2.0)	(3.7)			

Sources: The annual percentage change in the GDP price deflator is computed from Organization for Economic Cooperation and Development, *National Accounts of OECD Countries, 1950–78*, vol. 1: *Main Aggregates*; and OECD, *Main Economic Indicators* (December 1980). The index of primary commodity prices is from United Nations, *Monthly Bulletin of Statistics*, various issues. The aggregate demand is measured as a ratio of GDP to a quadratic exponential time trend for GDP in 1975 prices. The total of all ten countries is constructed by using 1975 GDP weights. The numbers in parentheses are *t*-statistics.
* Less than 0.05.
** Less than 0.005.

lagged inflation rate is not significant. But the magnitude of the coefficient is also relatively small for West Germany and largest for the United States. This result seems to accord well with studies that emphasize the greater inertia of inflation in the United States, which stems from long-term wage contracts negotiated at a more disaggregated level of the industry or firm. Second, the excess demand variables are significant for only half the countries. This was, however, a far better result than could be obtained from using an unemployment rate to measure demand pressures. The weak role for demand variables is in accord with the findings of other studies.[15] Third, the combination of current and lagged commodity prices was significant in all countries, but the timing of the effect varied considerably.

The contrasts are highlighted by comparing the results for several economies. West Germany has relatively small problems with the carry-over of inflation from previous periods; the inflation rate is sensitive to aggregate demand, and the lag is shorter than in the United States. In addition, primary commodity price fluctuations have less effect on West Germany than on any other country. Since the German revaluation against the dollar between 1972 and 1974 exceeded that of the other OECD countries, the size of the price shock itself was also smaller. West Germany was therefore ideally situated to achieve a low inflation rate over the last half of the decade, and demand-management policies could be expected to be an effective way to reach that goal. On the other hand, this equation formulation cannot explain the surge of inflation in West Germany in 1970–71.

Japanese inflation does not have a high degree of inertia. Commodity prices have a very large impact, and aggregate demand seems to be insignificant. The equation formulation, however, fits only part of the Japanese experience—the sharp burst of price increases in 1973–74. Japan did not have a similar rise of domestic prices in 1979. In fact, the rate of rise in the domestic value-added deflator appears to have slowed.

For the United States all the coefficients show a high degree of statistical significance. The United States has the highest degree of wage inertia as measured by the lagged inflation-rate term, and variations in demand conditions have a significant effect. The coefficient on primary commodities sums to 0.06 over a two-year period.

15. See, for example, George Perry, "Determinants of Wage Inflation Around the World," *BPEA, 2:1975*, pp. 403–35; and Jeffrey Sachs, "Wages, Profits, and Macroeconomic Adjustment: A Comparative Study," *BPEA, 2:1979*, pp. 307–11.

Overall, the equations are able to track the pattern of inflation during the 1970s. The equations for the United States and for the total OECD countries have no major errors in individual years and do surprisingly well in the years of great change in commodity prices (1973–74 and 1979). But like the large overprediction of the Japanese inflation in 1979, the sharp rise within the United Kingdom is unexplained, and smaller but significant errors of underprediction exist for Canada and France.[16] The equation formulation also underestimates the worsening of inflation within West Germany and the Netherlands in the early part of the decade. The errors in predicting inflation rates of individual countries seem to cancel out in aggregation across countries instead of being cumulative. Finally, the coefficients on primary commodity prices are statistically significant over a two-year period, though there are substantial differences in timing.

A Disaggregated View

Price indexes for internationally traded commodities, such as the UN index, provide a useful approximation of the magnitude of raw material price increases. But a single world index does not reflect the important differences in the impact on specific countries. These differences among countries in their exposure to primary commodity price fluctuations can be illustrated by a closer examination of the inflation in the three principal industrial countries: the United States, Japan, and West Germany. The United States has a high degree of self-sufficiency in raw materials. Japan represents the opposite extreme, being highly dependent on foreign sources. West Germany also imports much of its primary commodity needs, but the effect of food price increases was buffered by the common agricultural policies of the European Community and the substantial upward revaluation of its currency during the 1970s.

In this section, domestic price indexes are used to measure raw material price changes. For each country the relative importance of raw materials in final demand is determined from available input-output tables. The amount of domestically produced and imported raw materials is measured directly. An imputation for the raw material component of imports of intermediate and finished goods is made by assuming that the

16. The error for the United Kingdom should not be a surprise, since no account is taken of the sharp rise in value-added taxes in 1979.

Table 3-3. *Percentage Share of Raw Materials in Final Demand, United States, Japan, and West Germany, 1970*[a]

Raw material	United States[b] Consumption expenditures	Final demand	Japan	West Germany
Livestock and livestock products	4.9	2.7	⎫ 8.3	⎫ 9.3
Other agricultural products	3.5	2.0	⎭	⎪
Forestry and fisheries	0.3	0.6	2.7	⎭
Iron ores	0.1	0.2	0.5	0.3
Nonferrous metal ores	0.1	0.3	0.5	0.2
Coal mining	0.3	0.3	0.6	1.3
Petroleum and natural gas	2.2	2.2	1.3	1.2
Stone and clay quarrying	0.1	0.3	⎫ 1.1	⎫ 0.4
Other nonmetallic minerals	0.1	0.2	⎭	⎭
Total	11.6	8.8	15.0	12.7

Sources: See appendix A.
a. Final demand is defined as GDP or GNP (United States) plus imports.
b. Calculated with data for 1967, as explained in appendix A.

share is the same as for domestically produced goods. Where possible, the price indexes for raw materials reflect average transaction prices rather than spot market quotations. In addition, these raw material price changes are compared with prices of final demand (GDP or GNP plus imports) rather than to the more common value-added deflator, to measure the price actually paid by purchasers of the country's output.[17]

The distribution of primary commodity requirements for each of the three countries is shown in table 3-3. Even though the United States is a major exporter of agricultural products, it has the lowest share of output attributable to raw materials of the three countries. In part, this reflects the relatively lower share of all raw materials except fuels in the United States' structure of demand. But, in addition, the ratio reflects the lower relative prices for domestic raw materials in the United States. Furthermore, transportation costs are not included in the valuation of domestic materials production, which dominates the U.S. supply, whereas they are included in the valuation of imported materials.

17. A fuller explanation of the calculations for each country is given in appendix A. Raw material requirements per unit of final demand were assumed constant in real terms for all years. The final demand price index is that for GDP or GNP plus imports and thus reflects the price of goods and services sold in or by the individual country. The U.S. estimates are drawn from a special Commerce Department study of raw materials, but the total amount of raw material requirements is similar to the amount estimated from the input-output table.

The extent to which agricultural products and fuels dominate the raw material requirements of all three countries is also of interest. Other mineral requirements range from 1 percent of final demand in the United States and West Germany to 2 percent in Japan. For all three countries, about 90 percent of the requirements for raw materials could be accounted for directly. The other 10 percent, which represent the estimated raw material component of other imports, were distributed proportionately.

That Japan is more dependent on world markets for basic commodities is evident, for one-third of the raw materials used within Japan are imported (1970 price structure), as against 15 percent for the United States. Over 80 percent of crude fuels are obtained from foreign sources. Since these imported materials are presumably valued at world market prices plus transportation costs, the overstatement of Japan's relative intensity in the use of raw materials is likely to be concentrated in the agricultural component, where high-cost domestic production is significant.

Total raw material requirements per unit of final demand in West Germany (12.7 percent) lie midway between those in the United States and Japan. Again, the higher share of agricultural materials relative to the United States is caused by higher prices for domestic farm products and those imported from other countries in the European Community. In addition, West Germany depends less on petroleum than does the United States, because of lower overall energy requirements and greater reliance on coal. About one-half of the commodities used in their raw form within West Germany were imported in 1970.

United States

The impact on U.S. final demand prices anticipated from a full dollar-for-dollar pass-through of primary commodity price increases from 1971 through 1979 is shown in table 3-4. The unprecedented magnitude of the increases in the prices of raw materials is clearly evident from the 69 percent rise in the weighted average price between 1972 and 1974. This increase is, however, less than half as large as the increase shown in the UN index of world raw material prices discussed earlier (171 percent).

The lower estimated increase in raw material prices in the United States reflects two factors. First, the composite index for the United States has a much greater weight on livestock products than does the

Table 3-4. *Contribution of Primary Commodity Prices to Inflation, by Major Component, United States, 1971–79*
Percent

Year	Component				Final demand[a]
	Agriculture	Energy	Other	Total	
	Change in price index				
1971	3.1	7.5	2.4	4.2	5.1
1972	11.3	1.6	9.2	8.1	4.3
1973	41.8	14.1	15.6	29.2	6.6
1974	5.9	97.2	20.1	30.6	12.0
1975	−3.0	17.9	10.1	6.7	9.3
1976	0.6	8.2	11.1	5.4	5.3
1977	−1.8	14.3	9.4	6.8	6.3
1978	15.8	7.9	8.4	11.0	7.3
1979	14.9	34.6	16.1	23.6	9.5
	Contribution to final demand price[b]				
1971	0.1	0.2	0.0	0.4	5.1
1972	0.5	0.0	0.1	0.7	4.3
1973	2.0	0.3	0.3	2.6	6.6
1974	0.4	2.5	0.4	3.3	12.0
1975	−0.2	0.8	0.2	0.8	9.3
1976	0.0	0.4	0.2	0.6	5.3
1977	−0.1	0.7	0.2	0.8	6.3
1978	0.7	0.4	0.2	1.3	7.3
1979	0.7	1.9	0.3	3.0	9.5

Source: Authors' calculations, as described in appendix A.
a. GNP plus imports.
b. Contribution equals the percentage change in the price of the component multiplied by its relative share in final demand in the base period. The relative share is from table 3-3.

UN index. Although livestock prices rose sharply in 1973, they actually declined in 1974, whereas the food component of the UN index continued to rise. Thus individual domestic agricultural prices did move in line with world prices, but the emphasis on crops in the UN index overstates the impact on the U.S. domestic price level.

Controls on petroleum and natural gas prices were the second main factor that contributed to a lower rate of price increase in the United States than in other countries in the middle of the decade. Between 1972 and 1975 domestically produced petroleum costs to refiners increased by about 125 percent, whereas petroleum prices in international markets increased fourfold. At the end of the decade, domestic prices were still limited to two-thirds of the cost of imports. Interstate natural gas prices were also subject to controls, and effective price increases for both coal and natural gas were further moderated by the existence of long-term contracts.

The estimated impact on final demand prices shown in table 3-4 does not allow for lags in the pass-through of increases in the prices of raw materials. Nor does it include any induced effect of higher prices leading to adjustments in wages and thus a secondary round of further price increases. But during the 1972–74 period the direct effects of higher raw material prices represent nearly one-third of the rise in final demand prices, compared with an average share in demand of 9 percent.[18] Again in 1979 the contribution of commodity prices equals nearly one-third of the overall inflation rate. In terms of fluctuations in inflation, commodities directly accounted for about one-third of the surge in 1972–74, 40 percent of the deceleration from 1974 through 1976, and two-thirds of the acceleration between 1977 and 1979. In each of these episodes, the effect on consumer goods was more pronounced than on total final demand.

The contribution of individual components of the raw material group is also of interest. Agricultural and energy prices dominate the movements in the index. Other raw material prices rose by 39 percent over the two-year period 1973–74, yet they added relatively little to overall inflation—averaging 0.3 percentage point annually. Agricultural prices were important in 1973, with a 2.0 percentage point contribution; and energy prices added 2.5 percentage points in 1974, and 1.9 percentage points in 1979.

Japan

The greater importance of raw materials to the Japanese economy would imply that the explosion of raw material prices in 1973–75 would have greater inflationary effects in Japan than in the United States. But several factors operated to moderate the impact of higher world market prices. First, the dollar value of the Japanese yen appreciated by 28 percent, relative to the dollar, between 1971 and 1973. Second, the sharp rise in world agricultural prices in 1972–73 had less effect on the level of domestically produced products within Japan, since the prices of those

18. The share of raw materials in final demand is adjusted in the years after 1967 for differential rates of price increase for raw materials and final demand. Thus, though the share is assumed constant in real terms, the nominal dollar share declines to 8.5 percent in 1971 and then rises to 14.2 percent in 1976. Most statistical studies of pricing behavior indicate that materials costs are largely passed through within four to six quarters. See, for example, Popkin, "Commodity Prices and the U.S. Price Level," pp. 249–59.

Table 3-5. *Contribution of Primary Commodity Prices to Inflation, by Major Component, Japan, 1971–79*
Percent

Year	Component				Final demand[a]
	Agriculture	Energy	Other	Total	
	Change in price index				
1971	3.0	13.2	−3.5	2.6	4.3
1972	2.3	−1.2	−2.5	0.7	3.9
1973	17.9	8.7	25.9	18.4	11.3
1974	15.6	192.9	26.8	39.8	23.7
1975	18.1	20.2	−4.5	13.8	8.3
1976	5.7	8.3	4.2	6.1	5.3
1977	3.3	−3.2	−0.8	0.8	4.5
1978	−2.8	−18.0	−5.7	−7.3	2.5
1979	2.1	29.7	28.3	13.3	3.2
	Contribution to final demand price[b]				
1971	0.3	0.2	−0.1	0.4	4.3
1972	0.2	0.0	−0.1	0.1	3.9
1973	1.5	0.2	0.8	2.5	11.3
1974	1.4	3.3	0.9	5.6	23.7
1975	1.5	0.8	−0.2	2.2	8.3
1976	0.5	0.4	0.1	1.0	5.3
1977	0.3	−0.1	0.0	0.1	4.5
1978	−0.3	−0.8	−0.2	−1.2	2.5
1979	0.2	1.0	0.8	2.0	3.2

Source: Authors' calculations, as described in appendix A.
a. GDP plus imports.
b. Contribution equals the percentage change in the price of the component multiplied by its relative share in final demand in the base period. The relative share is from table 3-3.

goods, which account for 80 percent of Japanese agricultural consumption, already exceeded world market prices. Whereas in 1973 raw material prices rose 29 percent in the United States, they rose only 18 percent in Japan (see table 3-5). But since this slower rate of increase was combined with a larger role for raw materials, the impact on final demand prices in Japan was 2.5 percentage points, almost the same as in the United States.

The raw material inflation, however, hit Japan hard in 1974, when world oil prices rose by over 300 percent. Lacking domestic sources, Japan was unable to moderate the immediate impact by holding down domestic prices as was done in the United States. The pressure on prices was also heightened by a 7 percent decline in the value of the yen. As indicated in table 3-5, the raw material inflation greatly worsened in 1974;

and, for Japan, it was largely due to petroleum prices rather than to a mixture of food and fuels, as in the United States.

For the three-year period 1972–75, raw material prices accounted directly for about 20 percent of the inflation of final demand prices. This is somewhat less than the overall contribution of raw material prices to the inflation in the United States. Raw materials did not play as dominant a role in the Japanese inflation, since much of the rise in final demand prices preceded the increase in raw material prices. In particular, the acceleration of the inflation rate to 11.3 percent in 1973 is far greater than could be accounted for by the rise of raw material prices, even if a generous allowance for secondary effects on wages were made.

The pattern of commodity price increases in the latter half of the decade was also quite different for Japan than for the United States. The strong appreciation of the yen in 1977 and 1978 was largely responsible for the decline of 7 percent in the cost of raw materials in 1978. On the other hand, the reversal and decline in the exchange rate in 1979 coincided with sharply higher oil price increases, and raw material prices rose by 13 percent. Still, the rise in those prices in 1979 was less than that experienced by the United States.

West Germany

The composition of raw material consumption in West Germany, together with a sharp revaluation of the mark, limited the impact of the 1972–74 rise in raw material prices (table 3-6). The 36 percent rise in those prices was slightly more than half the increase experienced by Japan and the United States. Much of this difference can be attributed to the 23 percent increase in the value of the mark relative to the dollar between 1972 and 1974 (the yen appreciated only 4 percent). But also agricultural prices within the European Community rose far less than in world markets. This difference was particularly evident in 1973, before the oil price increase, when raw material prices rose by 11 percent in West Germany and 29 percent in the United States. In prior years domestic agricultural prices in Germany were maintained above the world level by a variable levy on imports equal to the difference between the domestic target price and world prices. As world prices moved up to those of the European Community in 1972–73, the import levy was reduced, and when world prices for cereals ultimately moved above those of the Community, the agricultural commission switched to a tax on exports rather than imports.

Table 3-6. *Contribution of Primary Commodity Prices to Inflation, by Major Component, West Germany, 1971–79*
Percent

Year	Component				Final demand[a]
	Agriculture	Energy	Other	Total	
	Change in price index				
1971	-1.2	13.5	0.6	1.8	6.6
1972	8.7	0.4	-2.2	6.2	4.7
1973	12.2	8.1	7.7	11.1	6.6
1974	2.4	94.3	17.8	22.0	9.3
1975	-0.9	11.6	0.8	3.3	5.6
1976	13.4	38.2	1.9	10.9	3.5
1977	9.1	0.3	-3.7	5.4	3.3
1978	-7.4	-4.4	-6.7	-6.4	2.6
1979	1.0	14.1	7.6	5.7	4.3
	Contribution to final demand price[b]				
1971	-0.1	0.3	0.0	0.2	6.6
1972	0.8	0.0	0.0	0.7	4.7
1973	1.1	0.2	0.1	1.4	6.6
1974	0.2	2.4	0.1	2.8	9.3
1975	-0.1	0.5	0.0	0.5	5.6
1976	1.1	0.4	0.0	1.5	3.5
1977	0.8	0.0	0.0	0.8	3.3
1978	-0.7	-0.2	-0.1	-1.0	2.6
1979	0.1	0.6	0.1	0.8	4.3

Source: Authors' calculations, as described in appendix A.
a. GDP plus imports.
b. Contribution equals the percentage change in the price of the component multiplied by its relative share in final demand in the base period. The relative share is from table 3-3.

Similarly, the impact of the OPEC price increase was also moderated by West Germany's reliance on high-priced domestic coal. Before 1974 coal prices were held at artificially high levels, with heavy taxes on imported coal and petroleum. After the oil shock, therefore, the price of coal did not rise in step with that of petroleum: crude petroleum prices rose 190 percent between 1972 and 1974, whereas coal prices rose only 35 percent. Thus, in domestic currency terms, the average price increase for fuels was limited to 110 percent, as against 218 percent in Japan and 125 percent in the United States.

The more modest rate of commodity price inflation is reflected in a much lower rate of overall inflation within West Germany than in other countries. The difference is particularly marked in a comparison with Japan, where raw materials have a larger relative importance and showed a greater increase in their average price. In West Germany the exogenous shock to final demand prices over the 1972–75 period was 4.7 percentage points; in Japan it was 10.6 percentage points.

The direct impact of higher raw material prices represented about 20 percent of the rise in final demand prices in West Germany over the three-year period—about the same as in both the United States and Japan. On the other hand, if the comparison is limited to the acceleration of the inflation rate between 1972 and its peak in 1974, the direct effect of the commodity inflation amounted to about one-half the total rise in final demand prices.

The continued strong appreciation of the deutsche mark over the second half of the decade sharply limited the impact of primary commodity price increases. A poor crop pushed up food prices in 1976, but import prices declined sharply in 1978, and the rise in food and energy prices in 1979 was less than half of that experienced by the United States. Overall, the rise in primary commodity prices in West Germany was limited to 16 percent between 1975 and 1979, compared with 54 percent in the United States and 12 percent in Japan.

Qualifications

The above measures of the contribution of primary commodity prices to the accelerating inflation of the 1970s ignore two issues. First, if wage rates are very sensitive to changes in the cost of living, the rise in domestic wages, and thus prices, will amplify the effect of the price shocks on the overall price level. So the commodity price shocks should be charged with an additional responsibility for the rise of inflation. Second, since much of the difference in primary commodity price changes among these countries reflected divergent movements of exchange rates, the cause of the exchange-rate adjustments is critical to the interpretation of the events.

THE ROLE OF DOMESTIC WAGE RATES. The secondary effect of price shocks on the overall inflation rate through their impact on domestic wage rates continues to be a controversial subject. Although it is generally agreed that higher prices exert an upward effect on wage rates, the empirical estimates vary greatly. One difficulty has been the lack of structural stability in the empirical models. In regard to the United States, empirical investigators seem to find a continual need to augment their estimates with the passage of time and the addition of new observations. This problem is compounded when the studies are extended to other industrial countries. In particular, empirical formulations that fit the U.S. experience perform poorly when extended to West Germany or Japanese inflation. Perry found that import prices and the GDP deflator affected wage behavior in West Germany, but that prices had no such effect in Japan. That result for West Germany was supported in a recent study by Sachs.[19] But in both studies the basic statistical relationship explained a far smaller proportion of wage inflation in West Germany and Japan than in the United States.

Labor market institutions in West Germany and Japan differ markedly from those in the United States. Long-term contracts do not extend from one year to the next, there are no formal cost-of-living escalator provisions, and bargaining is far more centralized than in the United States. Also, the government and its economic policies play a more prominent role in the wage determination process. Negotiations over wages are likely to focus on a relatively short time horizon and on the problems of the moment rather than on longer term expectations. As a reflection of the shorter term of contracts, average annual wage-rate changes show greater variability in both Japan and West Germany than in the United States.

On the basis of the currently available studies, we conclude that the secondary effect of commodity price shocks on wages is a significant part of the inflation process in the United States. The initial effect is small—about 10 to 30 percent of the rise in prices—since it is limited primarily to workers with formal cost-of-living clauses in their contracts, but it increases over time as other wage rates adjust to the change in the relative wage situation. There is some evidence that price inflation affects wage behavior in West Germany, but because of the flexibility of the wage determination process and its greater sensitivity to demand-management policies, there is less of a conflict between the goals for inflation and unemployment than in the United States. The evidence that prices have cost-of-living effect on wage rates is weaker for Japan. Thus the institutional arrangements for wage determination imply that commodity price disturbances create a more serious problem for anti-inflation policy in the United States than in either West Germany or Japan. In addition, a comparison of the 1973–74 experience with that of 1979–80 shows less response of domestic inflation to external shocks in

---

19. Perry, "Determinants of Wage Inflation," pp. 403–35; and Sachs, "Wages, Profits, and Macroeconomic Adjustment," pp. 269–319.

the second episode—particularly for Japan. This suggests that domestic economic agents have learned that they cannot all be compensated for changes in the external terms of trade.

THE ROLE OF EXCHANGE RATES. Much of the difference in commodity price trends among the countries, particularly after 1975, is associated with the improvements of the Japanese and West German exchange rates relative to the dollar: 63 percent for Japan and 99 percent for Germany between 1970 and 1979.

If we assume that the movements in exchange rates were simply a reflection of differences in relative inflation rates among countries, the differences in raw material price increases could be the result of rather than the cause of differences in domestic inflation rates. The failure to control inflation within the United States led to a fall in the exchange rate and a relative increase in the costs of imported raw materials.

If we also assume that primary commodities trade at a uniform world price, adjusted for exchange rates (contrary to the argument of the previous section), the raw material price increases for Japan and West Germany could be adjusted for the full amount of the change in exchange rates relative to the dollar. Such a computation would raise the increase in costs for Japan from 118 percent to 256 percent over the decade and for West Germany from 75 percent to 248 percent. For both countries this dollar-equivalent increase is slightly larger than the increase for the United States. On this basis, primary commodity price changes were no greater inflation problem for the United States than for Japan and West Germany, and the larger domestic price rise for these commodities in the United States simply reflects its failure to deal as well with inflation as did the other two countries.

Our two assumptions, however, do not hold up: differences in domestic inflation rates do not account for all the change in the exchange rates, and primary commodities are not traded at a uniform world price.

With respect to the first issue, differential movements in domestic inflation rates (purchasing power parity) account for 12 percentage points of the 99 percent appreciation in the West German exchange rate, and inflation in Japan (measured by the GDP deflator) actually exceeded that of the United States by 8 percentage points between 1970 and 1979. Therefore, differing degrees of success in controlling domestic inflation would seem to be a minor cause of the divergent exchange-rate movements.

As for the second issue, other factors contributed to different raw

CONTRIBUTION OF COMMODITY PRICE INCREASES 59

material price increases in the three countries. In particular, governmental policies often operated to protect domestic producers. The assumption of a single price is possible only for commodities that are not produced in the industrial countries and that must be bought from a third party. But even in the case of energy prices, controls on domestic oil and gas in the United States and the protectionist coal policy of West Germany contributed to substantial differences in relative prices.

Examples of governmental barriers to price equalization are most evident within agriculture. The United States sets a minimum support price for many grains and maintains a quota for beef imports. The variable import levies of the Common Agricultural Policy in Europe were discussed earlier; but even within the European Community, agricultural trade takes place at "green exchange rates," which can differ sharply from those used to exchange other commodities. In August 1973, for example, agricultural prices in West Germany and Italy differed by over 40 percent, and in West Germany and the United Kingdom they differed by 31 percent.[20] In the early 1970s rice prices paid to producers were reported to be 30.7 cents per kilogram in Japan, 18.4 cents in South Korea, and 11.7 cents in Taiwan.[21]

A more structured illustration of the divergence of prices is provided by comparing domestic price changes for eighteen basic commodities in the United States, West Germany, and Japan over the period 1952–75. These commodities constitute 59 percent of the trade-weighted UN index of primary commodity prices. After adjustment for exchange rates, price changes in the United States were correlated with those in West Germany and Japan, and price changes in Japan with those in West Germany. Thus, after adjusting for a few missing price indexes, we obtained forty-eight pairings of data on annual price changes that were correlated with one another in the relationship

$$\Delta P_{ij} = a + b\Delta p_{ik},$$

where Δp_{ij} is the change in the price of the ith commodity in the jth country. If the two price series reflected common market factors, one would expect the coefficient, b, to equal 1.0. In thirty-four of the cases

20. Tim Josling and Simon Harris, "Europe's Green Money," *Three Banks Review*, no. 109 (March 1976), p. 61.
21. C. Peter Timmer and Walter P. Falcon, "The Political Economy of Rice Production and Trade in Asia," in Lloyd G. Reynolds, ed., *Agriculture in Development Theory* (Yale University Press, 1975), p. 376.

the assumption that *b* equals 1 could be rejected at a 95 percent confidence level. The greatest evidence of a single price seems to exist in those cases, such as tin and cocoa, where domestic production is absent. But the general impression is that considerable market fragmentation exists.

Conclusions

Although primary commodity price increases were a strong inflationary force in all three countries, the magnitude and timing of the primary commodity price increases and their effect on domestic inflation rates differed considerably. The UN index of primary commodity export prices rose 225 percent between 1970 and 1975, but the increases ranged from 51 percent for West Germany to 95 percent for Japan and 103 percent for the United States. In part, the differences reflected exchange-rate adjustments and differences in the mix of raw material requirements. But also individual product prices rose at quite different rates within the three economies. West Germany was largely insulated from the worldwide rise in food prices in late 1972, because of its membership in the Common Agricultural Policy. Likewise, in Japan a program to support agricultural prices above world market levels limited the impact of the world food shortage to the imported component of agricultural products.

In 1973, because of its greater exposure to world price fluctuations in agricultural products, the United States suffered the largest increase in primary commodity inflation. The average increase of 29 percent in primary commodity prices was far above the 18 and 11 percent increases experienced by Japan and West Germany

But the situation was sharply reversed when world petroleum prices soared in late 1973. Both West Germany and Japan import nearly all their petroleum, whereas at that time the United States produced over half its needs domestically and relied heavily on other energy sources. By limiting the impact of the world price increase on domestic prices through controls on petroleum and natural gas, the United States experienced a far smaller rise in fuel costs than did Japan. In West Germany the impact was moderated by the limited increases in the price of coal. Thus, for both Japan and West Germany, the commodity price inflation was dominated by the enormous rise in world petroleum prices in 1974, but its effect was far more severe for Japan. For the United States, food and fuel were of roughly equal importance.

The effect of energy price increases on the U.S. inflation rate in 1979 was comparable in magnitude to the shocks of 1973 and 1974, since both domestic and imported oil prices increased sharply. Oil prices also rose in West Germany and Japan, but to a lesser extent. A 9.8 percent appreciation of the deutsche mark explains part of the difference, but the move away from price controls in the United States was an important factor. In fact, the increase in crude fuel prices understates the impact on retail prices because the margins of domestic refiners and distributors widened sharply in the face of gasoline shortages.

Over the decade as a whole, raw material price increases were a much greater problem for the United States than for West Germany and Japan. Between 1970 and 1979 the U.S. crude material index rose 213 percent and contributed 21 percentage points to final demand prices. Within Japan, raw material prices rose 188 percent and added 17 points of inflation. For West Germany, the corresponding figures were 75 percent and 9.5 percentage points.

Finally, for all three countries, it is evident that raw materials other than food and energy constitute a relatively minor inflation threat. Even though their prices fluctuate sharply, such commodities make up a small share of total output. Since agricultural prices in Japan and West Germany are not determined by world markets, inflation shocks in those countries are dominated by energy prices. But because oil is largely imported and its world price is set in dollars, exchange-rate changes are also important to West Germany and Japan. On the other hand, the United States, which relies more on domestic raw material supplies, is less concerned about exchange-rate changes but, as the world's principal grain exporter, is more vulnerable to disruptions in agricultural markets.

CHAPTER FOUR

Sources of Commodity Price Fluctuations

THE EFFECTS on inflation in industrial countries of fluctuations in primary commodity prices were examined in the last chapter. This chapter focuses on the causes of the extreme volatility of these prices during the 1970s. The various explanations for this volatility differ sharply in their implications for the probability of a recurrence and the lessons for future policy. Here we distinguish four competing explanations.

The first emphasizes general factors. Primary commodity prices are viewed as an indicator of aggregate demand conditions. Since they constitute the main part of the flexible-price sector of the economy, price changes in these markets are the counterpart of variations in order backlogs and delivery lags in fixed-price markets. From this perspective the surge of commodity price increases in 1972–74 were the result of a synchronized and excessive growth of aggregate demand in the principal consuming nations and did not constitute a special problem in and of themselves.

Alternatively, students of the individual markets tend to tell more specialized stories, involving supply disruptions (crop failures, strikes, and political turmoil in producing countries), long lags in the response of new supply to the cyclical ebb and flow of economic incentives to expand capacity, and the role of government policies in restricting production. Under this interpretation the price increases of 1972–74 resulted from an unusual combination of several events: natural disasters, the end of an extended era of excess capacity and depressed prices, and a series of government actions to reduce production and reserves.

A somewhat more aggregative supply-side interpretation is put forth by those observers who saw the rise in relative prices as evidence of a long-term trend toward exhaustion of natural resources. Such fears about the adequacy of resources can be traced back at least to the time of Malthus, but those concerns are invariably heightened in each episode of sharp increases in commodity prices. Whereas Malthus emphasized the pressure of a growing population on food supplies, the current concern is with the pressure that industrial growth places on the supply of energy and minerals.[1]

The fourth explanation emphasizes the demand for commodities as an asset in investment portfolios—particularly as a hedge against inflation and sharply changing relative values of national currencies. Here an important role is given to speculation or monetary factors that do not operate through the derived demand for primary commodities as inputs into the production of industrial products.

In subsequent sections these competing explanations are examined in more detail as they apply to three major components of basic materials: metals, foods, and nonfood agricultural products. This disaggregation of markets is important because the determinants of supply and demand differ in each of the three areas. We do not attempt a statistical analysis of fuel prices, because the sudden emergence of a producer organization (the Organization of Petroleum Exporting Countries) sharply changed the market structure.

The relation of the demand for these commodities to aggregate industrial production is the subject of the next section, followed by a review of the developments on the supply side and the role of inventory stocks. Next these "fundamental factors" of demand and supply are combined in a statistical analysis to determine if they provide an adequate explanation of the pattern of price change during the 1970s. In the fourth section price behavior is examined in a broader context, in which these commodities serve not only as an input into production but also as an investment asset. A more specific discussion of the markets for grains and petroleum is delayed until chapter 5.

Demand

The most common macroeconomic explanations for commodity price fluctuations focus on major global fluctuations in industrial production and therefore on the derived demand for material inputs. In particular,

1. This study does not focus on the issue of long-run scarcity. A recent book that deals with this subject and has extensive references is V. Kerry Smith, ed., *Scarcity and Growth Reconsidered* (Johns Hopkins University Press for Resources for the Future, 1979).

the 1972–73 rise in raw material prices is seen as the result of an unusual degree of coordination of the business cycle in the major industrial economies.

In the years 1972–75 all seven major industrial countries—Canada, the United States, Japan, France, Italy, West Germany and the United Kingdom—experienced a common business cycle. Industrial production in each country rose rapidly between 1972 and 1973, and in 1973–75 each slumped into the deepest recession in its postwar history.[2] For individual countries the rise in demand was not extreme by historical standards, but in the aggregate it generated an unusually high level of global production.

The synchronization of the cycle was singled out as the main cause of the size of the commodity boom and the subsequent decline.[3] It also raised several questions about the forces that generate a common pattern of expansion and contraction among national economies and the need for a greater coordination of economic policies. Was the 1972–75 cycle exceptional? Or did it represent the culmination of a trend toward a more synchronized international business cycle and thus a portent of what lies ahead?

The International Business Cycle

The period between World War II and 1972 showed only weak evidence of a common global business cycle, since the correlation of movements in economic activity across major industrial economies was much less pervasive than that across regions or cities within a single national economy.[4] In fact, the degree to which national cyclical movements have offset one another has contributed toward making percentage deviations of industrial production from trend considerably smoother on a world scale than in most countries. And it has also implied that the

2. As measured by indexes of industrial production.
3. For example, Richard N. Cooper and Robert Z. Lawrence, "The 1972–75 Commodity Boom," *Brookings Papers on Economic Activity*, 3:1975, pp. 671–715 (hereafter *BPEA*).
4. This conclusion results from examining either inflation rates or output movements. Whereas the variance in annual inflation rates across fifteen cities in the United States over the period 1956–71 was 0.3 percent, the variance across OECD countries in the same period was 4.0 percent. Similarly, the average correlation of the annual growth rate of manufactured production among regions in the United States over the period 1950–71 (0.74 percent) was considerably greater than the average correlation of all possible pairings of industrial production growth rates among the major industrial countries (0.37 percent).

largest economy, the United States, provides the global aggregate with its principal fluctuations.[5] Since 1975 there have again been marked differences in the cyclical experiences of the United States, Japan, and Europe.

Nor is there evidence of a continuous postwar trend toward a more synchronized cycle. Certain periods like the early 1950s, 1958–59, and 1971–75 were marked by a high degree of synchronization while others were not. Over the postwar period the world economy would seem to have become more integrated, trade has expanded as a percentage of gross national product, and capital is more mobile. Yet these structural changes need not necessarily lead to the convergence of cyclical movements. In theory, the degree of synchronization will be influenced by the kinds of disturbances that induce the cycle (for example, financial or real, supply-side or demand-side), the structure of the economies affected by them, the means by which the cycle is propagated, and the type of exchange-rate regime.

There are two traditional mechanisms for the synchronization of national expansions. The first is the simple trade multiplier by which an expansion in one country leads to increased exports and expansion in another. The second is the Humian mechanism by which an increase in one country's money supply leads, via the balance of payments, to an increase in the money supply abroad. Empirical studies suggest that the trade multiplier alone could not have induced a cycle of the kind experienced in the major industrial economies in 1972–75; and the evidence that these economies had adopted expansionary *fiscal* policies in 1971 and 1972 indicates that they were not being unwillingly swept into an expansion that was beyond their control. Had that been the case, at a minimum one would have expected contractionary fiscal measures.[6]

---

5. The U.S. economy has had smaller fluctuations (standard deviation from the exponential trend of 5.4 percent over the period 1950–74) than West Germany (7.4 percent), Japan (7.3 percent), and Italy (6.7 percent). But movements across Europe and Japan have been sufficiently unsynchronized to make the production index for the United States more volatile than that of Europe plus Japan (standard deviation from trend of 3.0). As a result, over the period 1950–74 the correlation between deviations from trend industrial production between the United States and the OECD as a whole was 0.90, and the corresponding correlation for Europe and the OECD was 0.23.

6. Bert G. Hickman and Stefan Schleicher, "The Interdependence of National Economies and the Synchronization of Economic Fluctuations: Evidence from the Link Project" (Stanford University, August 1978), p. 67; and Paul McCracken and others, *Towards Full Employment and Price Stability* (Paris: Organization for Economic Cooperation and Development, 1977), p. 280.

Figure 4-1. *Indexes of Industrial Production in the Market Economies, 1953–79*

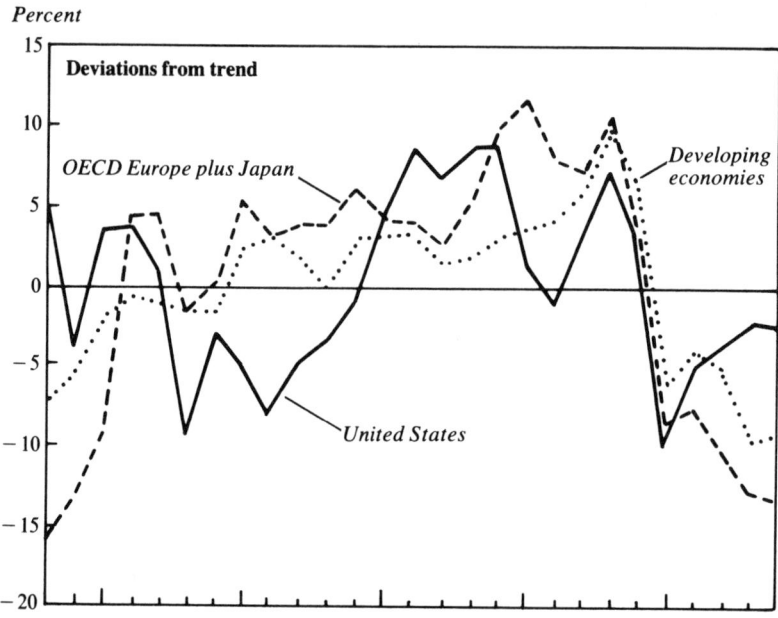

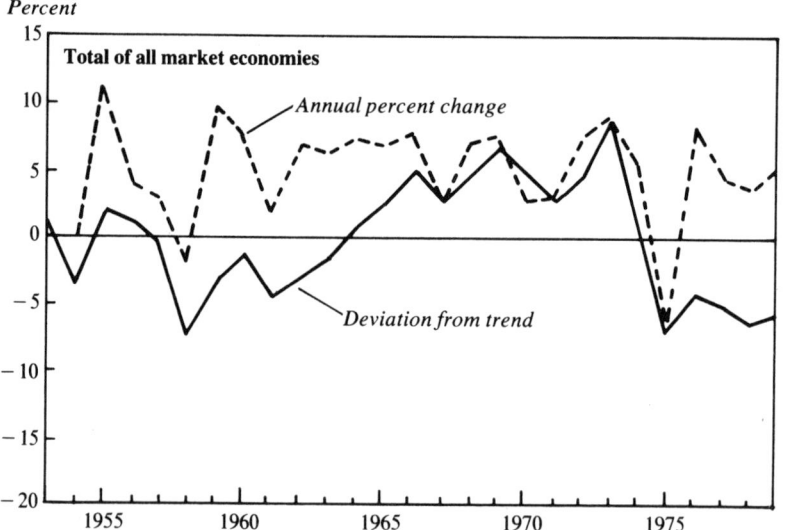

Sources: Original data are from United Nations, *Monthly Bulletin of Statistics*, vol. 34 (May 1980), and previous issues; and U.S. Department of Commerce, *Business Cycle Developments* (December 1979), and previous issues.

The relation between global movements in industrial production and production in the market economies is illustrated in the top part of figure 4-1. The presentation of industrial production as a deviation from an exponential growth trend allows one to abstract from the secular factors and to focus on cyclical patterns. The figure shows a substantial degree of independent movement in year-to-year growth rates, and even the cumulative growth patterns are quite different, because the United States expanded rapidly in the early and middle 1960s, whereas Japan and Western Europe had a strong sustained expansion late in the decade. Evidence of a common cycle is limited to 1958–59 and 1972–75. The slowdown in growth after 1975 in these regions and in the developing economies is obvious, with only the United States approaching a return to its previous trend line.[7] The degree of common movement that is evident for 1972–75 is unusual both by the standards of previous or subsequent experience.

The aggregation of industrial production to the level of the total of all market economies (bottom part of the figure) provides a perspective on the demand for primary commodities if one accepts the idea of an integrated world market. The result is a pattern of production growth considerably less volatile than that of any of the underlying economies. The 1972–73 period is clearly one of strong growth. Most evident is the magnitude of the 1975 recession and the incomplete recovery afterwards.

The 1972–73 Expansion

The lack of either a secular trend toward cyclical convergence or strong theoretical arguments favoring increased synchronization suggests that the economic cycle of 1972–75 had its roots in a set of unique historical events rather than in permanent features of the international economy.

One of those events was the collapse of the Bretton Woods international monetary system.[8] The balance-of-payments adjustment mechanism embodied in this system was seriously flawed. It failed to place

---

7. The correlation coefficients for paired annual changes in growth rates in the United States, Japan, Europe, and the developing economies all fall within the range of 0.1–0.5 for the 1954–71 period, but rise to 0.4–0.6 when the 1972–75 period is included and decline slightly if the period is extended through 1979.

8. This system was characterized by fixed exchange rates, except in the event of fundamental disequilibrium, and the use of the dollar as the major reserve asset, which was in turn convertible into gold.

symmetrical adjustment pressures on surplus and deficit countries. Whereas deficit countries were eventually compelled by a loss of reserves to take adjustment measures, surplus countries that were prepared to accumulate reserves could avoid adjustment and concentrate on domestic macroeconomic targets. Furthermore, the United States, able to print international reserves, could ignore the balance of payments as a policy constraint. In effect, other countries were required to take actions to cure a fundamental disequilibrium in international accounts.

These asymmetries led to a serious overvaluation of the U.S. dollar in the late 1960s that was camouflaged for a time by the large volume of foreign capital attracted by high U.S. interest rates. Countries with substantial deficit problems—the United Kingdom in 1967, France in 1968, and Italy in 1969—were forced to adopt contractionary policies. Countries with surpluses, however, like Japan and West Germany, by and large neglected the demands of their external disequilibrium and in 1969 and 1970 concentrated on fighting inflation with contractionary monetary policies.[9]

When U.S. monetary policy eased in 1970, its balance of payments came under tremendous pressure. The economy was expanding with an overvalued dollar while the principal foreign economies were slowing and U.S. interest rates were falling relative to those abroad. As the expected yield on holding dollars declined through 1970 and 1971 (because of lower U.S. interest rates and the prospect of a dollar devaluation) private holders began to reduce their dollar assets and foreign official holdings grew at an unprecedented rate (from $16 billion at the end of 1969 to $51 billion at the end of 1971). Although the explosion of international reserves was partly due to the adoption of expansionary policies in the United States, it is better viewed as stemming from a fundamental problem in the world payments system than from a highly inflationary U.S. monetary policy.[10]

By 1971 the Japanese and major European economies had also switched to expansionary policies. In the United States, West Germany,

9. Although the West Germans did allow the mark to appreciate in 1969 and 1970, this step was not reinforced by expansionary aggregate demand policies.

10. Studies by Lawrence and others suggest that when major industrial economies wanted to prevent an increase in foreign exchange reserves from causing a rise in their domestic money supplies, they were able to do so. See Robert Z. Lawrence, "The Measurement and Causes of the Synchronization of the International Business Cycle" (Ph.D. dissertation, Yale University, 1978).

SOURCES OF COMMODITY PRICE FLUCTUATIONS 69

Japan, and the United Kingdom—possibly because of undue attention to monetary factors, and possibly because of ignorance of the lags with which monetary stimulus operates—the forecasts for 1971 had badly overestimated the strength of economic activity. Chastened by their misplaced optimism, concerned about low levels of employment, and (except for the United States) comforted by their strong balance of payments, national governments moved impatiently and simultaneously from mid-1971 to mid-1972 to bolster the recovery with additional fiscal measures and to control the adverse price movements with incomes policies.[11]

Initially the expansion was marked by slow export growth, with domestic demand (construction and consumption expenditures) providing the expansionary stimulus. Large wage increases, low interest rates, and expectations of further inflation induced consumers to acquire consumer durable goods and houses as hedges against inflation, and investors to protect themselves by purchasing equities. Stock markets boomed. Private business, on the other hand, was pessimistic at first, and plant and equipment expenditures were particularly weak: the perceived glut of capital formation in the late sixties, low utilization levels, depressed profits, currency uncertainties, and fears about inflation all acted as dampers on investment.

In the second half of 1972, however, the expansion accelerated and changed in character as the full interactive effects of the policies were felt. Fears of shortages at home impelled a rush to buy abroad. As worldwide bottlenecks appeared, the pattern of demand shifted, and in many countries rising exports and investment in inventories and plant and equipment added to the expansion.

How large was the expansion? If the annual percentage increase in industrial production is used as a criterion, 1973 indeed saw a large boom. The 9.2 percent increase in the UN index for market economies was the largest annual increase since 1959, and it began from a relatively higher level of utilization of industrial production. And because the growth was concentrated in the last half of 1972 and the first half of 1973, the annual figures understate the size of the expansion.

11. An important factor in many countries was the need to face an election in 1972. In fact, five of the seven major countries had elections in 1972, and four of these (Canada, the United States, Japan, and West Germany) had them within a forty-three-day period at the end of 1972.

Supply

In 1972, when the commodity boom occurred, many commodity markets were at cyclical stages that made them extremely vulnerable to disturbances. The late 1960s had been a period of bountiful supplies, high inventories, and low prices for most agricultural commodities. By the early 1970s, government policies, economic incentives, and natural disasters prompted a reduction in the growth rate of supply and a depletion of inventories. At the beginning of 1972, stocks as a percent of trend production were lower than their 1965–70 averages across a wide spectrum of storable commodities, ranging from grains, oilseeds, and fats to beverages (like coffee, tea, and cocoa) and industrial raw materials (like rubber, cotton, and tobacco). U.S. policies directed toward reducing government-supported holdings of commodities were important in lowering stocks of grains, oilseeds, and cotton. The official Brazilian policy of coffee tree eradication in the mid-1960s and a frost in Brazil in 1970 contributed to the depletion of coffee stocks. Lower sugar prices—the result of an overenthusiastic response to high prices in the mid-1960s—initiated a period that was to last from 1970 to 1974 during which sugar consumption outran production.

Vulnerability to disturbances was not confined to storable agricultural commodities. Worldwide markets for meats and fish were becoming tighter. A combination of relatively high beef prices and low feed grain prices had pushed the global cattle cycle into the herd-buildup phase—producers reduced slaughter in order to expand their breeding stock. Between 1970 and 1972 the ratio of the UN index of beef prices to the corresponding price index for corn rose by 35 percent.[12] In the United States the cattle herd expanded by 8 percent between 1970 and 1973, while the amount of beef supplied to the market remained constant.[13] The by-product of lower slaughter rates was, of course, a decline in the supply of hides.

Fishing yields also follow a cyclical pattern. In theory there is an optimal rate at which shoals should be harvested. In practice overfishing depletes the fish stock, thereby reducing the profitability of fishing,

---

12. United Nations, *Monthly Bulletin of Statistics*, various issues.
13. U.S. Department of Agriculture, *Agricultural Statistics, 1976* (Government Printing Office, 1976), pp. 297, 341.

which in turn provides a respite for shoal replenishment. In the 1960s fully a third of the increase in global fisheries production (from 40 million tons in 1960 to 70 million tons in 1970) had originated in Latin America. And in 1970 Peru accounted for over 40 percent of total global fishmeal production. From 1970 to 1973, however, Latin American production fell (from 15.5 million to 5.4 million tons), and by 1973 Peruvian fishmeal production was only 11 percent of the world total.[14]

In metal production, both inventory levels and production capacity influence the sensitivity of prices to a surge in demand. Inventory data for the beginning of 1972 present a mixed picture. Inventory stocks, in comparison with their historical levels, appeared adequate for aluminum, copper, and lead, whereas they were particularly low for zinc and tin. The slow growth of the capacity to process primary metals in the 1970–75 period is evidence of the pessimism that existed at the beginning of the decade. As reported in table 4-1, noncommunist refining capacity of nonferrous metals, with the exception of aluminum, grew at less than half the rate of growth maintained during the last half of the 1960s.[15] Only for aluminum was the rise in refining capacity more rapid than its long-run (1955–70) average.

The decline in capacity growth can be ascribed to many factors: metal processing is especially capital-intensive, and an environment clouded with uncertainty particularly affected investment in long-lived assets. The widespread slowdown in 1970 and 1971 was a rude shock to those who had come to believe that recession was something in the past, sharply altering expectations of the future growth in demand. In large metal-producing economies like West Germany and Japan, the prospect of exchange-rate appreciations increased the uncertainty and lowered the expected profitability of metal production, and environmental and safety regulations raised the cost of investment in new capacity in many countries. And as a perusal of the industry publications of the period will bear out, it was widely felt that the capacity growth in the late 1960s had

---

14. The crisis in the Peruvian anchovy industry was originally attributed to a warming of the waters because of a change in the Humboldt current. The failure of the catch to return to normal levels by 1977 despite the restoration of oceanographic conditions, however, has strengthened the argument that the stock had been overfished. For an analysis see "The Peruvian Anchovy Industry," *CIPEC Quarterly Review* (April–June 1978), pp. 40–44.

15. The 1970–75 change in capacity is used to represent decisions on capacity expansion that were made before the boom of 1972–74. This use seems reasonable in view of the long lags in creating new capacity.

Table 4-1. *Change in Capacity for Processing Nonferrous Metals within Western Economies, Selected Periods, 1955–79*
Average annual percentage change

Period	Aluminum	Copper	Lead	Zinc	Total
1955–65	7.8	4.0	0.1	3.4	4.5
1965–70	6.4	6.2	3.9	5.3	6.0
1970–75	9.5	2.8	0.3	0.6	4.6
1975–79	4.4	0.8	1.4	0.8	2.2

Source: Leonard L. Fishman and others, *Major Mineral Supply Problems*, a study prepared by Resources for the Future for the Nonfuel Minerals Policy, Executive Office of the President (Washington, D.C.: RFF, 1979), chap. 7; available from National Technical Information Service, Springfield, Va. Data are based on refining capacity.

been excessive.[16] Although production levels for copper, aluminum, tin, and zinc were near normal in 1973 and 1974—given historical trends and the phase of the business cycle—the processing capacity for these metals was utilized at very high rates in most of the major producing countries.

In late 1972, therefore, the normal mechanisms for buffering sudden disturbances were lacking in important markets: inventories of many commodities were exceptionally low, marine stocks were depleted, beef herds were in a buildup phase of their production cycle, and metal-processing capacity was in short supply. And at precisely this time production shortfalls occurred for many agricultural commodities, while a rise in demand pushed utilization rates in metal processing to unusually high levels. Whereas weather conditions in different parts of the world are usually offsetting at any one time, in 1972 and 1973 many important producing areas experienced unfavorable conditions. Droughts reduced the production of wheat, sunflower seeds, and sugar in the Soviet Union; wheat and rice production in south and east Asia; and the production of cocoa, coffee, and groundnuts, sisal, and corn in Africa. At the same time, floods in the United States affected output of both cotton and corn, and frost damaged Brazilian coffee trees. Surprisingly, climatic factors also reduced the output of metals. In 1973 too much rain in Malaysia led to a flooding of the tin mines, while too little rain created a power shortage that forced the shutdown of aluminum refineries in the Pacific Northwest.

Political factors also played an important role. In the United States, to cultivate the farm vote, the administration continued its acreage set-aside program despite severely depleted grain inventories. In 1973

16. See, for example, a report on the problems of the aluminum industry: Organization for Economic Cooperation and Development, *Problems and Prospects of the Primary Aluminum Industry* (Paris: OECD, 1973).

copper supplies were curtailed because of political chaos in Chile and the decision of the Zambian government not to use the Rhodesian railways for shipping copper. An increased sensitivity to consumers' needs led Soviet and Chinese governments to enter the grain, soybean, and sugar markets in a substantial way.

Cumulatively, these events led to severe market disruptions. Although world agricultural production fell only 2 percent below trend in 1973, it was the largest shortfall since 1957. Capacity utilization rates in each of the major metal-refining industries met or exceeded historical peaks, and conditions of full utilization of available capacity existed throughout most of 1973 and the first half of 1974.

Quantitative Evaluation

A small model of price determination applied to historical data provides a quantitative basis for evaluating the conventional supply and demand factors in commodity markets. In this exercise demand is specified to be a function of free-world industrial production, relative prices, and a trend for technology. Supply is treated as exogenously determined in the short run and measured by actual production (agriculture) or capacity (metals). Where inventories are an element of short-term supply, the desired stock is related to expected prices. A rational expectations formulation is used to express anticipated prices as a linear function of the remaining exogenous variables. This model is reduced to a single equation that relates the relative price of a commodity to world industrial production, production of the specific commodity, initial inventory stocks, and a trend term. UN price indexes for each commodity were deflated by the export price index for manufactured commodities to provide a measure that is largely free of the influences of general inflation and changes in exchange rates.[17] Industrial production in market economies is used as a global income measure, and the production and inventory data are global aggregates. All the equations are estimated in logarithmic form.

The results for the major categories of food and nonfood agriculture,

17. The interpretation of this variable as a proxy for general inflation is supported by our finding that in most individual equations its coefficient is not significantly different from unity when used as an independent variable in an equation explaining the nominal price of the commodity.

Table 4-2. Results of Equations for the Relative Price of Agricultural Commodities

Commodity	Period	Independent variable						Summary statistic		
		Production	Inventory stock	Industrial production	Trend	1973 shift	Constant	R^2	Standard error	Durbin-Watson
Food	1961–79	−1.68[a] (3.2)	−0.66 (5.0)	0.99 (3.7)	...	...	9.3 (4.4)	0.78	0.06	1.6
Beef	1960–79	−1.86 (4.1)	...	1.90 (6.1)	−0.03 (−1.4)	...	49.7 (1.4)	0.80	0.06	1.8
Cereals	1962–79	−1.25 (1.1)	−0.36 (1.41)	0.72 (1.0)	...	...	7.0 (1.4)	0.16	0.15	1.2
Sugar	1955–79	−3.28 (3.0)	−1.62 (4.5)	3.60 (4.4)	...	...	1.7 (1.2)	0.61	0.27	1.5
Coffee	1961–78	−2.79[b] (3.4)	−0.59 (2.3)	...	0.02 (1.7)	...	−32.1 (1.1)	0.72	0.19	2.4
Cocoa	1955–79	−2.51 (7.3)	−0.26 (2.6)	...	0.10 (11.9)	...	−199.4 (11.6)	0.91	0.14	1.8
Fish	1956–78	−0.79 (4.3)	...	1.36 (9.0)	...	...	−2.7 (12.9)	0.94	0.07	1.9
Nonfood agriculture	1964–79	−3.90[a] (5.5)	−0.42 (4.4)	1.25 (4.6)	...	0.33 (7.8)	13.4 (6.1)	0.90	0.04	1.8
Fats and oils	1964–79	−2.33 (2.8)	−0.93 (2.0)	1.64 (2.5)	...	0.54 (3.0)	11.2 (3.5)	0.71	0.17	2.2
Cotton	1953–79	−0.67 (1.7)	−0.12 (1.0)	1.87 (3.7)	−0.11 (−4.8)	0.56 (8.0)	220.7 (4.9)	0.81	0.08	1.5
Wool	1960–79	−6.49 (5.5)	...	2.56 (3.6)	−0.13 (−3.9)	...	256.4 (4.0)	0.77	0.14	2.1
Rubber	1962–79	−1.33[a] (1.5)	−0.41 (1.4)	0.47 (0.7)	...	0.59 (4.7)	10.9 (2.1)	0.66	0.14	1.7
Hides	1960–79	−5.07 (6.1)	...	0.39 (0.6)	0.13 (3.2)	...	−207.3 (2.9)	0.73	0.13	2.3

Sources: See appendix B. Relative prices, production, and stocks are expressed as logarithms. The numbers in parentheses are t-statistics. The data are obtained from the sources listed in the appendix.
a. Production of previous year.
b. Current plus subsequent year.

together with important individual crops, are shown in table 4-2. They indicate some interesting features of commodity market behavior. First, much of the variation in relative prices can be explained by these simple formulations that emphasize the fundamentals of demand and supply. The coefficients on production and inventory stocks are consistently negative and of statistical significance. They also indicate that prices are highly sensitive to production changes. For total food, for example, a 1 percent reduction in production raises prices by about 1.5 to 2 percent. For nonfood agriculture the effect is even larger (4 percent). Income also shows a similar strong positive effect on prices, though the absolute size of the coefficient is usually smaller than for production, as one would expect for products that tend to have less than unitary income elasticity.

In contrast, these equations consistently underestimate the sharp surge of prices in 1973–74. For total food, relative prices averaged 24 percent above trend in 1973–74; yet the equation estimates the increase at 16 percent. About two-thirds of the predicted increase is the result of higher demand and one-third of supply and stocks. In fact, because relative prices were predicted to be higher than they actually were in 1972, the equation accounts for only about one-third of the *change* in prices between 1972–73. Although the individual equations track prices for beef, cocoa, and fish, the surge of cereal prices in 1973–74, high sugar prices in 1974–75, and the up-and-down movement of coffee prices in 1974–75 are largely unexplained. For many categories of nonfood agricultural products, one must allow for a permanent upward shift of relative prices in 1973 and later years to obtain any semblance of a reasonable statistical result. In several cases, such as rubber and cotton, this shift may reflect the effect of higher energy prices on the costs of synthetic substitutes, but the magnitude seems excessive.

On the other hand, the equations for the prices of nonferrous metals, presented in table 4-3, perform better during the 1970s. The aggregate equation performs particularly well, since it fully tracks the surge of prices in 1973–74, the 1975 collapse, and the smaller price rise in 1979. It does so primarily by assigning a very large weight to industrial production and beginning-of-period inventory stocks.[18] But the result is a little misleading because of the dominant weight of the copper and aluminum markets in the index. Copper prices (representing 45 percent of the index) have historically been very cyclical, and the equation predicts all

---

18. In all these markets the role of supply is probably understated because of our inability to adjust for strikes and similar production disruptions.

Table 4-3. Results of Equations for the Relative Price of Nonferrous Metals

Commodity	Period	Independent variable					Summary statistic		
		Industrial production	Inventory stock	Capacity	Time	Constant	$\bar{R}^2$	Standard error	Durbin-Watson
Nonferrous metals	1961–79	2.78 (8.4)	−0.41 (−4.1)	−0.89 (−2.9)	0.07 (3.3)	134.7 (3.5)	0.92	0.05	1.6
Aluminum	1961–79	0.31 (0.9)	−0.17 (−1.5)	−1.16 (−4.6)	0.07 (3.9)	−144.8 (−3.9)	0.74	0.06	1.7
Copper	1956–79	4.45 (6.7)	−0.27 (−2.9)	−0.64 (−1.3)	−0.18 (−4.7)	342.2 (4.8)	0.90	0.10	2.2
Lead	1957–79	0.06 (0.1)	−0.38 (−2.1)	...	0.02 (0.3)	−29.4 (−0.3)	0.41	0.17	1.2
Zinc	1959–79	2.70 (1.6)	−0.35 (−1.2)	−0.85 (−0.6)	−0.10 (−1.7)	188.8 (1.7)	0.45	0.22	0.9

Sources: See appendix B. Relative prices, production, stocks, and capacity are expressed as logarithms. The numbers in parentheses are t-statistics.

the major price movements, though actual prices moved up more sharply than predicted in 1972. The nominal price of aluminum, however, remained constant in 1973, implying a fall in the relative price. The result is a large overprediction of prices in 1973–74. The large error for aluminum (constituting 25 percent of the index) serves to offset the underprediction of prices in other major metal markets during the same period. An examination of the smaller metal markets indicates that in many cases prices that had previously been insensitive to business cycle conditions moved up sharply in 1973–74. Thus the aggregate index was dominated during the 1970s by prices in the copper market, and the strong performance of that equation overstates the ability of a conventional analysis to explain developments in other metal markets.

Monetary Factors and the Demand for Commodities as Assets

The previous statistical estimates result in two somewhat countervailing conclusions. The conventional supply and demand framework emphasized by economists is strongly supported by the consistently significant and plausible magnitudes of the coefficients on demand and supply factors in the equations. Yet these "fundamentals" are not enough to account fully for the magnitude and pervasiveness of the primary commodity price increases in 1973–74 and their collapse in 1975. One area of the conventional analysis that has been frequently criticized is the treatment of inventories or the demand for commodities as assets.[19] One explanation links the boom with the international monetary explosion that took place in the early 1970s. As Hendrik Houthakker has argued:

My hypothesis is that commodity markets are inherently more sensitive to supply and demand changes. . . . What I think we are observing in these markets is the intensification of inflationary pressure that began in 1972. I would attribute this increase in general to the breakdown of the Bretton Woods system and in particular to the large accumulation of international reserves between 1969 and 1972. Such an accumulation created a tremendous amount of excess purchasing power. And, while in most markets, excess demand generally takes a long time to show up in prices, it showed up quite rapidly in sensitive commodity markets.

The full impact of the very strong inflationary pressures that culminated

19. For a more elaborate theoretical treatment of primary commodities as assets, see Carl Van Duyne, "The Macroeconomic Effects of Commodity Disruptions in Open Economies," *Journal of International Economics*, vol. 9 (November 1979), pp. 559–82.

during 1972 was concentrated on commodity markets as the inflationary pressures raised the demand for inventories of raw materials by users. This extraordinary rise in raw-materials demand is not captured by the normal relation between raw materials and the demand for final goods.... Then, as inflationary pressures were alleviated by general price increases, there was a corresponding negative reaction in commodity prices—the necessary sequel to what went before.[20]

This explanation is a departure from conventional economic analysis, which separates questions of (microeconomic) relative price determination from (macroeconomic) questions about the absolute price level. Traditionally, an increase in the money supply is assumed to leave relative prices unchanged. In Houthakker's explanation, however, the relative price of commodities with flexible prices will rise in response to an increase in the money supply, since prices of these commodities do most of the adjustment to the increased purchasing power. But in the long run, as the prices of other goods rise, they drain off purchasing power from the commodity markets, so that the rise in the money supply has no lasting effect on the relative prices of primary commodities.[21] This line of argument implies that monetary policy does not work only through interest rates and the level of aggregate demand. It suggests that commodity booms may stem from monetary factors as well as from changes in the basic determinants of commodity demands and supplies. This hypothesis may also explain why primary commodities (like gold) or any assets with flexible prices may provide an effective short-run hedge against an inflationary increase in the money supply and why commodity speculation responds positively to uncertainty about inflation. But the theory also implies that this hedge will not be permanent, and that, over the long run, commodity prices will rise as much as prices of other goods in response to inflation.

Allowance for such an asset demand for primary commodities implies the addition of a measure of world money supply to the equations of the previous section. We used both world reserves and the world money supply as measures of the monetary variable in a simplified test of Houthakker's hypothesis. Among the aggregate market groupings, positive statistical results were obtained only for food products—the coefficients on the monetary variable were insignificant or of an unexpected

20. Hendrik S. Houthakker, "Comments and Discussion," *BPEA, 3:1975*, pp. 718–20.
21. This exploration assumes we can ignore any of the long-lasting effects that the short-run changes in relative prices might have had on investment and other resource allocation decisions.

sign for nonfood agricultural and nonferrous metals. In the case of food, a substantial improvement in explanatory power was obtained for an equation using total world reserves, but not for the money supply.[22]

The results for food prices suggest that commodity price behavior is affected by asset demand, but one cannot ignore the negative results in other markets. The main difficulty with the Houthakker explanation as it applies to other markets is the timing between the change in world reserves and monetary growth and the surge of primary commodity prices. World reserves began to grow at a sharply accelerated pace in 1970 (they rose at a 22.9 percent annual rate between 1969 and 1974 as against a 3.3 percent yearly average in the previous decade), whereas commodity prices remained low until the end of 1972. Reserves also continued to grow rapidly in the last half of the 1970s—12.6 percent annually—whereas the relative prices of nonfood commodities fell sharply in 1975 to a level comparable to that of the 1960s. The emphasis on food markets as the primary area in which an asset demand for commodities emerges also seems implausible. One would expect to see more evidence of such behavior in nonfood markets.

These results are not encouraging for Houthakker's hypothesis, but they reflect a narrow interpretation of the asset demand for commodities because of the focus on a monetary-nonmonetary imbalance in portfolios. The full integration of primary commodities as assets requires a deeper examination of the motives for holding such stocks in a mixed economy. We can distinguish both a convenience yield and a speculative yield—expectation of future price changes—as motives for holding commodity inventories.

Convenience Yields

In the first instance producers and consumers hold physical inventories to smooth out production, economize on transactions, and avoid the threat that an unexpected shortfall in the delivery of a key input will

22. Data on reserves and the money supply were taken from *International Financial Statistics*, various issues. We used several different methods of aggregation, including weighting indexes for individual countries and regions by their GNP in 1975 and converting all data to U.S. dollars. In addition, we used a money supply index constructed by Ronald McKinnon that is based on rates of money growth in ten industrial countries and weighted by their GNP in 1970. See Ronald McKinnon, "Currency Substitution and Instability in the World Dollar Standard" (Stanford University, July 1981). Futures markets for grains and other food products are among the most active globally, and to find evidence of asset effects in these markets is not as implausible as it might seem at first.

disrupt production at higher levels of fabrication. Such precautionary holdings of inventories will be related to the expected variance in commodity consumption and production.

A consideration of these motives for holding inventories suggests that *desired* stocks would have increased during the first half of the 1970s. National governments constantly interfered with international commodity trade, thereby affecting both the efficiency with which commodity market disturbances were distributed internationally and the security of supplies. There were numerous cases in which governments of producer countries imposed embargoes or restrictions on primary commodity exports. The motivations behind such actions varied. The most famous embargo, placed on oil sold by Arab countries to the United States and the Netherlands in the aftermath of the Arab-Israeli war in October 1973, was imposed for political reasons. So, too, was the 1973 decision by the Zambian government to avoid the use of the Rhodesian railway system to convey its copper exports. But the OPEC cartel's decision to quadruple oil prices, and the supply restrictions this entailed, had economic reasons. It was widely predicted that OPEC would be emulated by other commodity producers, which cast doubts in several markets about the reliability of supplies.[23] And the entry of new consumer countries, most notably the Soviet Union and the People's Republic of China, that were capable of buying up a sizable portion of world supplies in one transaction also raised fears about shortages.

In sum, the widespread practices of defaulting on previous agreements and understandings, and the imposition of taxes on production and barriers on exports without regard for the difficulties imposed on dependent countries, created a situation in which prudence required higher inventory levels.

Speculative Yields

Commodities may be attractive as an asset both because of expectations about their own future prices and because of their usefulness in a portfolio to diversify the risks of holding other assets. That is, the attractiveness of commodity price speculation will depend positively

23. In some countries taxes on commodities were increased: in Malaysia on tin and in Jamaica on bauxite. In others, export restrictions were a way to ensure adequate commodity supplies and lower prices in the domestic market. Examples were the Argentinian government's restrictions on the export of cattle hides in 1971, the embargo imposed by the United States on soybean exports in mid-1973, and the controls imposed by Thailand on rice exports in 1974. For other producers, like the Caribbean sugar

upon the expected appreciation in the commodity price and negatively upon the expected return on other assets. Insofar as commodity prices can be expected to be inversely related to or independent of other asset prices, they are also useful in reducing the riskiness of the overall portfolio. Although it is true that speculators need not actively hold physical inventories, since their objectives can be achieved as well by transactions in the futures market, price increases in that market must be fully reflected in the current spot market outside a range determined by the costs of storage.

These speculative motives also suggest that major changes in the asset demand for commodities could have been expected in the 1970s, though, as with the convenience motive, their quantitative importance is difficult to measure. The most important factors were (1) the belief that a new era of commodity scarcity had begun, (2) an increase in the rate of inflation, (3) the widespread application of wage and price controls from which primary commodity markets were generally excluded, and (4) an increase in uncertainty associated with both inflation and exchange rates.

As to the first factor, in 1972 the Club of Rome had written a report forecasting shortages in many global primary resources.[24] Shortly afterwards, in an apparent heralding of the new era of shortages, primary commodity prices had exploded. To many, these events were linked, and the prospects of increasing the relative scarcity of primary commodities gave rise to expectations of higher trends for commodity prices. Given a particular rate of interest, the effect of an anticipated higher future price will be capitalized in the current price.

Second, primary commodity prices are very sensitive to changes in the inflation rate, and in the short run they usually rise in the same direction, and by proportionately more than the price level in general.[25]

---

producers, the attractions of selling at high world prices rather than honoring long-term contracts at lower prices proved irresistible. In early 1974, therefore, the United Kingdom experienced shortages of sugar supplies despite its having renegotiated and raised the price of sugar sold under the Commonwealth Sugar Agreement.

24. Donella H. Meadows and others, *The Limits to Growth,* A Report for the Club of Rome's Project on the Predicament of Mankind (Universe Books, 1972). For a critique of such analyses, see W. Beckerman, "Economists, Scientists and Environmental Catastrophe," *Oxford Economic Papers,* vol. 24 (November 1972), pp. 237–44; and William Nordhaus, "World Dynamics—Measurement Without Data," *Economic Journal,* vol. 82 (December 1973), pp. 1156–83.

25. In this respect, Hicks's distinction between fixed- and flexible-price markets and the argument that the flexible-price markets will bear a disproportionate share of the burden of adjusting to aggregate demand and supply conditions seems appropriate. Thus speculators who anticipate an acceleration in inflation will seek to enlarge the share of primary commodities in their portfolios.

Moreover, there are tax reasons why primary commodities become more attractive when higher inflation rates are anticipated. The gains from holding commodities will be taxed, if at all, at generally low capital gains tax rates, while borrowing costs are an offset to regular income.[26] By contrast, the reflection of higher expected inflation rates in bond yields will be taxed as regular income, and if tax brackets are not indexed, the returns to human capital, in the form of higher wages, will be subject to the income tax at higher marginal levels as wage earners are pushed into higher nominal income brackets. The effect of inflation on real corporate profits is ambiguous, however. On the one hand, higher inflation rates ease the real burden of debt service. On the other hand, historic cost depreciation methods lead to an understatement of costs and thus to an overstatement of profits and an overpayment of taxes.

Commodities therefore have a role as a hedge when most income sources are adversely affected by unanticipated increases in inflation. Since inflation accelerated sharply throughout the world during 1972–74, those who anticipated that development would have been induced to increase their desired commodity holdings.

The data also indicated that the inflation rate became more variable in that period.[27] Would a rise in the variability of the inflation rate raise or lower the relative price of primary commodities? Since commodity prices are so sensitive to inflation changes, commodities, held in isolation, will become more risky when uncertainty about inflation increases. On the other hand, since unanticipated inflation will adversely affect the returns from holding assets of fixed denomination, while raising those on primary commodities, commodities may actually serve to reduce overall portfolio risk and command a premium rather than a discount.

Third, in the presence of wage and price controls, primary commodities not subject to such will become even more attractive as investments. If wages and manufactured goods prices are regulated, expansionary

26. An exception would be the profits that occur to firms that use first in, first out (FIFO) accounting methods. But this is one reason many firms switched to the last in, first out (LIFO) system during the 1970s. This whole issue of inflation, taxes, and the return on assets has been extensively analyzed by Martin Feldstein and others. See, for example, Martin Feldstein, "Inflation and the Stock Market," *American Economic Review,* vol. 70 (December 1980), pp. 839–47.

27. For a discussion of this point, see Edward Foster, "The Variability of Inflation," *Review of Economics and Statistics,* vol. 60 (August 1978), pp. 346–50. For the United States, too, there is evidence that expectations of the variance of inflation increased sharply during the 1970s. See F. Thomas Juster and Robert Comment, "A Note on the Measurement of Price Expectations" (University of Michigan at Ann Arbor, April 1980).

monetary and fiscal policies will spill over into commodity prices with even greater effects than usual. It is noteworthy that in 1972 and 1973 such programs were in effect in several large industrial countries.[28]

Finally, the increased variability of exchange rates may have influenced the demand for commodities as assets. It is true that residents of a specific country can avoid the risks of exchange-rate changes by holding a diversified portfolio of domestic and foreign assets; and thus from a global perspective there is no presumption that commodity prices will be raised by anticipations of exchange-rate changes.[29] But if government barriers to the purchase of foreign currency assets exist (as they frequently do in countries with downward rate pressures), commodity markets are a way to avoid the restrictions.

Quantitative Evidence

These asset demand factors are difficult to evaluate quantitatively. The data for producers' stocks are incomplete and those for consumer inventories are largely nonexistent. Moreover, the motivations reflect expected future prices and changes in risk perception that are largely unobserved information. In addition, the complex issues surrounding the motivation for holding stocks have not been the focus of most of the econometric-model research on commodity markets. Instead, the econometric studies have emphasized disaggregation to the level of individual commodities and specific components of demand as a more promising way to improve the accuracy of predictions.

Yet some evidence exists that stock demand, rather than a strictly derived flow demand relation to industrial output, was important in the 1973–74 period. First, we examined data for the implied consumption of metals by individual countries.[30] Domestic consumption of six important metals in Japan, the United States, and Western Europe was statistically related to domestic production of fabricated nonferrous products for the

28. See Anne Romanis Braun, "Incomes Policies in Industrial Countries Since 1973," staff paper (International Monetary Fund, January 1978).

29. A recent paper that examines the issues of portfolio diversification in the face of exchange-rate risk is Rudiger Dornbusch, "Exchange Rate Economics: Where Do We Stand?" *BPEA, 1:1980*, pp. 143–85.

30. This estimate equals domestic production plus imports minus any known accumulation of inventories by domestic producers. Thus the accumulation of stocks by users is included in the estimate of consumption. See Metallgesellschaft Aktiengesellschaft, *Metal Statistics* (Frankfurt am Main: MAG), annual. We used this data for copper, nickel, lead, tin, and zinc.

Table 4-4. *Turnover of Futures Contracts in Selected Commodities, U.S. and U.K. Markets, as Percent of World Consumption, 1972–80*

Commodity	1972	1973	1974	1975	1976	1977	1978	1979	1980[a]
Cocoa	242	377	318	292	299	307	220	226	373
Coffee[c]	3	67	65	25	68	98	66	166	433
Copper	86	164	126	177	313	251	348[b,d]	512[b,d]	556[d]
Corn[c]	81	167	209	196	179	186	216	297	255
Cotton	65	78	66	94	161	142	198	282	583
Gold[c]	0	0	2	225	210	481	1,677	2,469[b]	2,105
Lead	35	48	37	43	42	40	38	. . .	. . .
Silver[c]	2,998	5,184	5,283	8,325	9,563	9,215	9,930	9,806[b,d]	3,020[d]
Soybeans[c]	1,056	599	679	798	1,232	1,412	1,490	1,490[b]	1,093
Sugar	46	53	40	41	51	54	53	93	220
Tin	111	101	155	157	225	295	280	. . .	. . .
Wheat[c]	50	76	117	121	130	93	110	164	193
Zinc	26	34	34	43	42	40	38	. . .	. . .

Sources: London Metal Exchange turnovers for copper, lead, silver, tin, and zinc from *Mining Annual Review*, various years; U.S. turnovers from Futures Industry Association, Inc.; gold and silver production from American Metal Market, *Metal Statistics, 1979: The Purchasing Guide of the Metal Industries* (Fairchild Publications, 1979); consumption of other metals from Metallgesellschaft Aktiengesellschaft, *Metal Statistics, 1968–1978* (Frankfurt am Main: Metallgesellschaft AG, 1979) (excludes communist countries); consumption of cocoa, cotton, and sugar, and production of coffee from U.S. Department of Agriculture, Foreign Agricultural Service; production of corn, wheat, and soybeans from Food and Agriculture Organization of the United Nations, *FAO Monthly Bulletin of Statistics*, various issues.
  a. Figures are annualized flows based on January–March turnover data.
  b. Figures based on projected consumption or production.
  c. Turnover as percent of production.
  d. Assumes that London turnover rate is constant at level of last known year.

1955–75 period. For Japan, actual demand exceeded predicted demand in 1973, except for nickel, by amounts ranging from 10 to 20 percent; this was followed by negative residuals in 1974–75. A similar pattern of positive residuals in 1973 followed by negatives in 1974–75 occurred for the United States, though the magnitudes were closer to 10 percent. There was no significant evidence of excess demand for Western Europe.[31] Thus it appears that in 1973 users in Japan and the United States purchased materials beyond current requirements.

Second, a tremendous growth in futures markets occurred in the 1970s, which could be attributed to the same concerns that underlay the speculative demand for physical inventories. As shown in table 4-4, the volume of futures trading on existing exchanges expanded dramatically after 1972, and the number of such markets greatly increased.

Third, on an ex post basis, one can examine the implications for asset holders of investing in commodities. Statistical correlations between

  31. Evidence of an abnormally high level of Japanese imports in 1973 and offsetting low levels in later years was also found by Edward R. Fried, "International Trade in Raw Materials: Myths and Realities," *Science* (February 20, 1976), p. 642.

SOURCES OF COMMODITY PRICE FLUCTUATIONS

Table 4-5. *Correlation Coefficients for Commodity Prices, Equities, and Inflation, 1952–79*[a]

Item	Anticipated inflation	Unanticipated inflation	Commodity prices
Unanticipated inflation	−0.17	...	...
Commodity prices	0.06	0.68	...
Common stock yields	−0.20	−0.53	−0.34

Sources: Authors' calculations using the following data sources: anticipated inflation is measured by the predicted values of an equation relating current percent changes in the consumer price index in the previous two years, corrected for first-order serial correlation; unanticipated inflation equals the actual change minus the predicted change in the consumer price index; commodity price changes are measured by the U.S. Bureau of Labor Statistics' spot market index for 22 sensitive commodities; the common stock yield is the change in the Standard and Poor's index of common stocks plus the dividend–price ratio.
a. Values of R greater than 0.38 are significant at a 95 percent level of confidence.

rates of returns on commodities, equities, and measures of anticipated and unanticipated inflation are reported in table 4-5. The results confirm the expectation that equity yields respond negatively and significantly to unanticipated increases in inflation (−0.53 correlation coefficient), while spot commodity prices respond in a positive fashion (0.68 correlation coefficient).

Does this negative covariance between commodity and common stock prices provide a reason for the increased asset holdings of commodities in the 1970s? To answer that question we must turn to the formal specification of portfolio theory with risky assets. Diversification of a portfolio of assets allows an investor to reduce risks by taking advantage of the tendency of yields on some assets to move in offsetting directions. Thus the attractiveness of an asset will depend positively on its return and negatively on its own price variance and the extent of its covariance with other asset prices. The importance of return relative to risk will depend upon the investor's relative risk aversion.[32]

32. It can be shown that, given the choice between two assets with yields r and r^* respectively, and variances V and V^* and covariance C, the risk-averse investor will hold x percent of his portfolio in asset a^*, where

$$x = \frac{(r^* - r)}{b(V + V^* - 2C)} + \frac{(V - C)}{(V + V^* - 2C)},$$

and b is the coefficient of relative risk aversion (a large value of b is indicative of high-risk aversion).

This equation shows that portfolio selection depends on the yield differentials, risk aversion, and the structure of rates of return. The first part of the equation is the speculative part of the portfolio, which depends on the yield differential and risk aversion. Since the amount of speculation in the other security will be the negative of $(r - r^*)/b(V + V^* - 2C)$, the speculative portfolio will sum to zero across assets. Although all those taking speculative positions will hold positive or negative positions in similar ratios, the degree to

To determine whether holding commodities has made a positive or negative contribution to portfolio riskiness, we calculated the mean real returns on holdings of bonds and of twenty-two spot commodities, and the yield from holding the Standard and Poor's common stock average. These results are reported separately for the periods 1960–69 and 1970–79 in the top part of table 4-6. The variances and covariances of these returns as well as their shares in the optimum ex post portfolio for an investor with a particular degree of risk aversion are shown in the bottom part of the table.[33] The results show a dramatic contrast between the 1960s and the 1970s. In particular, the variance of commodity prices increased substantially in the 1970s relative to that of stocks. Nonetheless, in both periods the yield on twenty-year bonds had a considerably lower variance, so that bonds dominate the minimum variance portfolio. It is noteworthy, moreover, that even though commodities had a negative covariance with bond and equity yields in the 1970s, they form a smaller share of the minimum variance portfolio in the 1970s (0.01) than in the 1960s (0.02). In other words, even when viewed in a portfolio context, the risk associated with holding primary commodities increased in the 1970s because their own variance tended to dominate the negative covariance between commodities and other assets. Similar results were obtained for other portfolios that expanded the categories of commodities and added treasury bill yields rather than bond yields.

In sum, therefore, an ex post examination suggests that adding commodities to one's assets increased portfolio riskiness in the 1970s. This may explain why commodity stocks in some markets have not been rebuilt, and why futures markets greatly expanded as users who wished to hold commodity stocks for reasons of convenience sought to attract other investors who were willing to accept the risks. We are tempted to argue that the demand for commodities as an asset and as speculation are important elements in the behavior of commodity prices during the

---

which participants engage in speculation will depend upon their risk aversion. In the two-asset case, speculators will borrow by issuing the relatively lower yielding asset and will purchase the asset with the higher yield insofar as they are willing to tolerate risk. The second part of the equation indicates the minimum variance portfolio. This combination of assets is independent of risk aversion and depends solely on the variances and covariances of the assets. This discussion is based on Dornbusch, "Exchange Rate Economics," pp. 163–68.

33. For a description of how this is done, see Pentti J. K. Kouri and Jorge Braga de Macedo, "Exchange Rates and the International Adjustment Process," *BPEA, 1:1978*, pp. 111–50.

Table 4-6. *Variance and Covariance in Real Returns for Alternative Assets, 1960–79*[a]

Item	1960–69			1970–79		
	Commodities	Bonds	Stocks	Commodities	Bonds	Stocks
Commodities	30.80	...	...	192.60	...	...
Bonds	−0.43	0.29	...	−4.80	3.30	...
Stocks	2.77	3.30	102.60	−65.70	15.70	181.00
Mean real returns (annual average)	−1.60	2.50	3.90	2.40	1.00	−2.30
Share in minimum variance portfolio	0.02	1.01	−0.03	0.01	1.06	−0.08
Share in speculative portfolio[b]	−1.29	1.14	0.15	−0.02	0.25	−0.23

Sources: Authors' calculations from sources in table 4-5, and the twenty-year bond rate from *Federal Reserve Bulletin*, various issues.
a. Real returns are calculated as yields minus change in the U.S. consumer price index.
b. $b = 0.01$.

1970s. However, the dependence of asset behavior on expectations creates difficulties for statistical modeling, and the theoretical framework is limited.

We have found in this chapter that the fundamentals of demand and supply partly—but not entirely—explain commodity price fluctuations.[34] The aggregative world market approach is particularly unsatisfactory for two major markets—grains and petroleum—where institutional arrangements and government policy largely control prices. These markets are the subject of the next chapter.

34. E. C. Hwa, "Price Determination in Several International Primary Commodity Markets: A Structural Analysis," *IMF Staff Papers*, vol. 26 (March 1979), p. 157.

CHAPTER FIVE

Grains and Petroleum: The Role of Institutional Changes

THE ANALYSIS in chapter 3 of the inflationary effects of commodity price fluctuations in the 1970s emphasized the importance of food and energy prices. Yet it is for these two categories that the demand-supply framework of the preceding chapter is least satisfactory. In both markets institutional factors predominate, with governments being widely involved in the price-setting process. The sharp changes in price behavior in the two markets during the 1970s can be traced to changes in institutional factors rather than to changes in global demand and supply.

Grains

In the previous chapter we assumed that primary commodities adhere to the law of one price and that they can be examined within the context of a single global market. But for food products of the temperate zone, in particular, this assumption seems unreasonable. As discussed in chapter 3, national governments have frequently intervened in those markets to isolate domestic producers and consumers from the consequences of events in world markets. Also, a reduction in production or a rise in consumption within an individual country does not automatically translate into increased demand in international markets. Consumers in some countries may lack the necessary foreign exchange and thus suppress the effects of domestic conditions on world prices. In the 1960s excess U.S. grain reserves were made available to less-developed countries through the P.L. 480 (food for peace) programs, but such local currency sales were sharply curtailed in the 1970s. Finally, grain reserves are often controlled by governments, and only rarely will reserves in one consuming country be made available to another in the event of crop failure. Thus the impact of production shortfalls on market prices will largely depend on the distribution of these shortfalls among countries relative to the distribution of reserves. In the following section, therefore, we no longer make the assumption that there is a single global market for grains.

A Disaggregated View of the World Cereal Market

The crisis in world grain markets since 1972 has been the subject of several studies.[1] The factors cited in these studies as being responsible for the sharp rise in grain prices include a major crop failure, the depletion of grain reserves, the sharp drop in oilseed and fishmeal production, rising affluence, the effect of Russian grain purchases, the devaluation of the dollar, and the policies undertaken by individual countries to insulate their economies from conditions in world grain markets. The purpose of this section is simply to present these factors in a quantitative framework in order to assess their relative importance. In particular, we seek to explain why a scant 3 to 4 percent reduction from trend of world cereal (grains plus rice) production in the 1972–73 marketing year would trigger a near doubling of cereal prices on world markets.

CROP FAILURES. World production of the principal cereals, measured as deviations from trend levels of consumption, is shown in the first four columns of table 5-1. The decline in cereal production in 1972–73—principally the coarse grain and rice production of the Soviet Union and Southeast Asia—totaled about 41 million tons, or 3.4 percent below the normal trend level of world consumption. When judged by historical standards, however, the shortfall was only marginally greater than in such years as 1964 and 1966 when prices were fairly stable. Thus it is difficult to explain the sharp rise of cereal prices after 1972 solely in terms of crop failures. Prices rose by 40 percent in the 1972–73 marketing year (October 1 through September 30), tripled between the second quarter of 1972 and the peak in the first quarter of 1974, and continued at high levels throughout 1974 despite a strong recovery of production. And

1. See, for example, Dale E. Hathaway, "Food Prices and Inflation," *Brookings Papers on Economic Activity, 1:1974*, pp. 63–109 (hereafter *BPEA*); United Nations World Food Conference, *Assessment of the World Food Situation: Present and Future*, Item 8 of the Provisional Agenda, E/CONF.65/3 (Rome, November 5–16, 1974), pp. 15–24; D. Gale Johnson, *World Food Problems and Prospects* (Washington, D.C.: American Enterprise Institute for Public Policy Research, 1975), pp. 7–34; and Fred H. Sanderson, "The Great Food Fumble," *Science* (May 9, 1975), pp. 503–09.

Table 5-1. World Cereal Production, Reserves, and Prices: Deviations from Trend, 1960–61 through 1979–80[a]

Amounts in millions of metric tons

Marketing year[a]	Cereal production					"Excess" reserves of cereals[b] (6)	Available supply of cereals[c] (7)	Oilseed production (8)	Cereal price index	
	Wheat (1)	Coarse grains (2)	Rice (3)	Total amount (4)	Percent deviation (5)				Nominal (9)	Relative (10)
1960–61	11.3	21.1	–1.7	34.6	4.3	55.3	89.9	n.a.	94.7	107.3
1961–62	–10.2	–10.1	3.1	–13.3	–1.6	64.1	50.8	n.a.	101.8	116.0
1962–63	9.8	1.0	0.4	15.5	1.8	33.1	48.6	n.a.	102.3	116.6
1963–64	–17.2	–5.4	3.4	–14.9	–1.7	31.0	16.1	n.a.	104.7	117.9
1964–65	10.3	–15.7	9.5	8.7	0.9	25.0	33.7	–1.0	104.7	115.3
1965–66	–9.9	–19.7	–2.8	–27.4	–2.9	21.5	–5.9	0.5	102.9	111.5
1966–67	24.7	0.5	–5.2	24.8	2.5	–17.3	7.5	1.5	111.1	119.0
1967–68	2.1	13.2	3.8	24.1	2.4	5.4	29.5	0.7	105.8	112.7
1968–69	22.3	–3.7	–0.1	23.7	2.3	17.5	41.2	1.2	105.8	110.3
1969–70	–7.6	2.8	2.0	2.6	0.2	40.1	42.7	0.6	100.0	100.0
1970–71	–13.6	16.2	3.4	–20.9	–1.9	18.3	–2.6	–0.3	102.9	98.4
1971–72	7.3	17.7	1.4	32.3	2.8	–27.5	4.8	–1.2	94.7	85.2
1972–73	–11.0	–22.0	–13.8	–40.7	–3.4	–13.0	–53.7	–2.4	132.2	105.3
1973–74	4.9	16.9	–3.9	24.4	2.0	–55.0	–30.6	5.3	254.4	169.0
1974–75	–24.0	–44.6	–6.1	–68.0	–5.3	–58.6	–126.6	–3.0	254.4	144.9
1975–76	–45.0	–49.6	17.8	–69.7	–5.3	–79.8	–149.5	1.8	228.7	122.8
1976–77	5.6	–14.0	–3.5	–4.4	–0.3	–86.3	–90.7	–8.0	193.6	99.3
1977–78	–42.7	–36.3	3.2	–68.0	–4.8	–36.1	–104.1	0.0	212.9	97.7
1978–79	6.4	–16.1	5.4	3.9	0.3	–51.4	–47.5	1.0	250.9	100.7
1979–80	–38.5	–61.1	–9.4	–100.3	–6.7	–28.3	–128.0	10.5	304.7	107.8

Sources: U.S. Department of Agriculture, Foreign Agricultural Service, *Foreign Agriculture Circular: Grains*, August 13, 1980, and *Foreign Agriculture Circular: Oilseeds and Products* (August 1980); price data are from the United Nations, *Monthly Bulletin of Statistics* (August 1980), and previous issues. Quantities are shown as deviations from their exponential trend for 1961–72. The trends for 1961–72 were: wheat, 0.0367; coarse grains, 0.0319; rice, 0.0291; total cereals, 0.0328; and oilseeds, 0.0477. The cereal price is an average of the quarterly index on a July to June basis, and the UN export price index for manufactured goods is used as a deflator in the estimate of the relative price.

n.a. Not available.

a. The marketing year runs from October 1 of one calendar year through September 30 of the following year.

b. Beginning-of-period reserves minus "normal" stocks, as computed from the 1961–80 average ratio of stocks to trend production.

c. Available supplies equal total cereal production plus reserves.

even though far more severe crop failures took place in 1975 and 1976, prices actually declined slightly from the peak of early 1974. By 1979 the relative price (deflated by the price of manufactured goods) had returned to 1970 levels, though the historical pattern of a secular decline in the relative price of cereals was not resumed.

It is also clear from the table that the sharp fall in Peruvian anchovy (fishmeal) production and a smaller than normal rise in soybean meal output cannot explain the rise in cereal prices. Total oilseed production (including fishmeal) was severely depressed in the years 1971–73, but the market was not large enough to have much effect on the overall balance of demand and supply for grains.[2] Therefore, although the disappearance of the anchovy is an interesting story, it is a minor element in the grain price increase.

GRAIN RESERVES. Current production is an incomplete measure of the supply available to meet demand, because it ignores the carry-over of reserves from previous years. Grain reserves have a crucial bearing on why prices in 1973 behaved differently from prices in the 1960s. As shown in column 6 of table 5-1, the high level of reserves maintained during the 1960s was enough to cover most of the shortfall of production in years when crops were poor.[3] World reserves at the *beginning* of the 1972–73 marketing year were only marginally above the levels reached at the *end* of the previous periods of low production in 1966 and 1970. The initial reserve position was low in both 1967 and 1972, but in both years the world grain crop was relatively good and a serious supply shortage was avoided.

When beginning-of-year "excess" reserves are added to current production in column 7, the 1960s emerge more clearly as a period of high world grain supplies and the magnitude of the 1972–73 shortfall is far more evident. Thus the sharp shift in the reserve position from 21.5 millions tons in 1965–66 to −13 million tons in 1972–73 was of equal or greater importance than the slightly larger crop failure in the latter

---

2. Oilseed meal and fishmeal are interchangeable with coarse grains as high-protein animal feed. The higher protein content of the meals would imply a somewhat greater impact than that reflected by a straight tonnage measure (a multiplier of about 1.5), but such an adjustment would not greatly change the comparison.

3. The average ratio of stocks to trend production during the 1961–80 period (18.3 percent) is used as an estimate of normal carry-over requirements. The deviation in available supply is then the deviation of production from trend plus the excess of stocks above normal carry-over requirements. Estimates of rice reserves are not available for the full period.

period.[4] It is particularly evident in 1974, a year of high production, that the vulnerability of the reserve position had a dominant impact on prices.

RISING WORLD INCOMES. Affluence is often cited as a prime cause of the grain crisis. But the interpretation of this argument is difficult. It is true that rising incomes over long periods of time usually result in a decline in the direct consumption of cereals and greater reliance on meats.[5] It is also true that, when measured in terms of caloric content, the consumption of meats requires four to five times as much grain as consumption of cereals. Thus a given amount of grain would provide a higher caloric food supply if consumed directly.

Yet it seems unrealistic to cite the influence of increased affluence and industrialization on the demand for food, while ignoring the implications for supply. In the past, technological advancement has greatly increased crop yields, and for most industrial countries it has increased supply more than demand. This is evident in the almost universal practice within these countries of restricting agricultural production to boost farm prices. Therefore, the problem has more frequently been excess supply and depressed farm incomes.

If, on the other hand, reference is being made to cyclical fluctuations in income, it is difficult to see how the acceleration of world income growth in 1972–73 could have significantly affected the demand for feed grains in 1973, because of the lags in the adjustment of consumption patterns to income change plus the lag in building up livestock (the other main source of demand for grains). Certainly the fluctuations in the consumption of grains about the trend do not provide much support for such a demand-oriented explanation.

DEVALUATION. During the 1971–73 period the U.S. dollar was devalued 12.6 percent relative to currencies of the other OECD countries and 8.7 percent relative to the currencies of the forty-six major trading countries.[6] Since the price indexes discussed earlier are in dollar terms, some of the price increase can be attributed to devaluation. A lowering

4. As a share of total consumption, the 40.7 million ton shortfall of production in 1973 was only marginally larger than that of 1966 (3.4 percent as against 2.9 percent). It would therefore be improper to explain the 1973 price developments as being solely the result of an abnormally large decline in production.

5. In developed countries the income elasticity of wheat demand is estimated to be zero or negative, whereas that for feed grains is usually found to range between 0.3 and 0.6.

6. Exchange rates are weighted by bilateral trade flows with the United States and are published in U.S. Treasury Department, *Treasury Bulletin* (May 1977), p. 83. The forty-six main trading nations account for approximately 90 percent of U.S. total trade and are probably more representative for U.S. grain exports than the OECD alone.

of the U.S. price in foreign currencies would have stimulated a rise in U.S. exports and thus higher prices. One empirical study of the effect of devaluation on the U.S. price of wheat concludes that a 10 percent devaluation raises the domestic price of wheat by 7 percent.[7] This would imply an increase of 6 to 9 percent in wheat prices during the 1971–73 period. But while that analysis is instructive, it may not be appropriate to extend it to other grains. Moreover, the impact of devaluation is diminished by the fact that the dollar did not depreciate as sharply with respect to the currencies of other large grain exporters such as Canada and Argentina. Thus there was less improvement in the competitive position of the United States than is implied by the average amount of devaluation. In any case, it seems clear that devaluation accounted for a relatively small part of the rise in grain prices measured in U.S. prices.

Although the combination of reserves and production highlights the differences between 1973–74 and the 1960s, the problem remains of accounting for the decline in relative prices in 1975 and afterwards. Contrary to the general impression, the crisis was not resolved by the recovery of world grain production in the last half of the decade to a level consistent with the historical trend, and reserves continued to be limited. Clearly, something happened on the demand side to restore balance, and it was not simply a response to current prices, since relative prices fell back to pre-1973 levels despite production failures larger than those of 1973.

STRUCTURAL CHANGE. The events of the 1970s must be seen against the backdrop of a substantial change in the structure of the world grain market—a kind of change not reflected in the global demand and supply framework used earlier. Between 1947 and 1968 world grain prices were essentially controlled by governments under an international wheat agreement. While there have been many commodity agreements that have tried to stabilize prices and failed, this agreement lasted because it was consistent with the domestic policies of the two principal world exporters, the United States and Canada, which cooperated to maintain the price goals of the agreement.[8] Because of the large gains in yields, both countries were under pressure to buy up grain (holding the price at or above the cost of production) to slow the movement of the population

---

7. Thomas Grennes, Paul R. Johnson, and Marie Thursby, *The Economics of World Grain Trade* (Praeger, 1978), pp. 110–13.

8. The agreement may have simply reflected policies that the participating nations wished to follow anyway.

Figure 5-1. *Price Trends under the International Wheat Agreement, 1950–79*

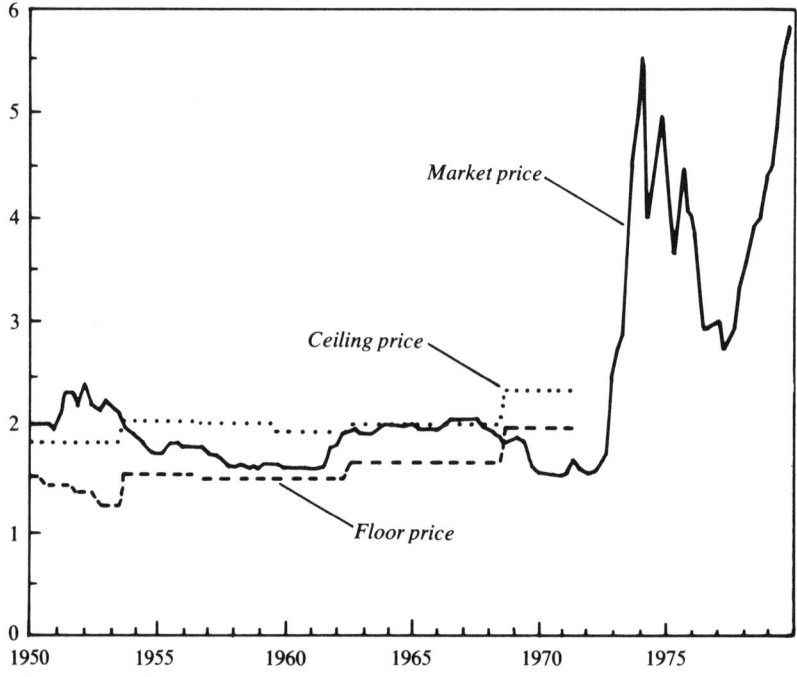

Sources: M. Hoffmeyer, "International Commodity Agreements as Instruments of Price Regulation," in W. Driehuis, ed., *Primary Commodity Prices: Analysis and Forecasting* (Rotterdam University Press, 1976), pp. 66–98; and *International Financial Statistics*, vol. 33 (December 1980), and previous issues.

off farms. In effect, domestic government policies created a floor under market prices, and the tremendous levels of accumulated reserves allowed them to ensure that prices would not exceed the ceiling. As shown in figure 5-1, market prices were controlled within a very narrow band during the 1960s. The wheat agreement broke down in 1968, and the exporting countries moved to reduce their stocks through restrictions on production. World acreage devoted to wheat production was reduced by 8 percent between the 1968–69 and 1970–71 marketing years and stocks were reduced by 35 percent.[9] Thus the reduction in reserves was the result of conscious government policies that, while maintaining a floor price, eliminated the ceiling on world market prices.

9. The combined wheat area of the United States, Canada, Australia, and Argentina declined by 35 percent. See U.S. Department of Agriculture, Foreign Agricultural Service, *Foreign Agriculture Circular: Grains*, August 13, 1980.

One must also drop the assumption of a single integrated world market. Analyzing the world grain balance of supply and demand in terms of aggregates can mislead one about the source of price increases, since it assumes that a single grain market exists and that shortages have the same effect on prices wherever they occur. This is obviously not true. Some of the least-developed economies lack the income and foreign exchange to make up domestic shortages through purchases in world markets. For others, like the Soviet Union, the balancing of demand and supply is not governed by prices. And if localized crop failures are severe, transportation bottlenecks may prevent imports from completely substituting for domestic supplies. Thus declines in domestic production do not always translate into increases of effective demand in international markets.

The failure of national demand and supply fluctuations to have their expected effects on international markets is well illustrated by the past variability of Soviet grain production and import requirements (see table 5-2). First, the variation of the Russian production about the trend is nearly as great as that of the world total. Since 1961 the deviation of Russian production from trend has ranged from a surplus of 24 million tons in 1967 to a shortfall of 82 million tons in 1980. This compares with a range of variation from a positive 37 million tons in 1964 to a negative 51 million tons in 1975 for the rest-of-world total. The instability of Soviet production can be traced to a combination of severe weather fluctuations and agricultural practices.[10] It is also evident that the Soviet Union accounts for nearly all the apparent slowing of the growth in production after 1972.

Except for a brief period in the late 1960s, however, the Soviet Union has not made use of grain reserves to smooth out supply. It has preferred either to reduce current consumption during years of low crop yields or to rely on purchases in the world market to make up the deficit. A comparison of fluctuations in domestic supply and net exports, as shown in table 5-2, indicates that during the 1970s the Soviet Union relied much more than before on imports as the means of adjustment. In 1964 domestic consumption was curtailed, and imports offset less than a third of the shortfall of domestic supply. In 1966 the carry-over from the previous year's good crop reduced the need to increase imports or cut

10. The Soviet agricultural system is discussed in some detail in D. Gale Johnson, *The Soviet Impact on World Grain Trade* (London: British-North America Committee, 1977). Johnson argues that farming practices could be modified to substantially reduce the fluctuation of yields in response to changing weather conditions.

Table 5-2. USSR Grain Balance: Deviations from Trend, 1961–62 through 1979–80
Millions of metric tons

Marketing year	Production (1)	Initial inventory (2)	Available supply[a] (3)	Domestic consumption (4)	Net imports (5)	Rest-of-world production[b] (6)
1961–62	15.9	−3.9	12.0	11.7	−8.1	−29.2
1962–63	16.6	−7.3	9.3	7.2	−8.0	1.1
1963–64	−21.9	−5.8	−27.7	−15.3	5.1	36.8
1964–65	13.6	−7.3	6.3	−4.4	−1.6	−4.9
1965–66	−19.3	9.1	−10.1	−2.1	3.7	−8.1
1966–67	24.1	−4.3	19.6	−3.3	−1.9	0.7
1967–68	−5.7	21.0	15.3	−6.5	−4.4	29.8
1968–69	7.9	17.4	25.3	−0.6	−6.2	15.8
1969–70	−7.0	19.7	12.8	7.5	−6.3	9.6
1970–71	10.3	−1.0	9.3	11.5	−7.5	−31.2
1971–72	−2.8	−9.7	−12.5	−4.0	1.1	35.1
1972–73	−24.0	−7.4	−31.4	−4.6	20.8	−16.7
1973–74	19.5	−6.2	13.3	10.4	5.1	4.9
1974–75	−16.7	8.0	−8.8	−6.7	0.2	−51.3
1975–76	−77.7	−1.9	−79.6	−42.7	25.2	8.0
1976–77	−7.9	−11.7	−19.7	−10.7	7.3	3.5
1977–78	−45.1	−1.7	−46.9	−12.9	16.3	−22.9
1978–79	−15.1	−17.7	−32.8	−20.5	12.6	19.0
1979–80	−82.5	0.3	−82.3	−34.5	30.2	−17.8

Source: *Foreign Agriculture Circular: Grains*, August 23, 1980. Production and consumption are shown as deviations from the 1962–72 exponential trend in consumption. 0.0464. Initial inventory is defined as beginning of period inventory minus normal stocks which are derived from the average ratio to trend consumption for the 1962–80 period. Net imports are actual values.
a. Equals production plus initial inventory.
b. Column 4 of table 5-1 minus column 1 of this table.

consumption, but in 1973 imports covered 75 percent of the supply shortage. In 1976 the import share was held down only because of the size of the crop failure. Transportation limitations would have prevented the supply shortage from being fully reflected in world markets even if the Soviet Union had been willing to spend the foreign exchange required. A similar constraint was evident in 1980. The emergence of the Soviet Union during the 1970s as a consistent net importer with wide year-to-year fluctuations, combined with the decision of the large exporting countries to reduce their reserve positions, represented a major shift in the structure of the grain market.

To highlight the changes in the world grain market during the 1970s, we examined the trends in the Soviet Union and the rest of the world from the perspective of the pressures they placed on the U.S. market (figures 5-2 and 5-3). In these figures the world market is divided into three groups: the United States, the Soviet Union, and the rest of the world. Demand for grains outside the United States is defined as Soviet net imports plus consumption of the rest of the world. A shortfall of production below demand in the rest of the world must be covered either by drawing down reserves in those countries or increasing imports from the United States. Consumption, production, and stocks are measured as deviations from a least-squares exponential trend for 1961–72. Trend levels of reserves and net imports are measured by their average ratios to trend consumption.[11]

The figures illustrate several developments in the 1970s. First, outside the United States, there was a growing imbalance between the consumption and production of grains (shown in the upper part of figure 5-2). Production (excluding that of the United States and the Soviet Union) was consistently below trend after 1972; and though consumption was also below trend after 1975, the drop in production was substantially larger. Second, the addition of Soviet net imports to the gap between consumption and production in the rest of the world gave rise to a large imbalance that could be met only by reducing reserves or by increasing U.S. exports.

The alternative means of meeting this excess of grain requirements is

11. The data underlying the figures is shown in the two tables in appendix C. The footnotes to those tables describe the procedures used to remove the trend. Normal imports and stocks are allowed for by defining the trend in production as trend consumption, minus the average ratio of imports from the United States to trend consumption, plus an allowance to maintain the increment to normal reserve requirements. Thus a growing imbalance implies a need to increase the share of imports in total consumption.

Figure 5-2. *Rest-of-World Supply and Demand Balance for Grains: Deviations from Trend, 1961–62 through 1979–80*

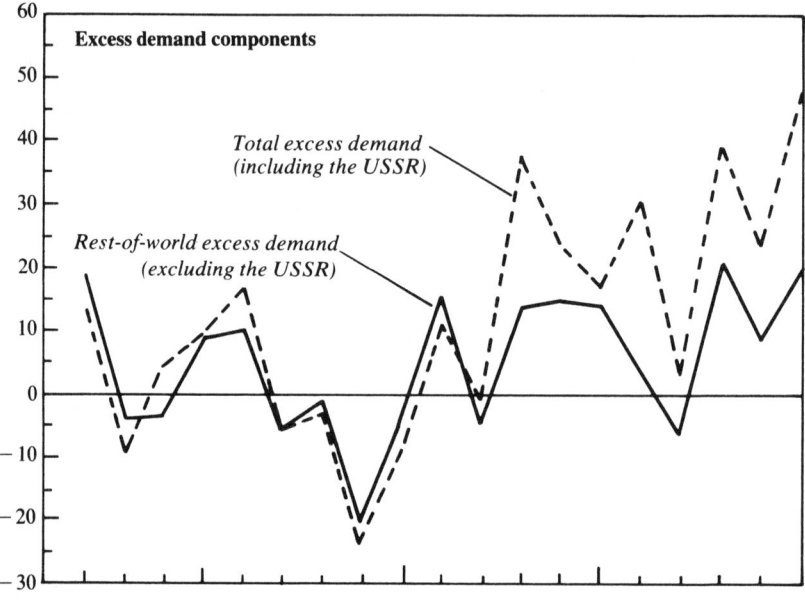

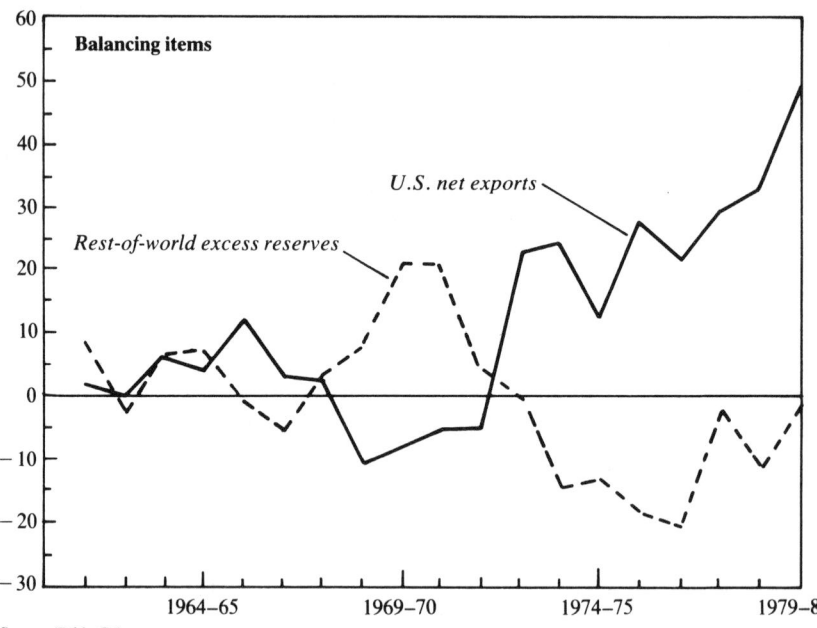

Source: Table C-2.

shown in the lower part of figure 5-2. Excess reserves outside the United States are shown as a deviation from the average 1962-72 ratio to consumption, and U.S. exports are also shown as a deviation from their normal share of trend consumption in the rest of the world. A high reserve position outside the United States at the beginning of the 1970s allowed the initial production shortfall in 1971 to be met by reducing stocks. Because 1972 was a relatively good crop year outside the United States, reserves did recover to some extent. The recurrence of a production shortfall in the 1972-73 marketing year, however, coincided with a large increase in Soviet import demand and an initial stock position no better than the historical average. Since consumption was below trend by a trivial amount, the burden of adjustment fell on reserves and U.S. exports. The continuing growth of the imbalance after 1973 was filled by increasing reliance on U.S. exports as reserves in the rest of world were gradually rebuilt.

The main surprise is the way in which the United States achieved the increase in grain exports. As shown in figure 5-3, higher export demand has not been matched by an above-trend level of production. Rather, the surge in exports was initially met by a depletion of U.S. reserves and later by a sharp fall in domestic consumption. Consumption fell by 23 percent (42 million tons) in 1975 and remained 10 to 15 percent below trend at the end of the decade. The United States increased its acreage under production (22 percent between 1969-71 and 1979-80), but because the annual increase in yields was slower, total production simply maintained the earlier trend.

The important role played by U.S. grain consumption is made even more evident when it is compared to consumption in other large countries and regions of the world, as in table 5-3. The percentage reduction in U.S. consumption was as much as three times the world average in the middle of the decade; and although the difference has narrowed in recent years, it remains substantial. In other words, the United States undertook a larger share than other countries of the adjustment to the agricultural crisis of 1973 and subsequent years—first by reducing its reserves and then by lowering consumption. In Western Europe consumption continued to grow rapidly throughout 1973-75, and both reserves and net imports were maintained at their previous rates. In 1976-77 Europe had its own crop failure, but much of the shortfall was offset by increasing net imports. The decline of consumption below trend was more gradual and of a smaller magnitude than the drop in production. The decline of consumption from trend in the United States, other grain-exporting

Figure 5-3. *U.S. Supply and Demand Balance for Grains: Deviations from Trend, 1961–62 through 1979–80*

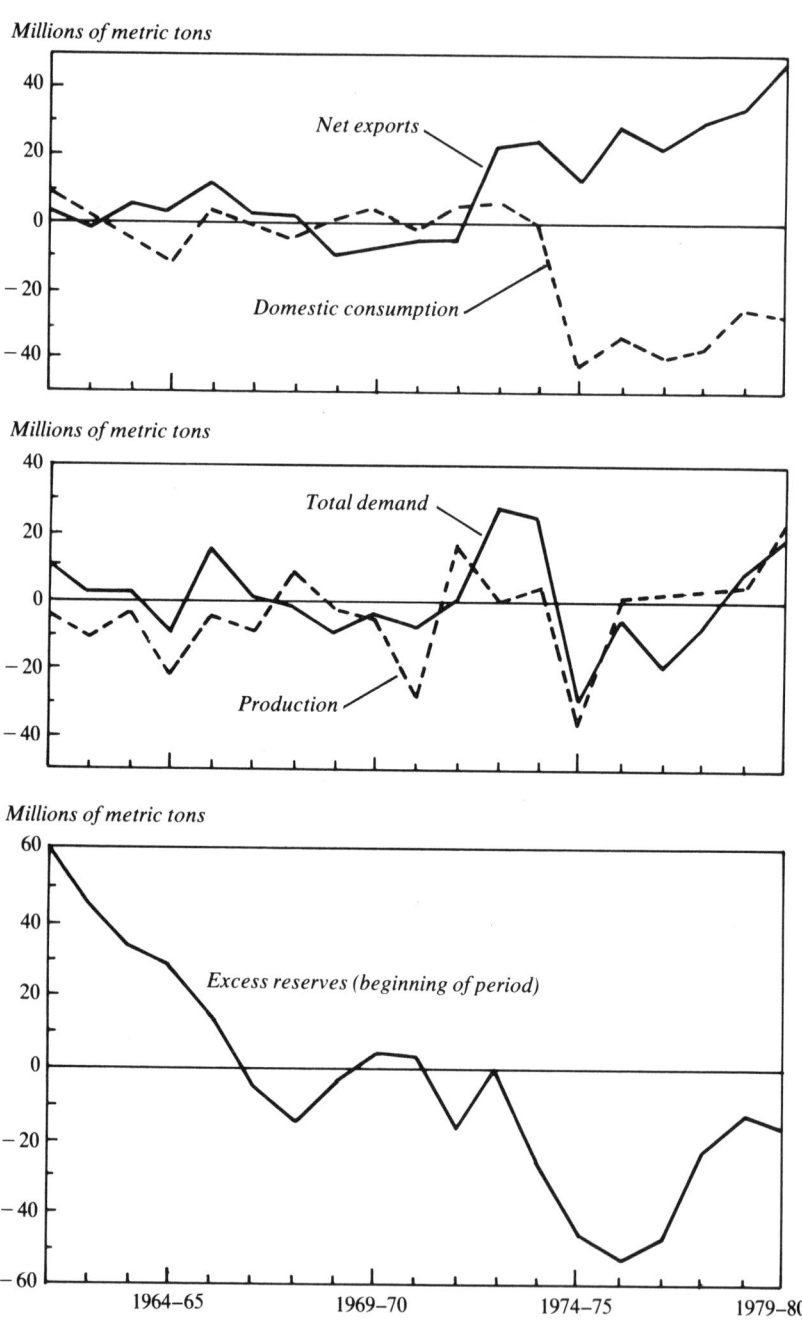

Source: Table C-1.

Table 5-3. *World Grain Consumption, by Selected Countries and Regions, 1970–71 through 1979–80*
Percentage deviation from trend[a]

Marketing year	United States	Other large grain exporters[b]	Western Europe	Soviet Union	China	Eastern Europe	Less-developed countries[c]
1970–71	−1.30	−3.34	−0.73	7.00	−2.12	−4.63	3.13
1971–72	3.00	6.66	0.57	−2.18	−7.54	8.96	−2.54
1972–73	3.63	−1.92	0.70	−2.27	−9.46	7.24	−0.36
1973–74	0.00	−0.54	−0.27	5.61	−9.97	4.40	3.55
1974–75	−23.02	−11.70	−1.43	−3.20	−10.98	7.89	0.50
1975–76	−17.96	−14.70	−5.75	−20.34	−14.33	5.88	0.71
1976–77	−21.03	−13.69	−7.44	−4.83	−15.31	8.05	2.47
1977–78	−18.66	−19.10	−7.47	−5.52	−14.20	4.68	1.62
1978–79	−12.28	−18.01	−7.37	−8.43	−7.03	6.80	5.68
1979–80[d]	−13.87	−19.29	−9.07	−13.62	−7.40	2.05	0.97

Source: *Foreign Agriculture Circular: Grains*, September 15, 1980.
a. Trend is the estimated exponential least squares line over the period 1961–72.
b. Canada, Australia, Argentina, Brazil, South Africa, and Thailand.
c. A residual, referring to those countries, including Japan, whose consumption is not dealt with individually.
d. Preliminary.

nations, and Western Europe was offset by a strong growth of demand in Eastern Europe and the less-developed countries. The Soviet reductions from trend were dominated more by the size of its crop failures and the physical impossibility of replacing such losses with imports.

The varying responses of consumption to world market prices can be largely explained by government policies that prevented the rise in price from being reflected in the price paid by consumers.[12] Between 1970 and 1974 the relative price of food actually declined in the European Community; in European countries outside the Community the rise was less than 5 percent, and in Japan it was 3 percent. The sharp increase in food prices in the United Kingdom was an exception, which reflected that country's devaluation and entry into the European Community. By contrast, in the United States and Canada the increases were above 10 percent because, as countries with major export interests, domestic prices were maintained closer to world market levels. Less-developed countries also experienced large increases in the relative cost of food, though there were wide variations among individual nations.[13]

12. This point has been emphasized by Johnson, *World Food Problems*, pp. 33–34.
13. For sixteen major less-developed countries we computed an average (weighted by 1972–75 grain imports) increase in the relative price of food of 18 percent between 1972 and 1974, and the relative price is computed as the food component of the consumer price index divided by the nonfood component. This exceeds the impact on U.S. consumers.

Individual countries employed a variety of measures to dampen the impact of world

The margin for moderating the world price increases was much greater, however, for Japan and Western Europe, where domestic prices had been far above world market levels, than it was for the United States and Canada. The European Agricultural Policy incorporates a variable import levy that equates import prices with those paid domestically. The size of this variable levy declined automatically as world prices rose to the level of domestic prices. In the 1972–75 import period, when wheat prices rose by $100 a ton, this levy declined from $55 to $0.39 a ton.[14] When foreign prices moved above internal prices in 1973–74, exports were restricted.

Similarly for Japan, the high level of internal agricultural prices (higher even than those of the European Community) made possible a considerable rise in foreign prices before domestic prices were affected. The Japanese system, however, operates somewhat differently from that of the Community. Domestic grains are purchased by the government and resold at a lower, subsidized price to consumers. In turn, all imports are purchased by the state and resold at a higher domestic price, the difference constituting an effective tariff. Thus the price paid by consumers lies between that received by domestic producers and the world market price. During the years 1973–75 the government stabilized consumer prices by not raising the resale price in line with higher world prices.[15]

At the same time, the United States had a greater capacity than Western Europe or Japan to reduce grain consumption, because of the importance in the United States of grains for animal feed as opposed to food grains and because of the structure of the U.S. livestock industry. Adjustments to higher feed-grain prices were reflected in (1) less feed per animal, (2) a shift to other feeding methods (a return to range-fed beef), and (3) a reduced animal herd.[16]

---

price increases. The United States subsidized exports in the years before 1973 at a level slightly below domestic prices. Both Canada and Australia employed a two-tiered price system, with domestic prices being maintained below world market levels. The domestic market was satisfied first at a lower price before grain was freed for export. For example, when the Canadian export price was $6.00 a bushel, the price charged domestic millers for wheat was $3.25.

14. Organization for Economic Cooperation and Development, *The Instability of Agricultural Commodity Markets* (Paris: OECD, 1980), p. 95.

15. The structure of Japanese agriculture is discussed more fully in Fred H. Sanderson, *Japan's Food Prospects and Policies* (Brookings Institution, 1978).

16. A model of the U.S. livestock and feed grain markets that incorporates many of

Figure 5-4. *Indexes of Feed Concentrate Consumption and Consuming Animal Units in the United States, 1955–79*

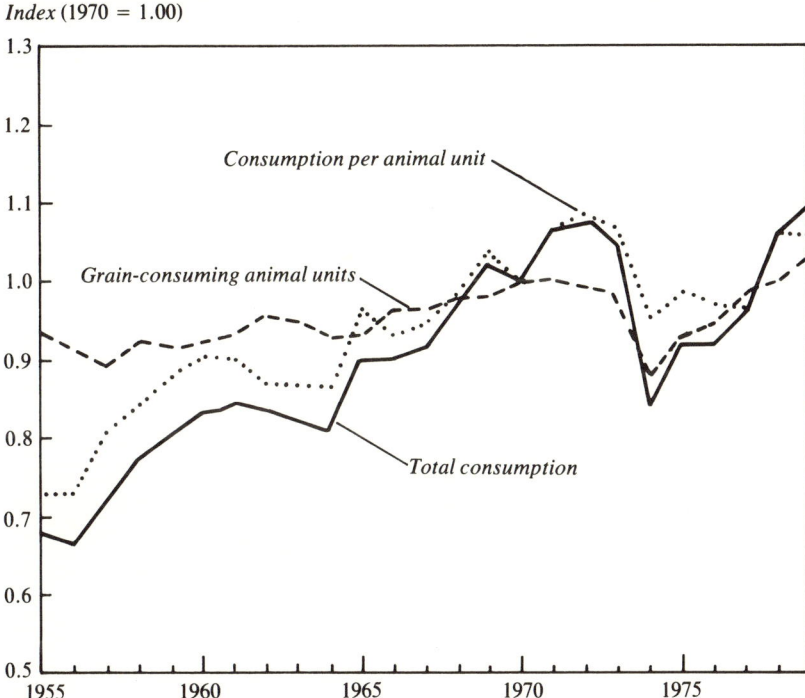

Sources: USDA, *Feed Situation* (November 1979), and previous issues. The animal population is defined in terms of units of equal grain-feed requirements.

The consumption of feed concentrates in the United States declined by 22 percent between 1972 and 1974, reflecting a 12 percent decline in the number of units of feed and a 12 percent drop in feed consumed per animal (figure 5-4).[17] In subsequent years, as feed costs declined, the number of animals on feed rose back toward the historical trend, but economies in the use of feed per unit continued. Thus in the 1978–80 period feed consumption was about 15 percent below its trend level. The

these adjustments is provided by Enrique R. Arzac and Maurice Wilkinson, "A Quarterly Econometric Model of United States Livestock and Feed Grain Markets and Some of Its Policy Implications," *American Journal of Agricultural Economics*, vol. 61 (May 1979), pp. 297–308.

17. The measures of feed use convert different animals to a common unit of feed consumption based on the average feed usage of 1969–71 and exclude cattle fed on range or roughage. The years are marketing years, which begin on October 1. The data are from U.S. Department of Agriculture, *Feed Situation* (November 1979), p. 17.

adjustment was most pronounced in the cattle sector, where the shift of animals back to grazing reduced the number of cattle on feed by 30 percent between the beginning of 1973 and 1975. Afterwards the proportion of marketing accounted for by fed beef recovered, but between 1975 and 1979 the severe price-cost squeeze induced a 15 percent reduction in total cattle herds and a 20 percent cutback in cows for breeding. Throughout the decade the supply of beef in the United States continued to be in disequilibrium as excessive slaughter reduced the size of the beef herd. To maintain such a supply on a sustained basis would require a much larger herd and thus a higher future demand for feed grains.

Econometric Analysis

The discussion above suggests that we drop the global framework of the earlier empirical model and focus on the market for trade in grain—effective, as opposed to potential, demand and supply. Several econometric models of the U.S. feed-grain and livestock markets that incorporate export demand have been developed in recent years. In contrast to our single equation these models are reasonably successful in explaining the pattern of grain prices during the 1970s and the implications of grain price fluctuations for retail meat prices. Even so, it is not easy to use the models to identify the sources of the disturbances in the 1970s. Much depends on what is treated as exogenous. Since the demand and supply of grains both affect and are affected by the prices of substitutes, for example, it is important whether these variables are treated as endogenous or exogenous. It is equally difficult to define a baseline case with which to compare them.

The most specific study that attempts to quantify the sources of the 1973 food price inflation is by Eckstein and Heien.[18] They use a small model of the feed-grain markets together with a highly disaggregated model of the livestock sector to attribute the change in price in the 1972–73 marketing year to changes in the exogenous variables. The decomposition of the 45 percent rise in corn prices is shown in table 5-4. According to this study, domestic rather than foreign factors were largely responsible for the rise in corn prices—a conclusion that is reinforced

18. Albert Eckstein and Dale Heien, "The 1973 Food Price Inflation," *American Journal of Agricultural Economics,* vol. 60 (May 1978), pp. 186–97.

Table 5-4. *Main Factors in U.S. Corn Price Increases, 1972–73 Marketing Year*

Factor	Contribution (percentage points)
Livestock prices	28.6
Livestock numbers	−1.1
Government policy	12.8
Other supply factors	−11.6
Foreign demand	3.2
Foreign supply	5.8
Soviet grain sales	9.1
Devaluation	2.2
Unexplained	−3.9
Total corn price change	45.1

Source: Albert Eckstein and Dale Hein, "The 1973 Food Price Inflation," *American Journal of Agricultural Economics*, vol. 60 (May 1978), p. 192.

when the authors examine the rise in livestock prices. Over a third of the latter rise is attributed to domestic demand.

There are, however, several difficulties with this analysis. The simple use of annual differences makes no distinction between anticipated and unanticipated changes in the exogenous variables. Demand, for example, can be expected to grow over time and is largely offset by an expansion of supply. It would therefore be more appropriate to look at deviations from trend. Such an adjustment would reduce the contribution of demand factors and raise that of supply. Second, the specific equations for grain prices ignore the role of inventories and imply a surprisingly low response of price to demand and supply fluctuations (relative to that found in other studies).

An alternative econometric model by Arzac and Wilkinson, though not used to decompose fully the causes of the 1973 price rise, places greater weight on exports, low inventories, and government limitations on production. The table of multipliers provided in their study indicates that the surge of export demand above trend in 1973–75 accounted for well over one-half the rise in corn prices during that period.[19] Still, the main point that emerges from both these studies is the importance of going beyond a global view of grain consumption and production. A crop failure in some part of the world does not have a great effect on prices unless it translates into effective market demand. In this regard, the increased willingness of the Soviet Union to make up domestic shortfalls

19. Arzac and Wilkinson, "Quarterly Econometric Model," p. 304.

in foreign purchases and the abandonment of a policy of holding large reserves in the United States would seem to be the principal developments of the 1970s. Econometric models that allow for these and similar structural changes appear to be able to explain grain price fluctuations in the 1970s.

Summary

In his review of the 1972–73 period, Dale Hathaway stressed the influence of an accelerating growth in world demand for grains—particularly feed grains—and the shortfall in production growth in the less-developed countries.[20] According to Hathaway, reserves were gradually drawn down by the growth of demand that could not be matched on the supply side, and the "flash point" came with the crop failure of 1972–73. But this interpretation ignores the fact that the land in production within the United States decreased in the immediately preceding years. In constrast, we would place much more emphasis on the supply side and regard the reduction of reserves as a direct outcome of specific government policies. The crisis was therefore the result of mistaken policies that allowed reserves (public and private) to fall below prudent levels. The price effects on world markets were then greatly magnified by the insulating policies of many nations, which discouraged any efforts toward conservation by their own consumers.

Concern about a growing imbalance between demand and supply seems more relevant, however, to the situation in recent years. Despite a great expansion of harvested land, actual production has remained below the trend growth rate. This slow growth has been primarily the result of a decline in the rate of improvement of production yields.

In the late 1970s world supply and demand were brought back into balance, prices fell sharply, and reserves were again being accumulated. But this restoration of balance resulted more from a decline in the demand for grains than from an increase of supply. If low grain prices stimulate a recovery of livestock herds and if slower improvements in yields continue, reserves will again come under pressure and prices will rise. The main question is whether the current low level of world cattle herds—particularly in the United States—is the result of a temporary low point in a long herd-rebuilding cycle or a reflection of a shift in consumer preferences. If it is the first, a recovery of beef herds will exert

20. Hathaway, "Food Prices and Inflation."

a steady upward pressure on grain demand and an inevitable surge in prices. The world lacks the former reserve of idle cropland in the United States, and existing grain reserves do not approach the levels of the 1960s. Nor is it likely that reserves will again be accumulated to those levels. The United States, at least, seems to be committed to maintaining a smaller reserve and relying more heavily on production restrictions to prevent price declines.

If the current leveling in the demand for beef reflects a shift in consumer preferences for meat, however, the downward shift in the consumption of grain can be maintained without significant increases in its relative price. In this case the threat of a future surge of prices would come primarily from the failure to rebuild reserves to meet the potential for future crop failures.

Petroleum Prices in the 1970s

The two surges in the price of crude petroleum, the world's most important primary commodity, were probably the most significant economic events of the 1970s. The rise in oil prices in 1973 had a devastating effect on the world economy. Coming at a time of high global aggregate demand and inflation, widespread commodity speculation, and instability in financial markets, it induced an acceleration in world inflation rates and large trade deficits in oil-importing nations. The inability of the members of OPEC to spend all the resulting increase in their new incomes gave a severe contractionary shock to a global economy that was already on the verge of recession.[21] And the decline in the terms of trade of the developed world brought about by the oil price hike lowered real incomes by about 2 percent.

After a four-year respite in which crude oil prices remained fairly steady in nominal terms and fell about 20 percent in real terms, the curtailment of oil exports from Iran, because of its domestic turmoil, touched off another surge of price increases. The 140 percent rise in oil

21. The contractionary mechanism was accurately described by Haberler in 1937: "Any very violent diversion of demand between countries, such as may occur in the course of world business cycle or as a result of war or large-scale harvest fluctuations, will probably be deflationary in its effect. The country losing money may be forced to contract, while the country gaining money will be unable at first to employ its new funds in investment." Gottfried Haberler, *Prosperity and Depression: A Theoretical Analysis of Cyclical Movements* (Geneva: League of Nations, 1937; Atheneum, 1963), p. 422.

prices between the end of 1978 and 1980 represented a real income loss to developed countries that was similar in magnitude to that of the first shock. But there were some important differences between the two episodes that made the industrial economies somewhat less vulnerable the second time: capacity utilization rates were lower, industrial activity was more moderate, and in other commodity markets speculative pressures were not so great. Moreover, there was an increased awareness of the need to absorb the decline in living standards caused by the oil price rise. Nonetheless, in every major industrial country the price level soared and economic activity declined.[22]

What lay behind the ability of the oil producers to raise prices with such impunity? And what determined the particular price strategy they chose?

OPEC's Ascent

Developments in the 1970s shocked most oil experts. For almost two decades—with a short interruption due to the Suez crisis—the real price of crude petroleum in international trade had gradually declined (see figure 5-5). (Adjusted for the inflation of world manufacturers prices, the real price of crude oil [Saudi Arabian light] in 1970 was 47 percent below its 1955 level; its nominal price had fallen by 33 percent). During the 1960s the discovery of proven global reserves had kept pace with consumption. In 1970 and 1971, when the first important price increases were negotiated, the world data do not suggest a particularly tight market. But this simply emphasizes the dangers of viewing commodity markets from too aggregative a level. The conclusion that "there is no oil shortage," based on an Olympian view of the oil market, ignored the crucial structural changes that had taken place in the 1960s: first, in the relation between the oil suppliers—the oil companies and the oil-producing countries—and second, in the growing importance of imported oil for meeting the energy requirements of consumers. In the short space of a decade the balance of power between oil companies and producing governments had been reversed.[23] In the 1950s the oil companies had

22. For a more extensive comparison between 1973–74 and 1979–80, see *OECD Economic Outlook*, no. 27 (July 1980), p. 124.

23. Adelman, writing in 1972, stated boldly, "There is no more basis for fears of acute oil scarcity in the next 15 years than there was 15 years ago—and the fears were strong in 1957. The myth that rising imports (of the United States) will 'turn the market around' is only the latest version of the myth that rising imports (of Europe and Japan) would dry out the surplus in 1957–70." See M. A. Adelman, "Is the Oil Shortage Real?" *Foreign Policy*, no. 9 (Winter 1972–73), p. 76.

Figure 5-5. *Petroleum Prices, 1950–79*

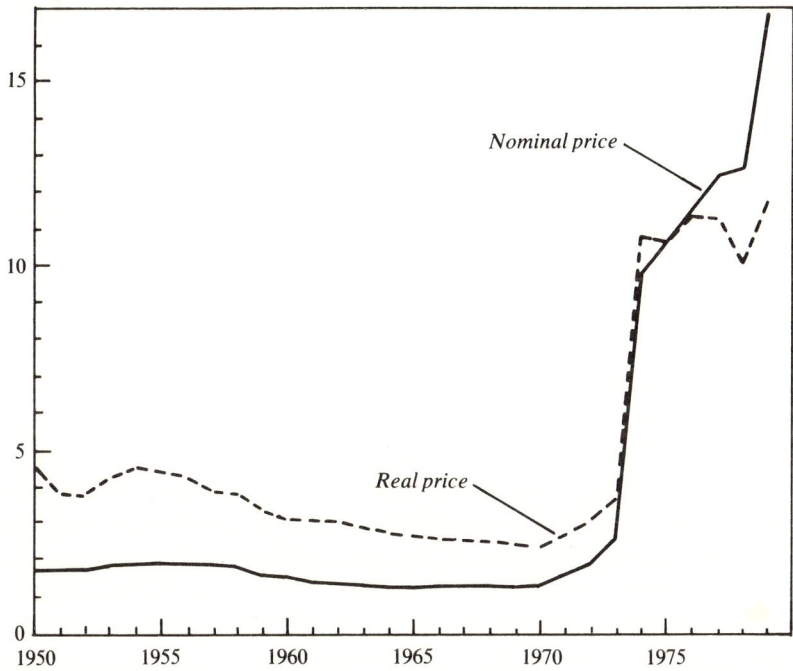

Sources: Nominal price is for Saudi Arabian light crude oil, f.o.b. Ras Tanura, from *International Financial Statistics*, vol. 33 (December 1980), and previous issues. Real price is nominal price divided by the UN manufactured goods export price index, from United Nations, *Monthly Bulletin of Statistics*, vol. 34 (July 1980), and previous issues.

been able to act without paying much attention to the producing countries. In the early 1970s the members of OPEC won a trial of strength, which allowed them to act unilaterally after 1973.

OIL COMPANY HEGEMONY. In the immediate postwar period, the seven major oil companies dominated all aspects of the exploration, production, refining, transportation, distribution, and marketing of petroleum.[24] Interlocking directorates and joint ventures—particularly for exploration and production—facilitated their explicit and implicit collabora-

24. They are Exxon Corporation, Royal Dutch/Shell Group, British Petroleum Company, Ltd., Gulf Oil Corporation, Texaco, Inc., Standard Oil of California, and Mobil Oil Corporation. Reviews of the history of the market are provided by Neil H. Jacoby, *Multinational Oil* (MacMillan, 1974); Anthony Sampson, *The Seven Sisters* (Viking, 1975); and M. A. Adelman, *The World Petroleum Market* (Johns Hopkins University Press for Resources for the Future, 1972).

tion.[25] The ability to present a united front, combined with the global diversification of supplies, allowed the seven companies to determine prices. The concession agreements they obtained from host countries gave them virtual sovereignty over the fields they discovered and developed. The nationalization of the Iranian oil fields in 1951 simply underscored the degree to which countries needed the companies. Iran was forced to grant an international consortium (which included all the major companies and a few independents) full control over all important operating decisions. The oil companies' strength was dramatically shown in 1959 and 1960, when they unilaterally lowered the posted prices that formed the basis for taxation of their profits. This action was not without cost, however, since it provoked the governments of oil-producing countries into forming OPEC despite their widely differing political persuasions.[26]

In the 1960s the members of OPEC were able to obtain several concessions. They prevented any further cuts in posted prices; separated royalty payments from tax payments (so that companies had to pay royalties as well as taxes); eliminated marketing allowances as a tax deduction; and regained control of unexploited territories. But several factors limited their power. First, there was considerable political enmity among the OPEC members. For example, when Iraq seized most of the Iraq Petroleum Company's concession territory in 1961, several Arab countries that mistrusted Iraq did not support its action.[27] Second, for many countries oil was the sole source of revenue and could not be forgone for any reason. And third, because of excess productive capacity in the non-U.S. market the major oil companies could "go slow" in countries displaying any recalcitrance. Thus both the loss of Iraqi production in the mid-1960s and the abortive attempt at an embargo after the six-day Arab-Israeli war in 1967 were relatively smoothly offset by increases in supplies elsewhere.

THE SHIFT IN POWER. In 1970 some long-run trends, reinforced by short-run circumstances, set the stage for a reversal of power. Now the

25. See Douglas R. Bohi and Milton Russell, *U.S. Energy Policy: Alternatives for Security* (Johns Hopkins University Press for Resources for the Future, 1975).

26. For a more thorough account, see Zuhayr Mikdashi, *The Community of Oil Exporting Countries: A Study in Governmental Cooperation* (Cornell University Press, 1972), chap. 1.

27. For a more complete description, see George Lenczowski, *Middle East Oil in a Revolutionary Age* (Washington, D.C.: American Enterprise Institute for Public Policy Research, 1976), p. 9.

Figure 5-6. *U.S. Consumption, Imports, and Domestic Supply of Petroleum, 1950–77*

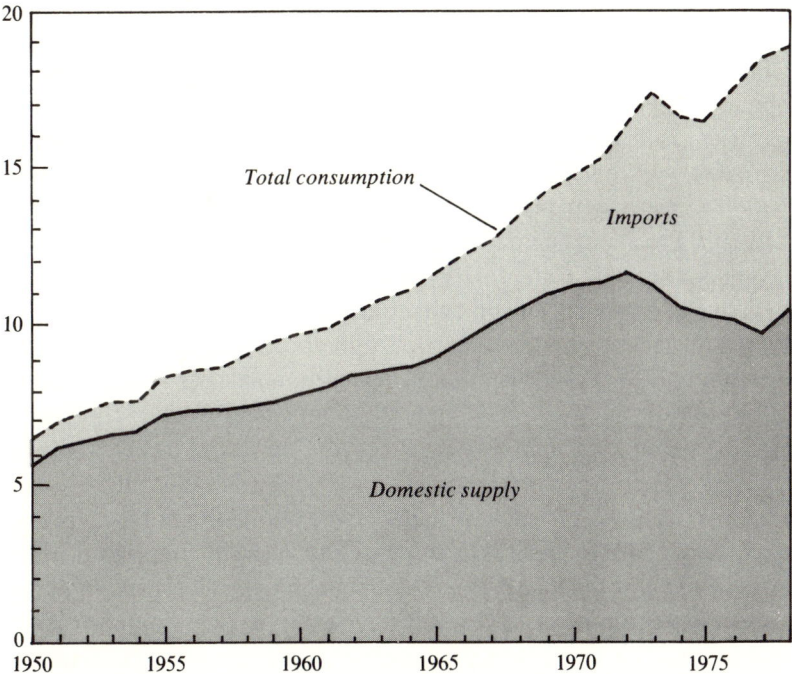

Source: American Petroleum Institute, *Basic Petroleum Data Book* (Washington, D.C.: API, 1979), sec. 7, table 3. Demand is domestic demand for refined products; domestic supply equals demand less total imports of crude oil and refined products.

members of OPEC would divide and rule. During the 1960s U.S. consumption had been growing faster than domestic production by 1 percentage point a year. New discoveries had not kept pace with consumption. Domestic reserves were equal to thirteen years' supply in 1960, but by 1970 they were equal to only nine years'.[28] Since the increase in domestic energy sources (natural gas, coal, and nuclear production) failed to meet the growth in energy demand, the shortfall between U.S. production and consumption was filled by a rise in U.S. petroleum import demand (see figure 5-6).

The growth in dependence on foreign oil was even larger in energy-poor Western Europe and Japan. The share of oil imports in total energy

28. See American Petroleum Institute, *Basic Petroleum Data Book* (Washington, D.C.: API, 1976).

consumption in Japan and the OECD countries of Europe had grown from 10 percent and 35.9 percent, respectively, in 1960 to 57.9 percent and 77.8 percent in 1970.[29] Although there was enough oil in the world to meet the needs of the consuming nations, the bulk of the imported oil had to come from the members of OPEC.

By 1970 many smaller, less geographically diversified independent companies, which were more vulnerable to actions taken by individual countries, had entered the market.[30] The OPEC members had not yet learned to work together, and it fell to a single country—Libya—to take the first steps toward changing the way in which oil prices were set.

In 1970 President Qaddafi found himself in an enviable position. The closing of the Suez canal in 1967 had made Libyan crude particularly attractive to the European oil consumers. By 1970 Libya was supplying about a quarter of Western Europe's oil imports. Demand was running particularly high in 1970 because of strong economic activity in Western Europe and Japan, a severe winter, the diversion of crude to the United States to mitigate a natural gas shortage, and a hydroelectric power shortage in Scandinavia. The pipeline carrying Iraqi oil to the Eastern Mediterranean was closed in a dispute over rates. And in May a Syrian tractor severed the Trans Arabian Pipeline, thereby cutting off about half-million barrels a day of Saudi Arabian oil from direct supply to the Eastern Mediterranean. Bolstered further by having enough foreign-exchange reserves to cover basic imports for several years, President Qaddafi ordered production curtailed until his demands for higher posted prices and tax rates were met.

The loss of almost all oil supplies normally available in the Mediterranean sent oil-tanker rates spiraling upward as Europeans sought to make up these deficiencies from the Persian Gulf. In September 1970 a vulnerable independent, the Occidental Oil Company, which depended on Libya for one-third of its revenue, agreed to the Libyan conditions; the other independent companies soon followed.[31] Faced with choosing

29. Guy De Carmoy, *Energy for Europe: Economic and Political Implications* (American Enterprise Institute for Public Policy Research, 1977), p. 11.

30. Some were the official companies of European countries, which had sought to escape their dependence on the U.S. majors for supplies. Bohi and Russell have estimated that between 1965 and 1970 the number of firms in the Middle East market grew from forty-four to seventy-five. *U.S. Energy Policy*, p. 34. For a complete historical tabulation of companies participating in Middle East oil, see also Frank R. Wyant, *The United States, OPEC and Multinational Oil* (Lexington Books, 1977), pp. 27–31.

31. Armand Hammer, chairman of Occidental Oil, had appealed to Exxon for alternative crude to help him resist Libyan demands but could not reach agreement on the price. See Sampson, *Seven Sisters*, p. 212.

GRAINS AND PETROLEUM 113

between the Libyan demands and paying the very high tanker rates for their European supplies, the major oil companies were forced to go along.[32] Since their agreements with many oil-producing countries contained a "most-favored nation" clause, committing them to extend favorable conditions granted one country to others, the companies were soon forced to make deals with other OPEC members. As soon as these agreements were signed, the Libyan government called for more concessions.

In December 1970, when a further round of demands was made by OPEC, the companies marshaled their forces and obtained from the U.S. Department of Justice special exemption from U.S. antitrust laws. The companies faced OPEC as a group in an attempt to reassert their positions and put an end to the leapfrogging process by which individual countries successively outdid one another in obtaining higher prices and taxes. But the members of OPEC also decided to unite. "In a special meeting of OPEC representatives on February 3, 1971, a resolution was adopted that pledged every country to enact (on February 15) the necessary legal or legislative measures to embargo (on February 21) shipments of crude and products to *any company* from *any source,* if that company did not meet the OPEC minimum demands for the Persian Gulf producing area."[33]

The Tehran agreement between six Gulf states and some sixteen companies signed on February 14 represented a significant OPEC victory in this clash between two united forces.[34] The agreement, which covered Gulf-exported oil only, did, however, provide the companies with some comfort: it pledged the six countries not to reopen the negotiations should other OPEC members secure better conditions; it contained

---

32. They also may have feared that independent European companies stood ready to pick up their Libyan concessions if they failed to accede to Libyan demands. See ibid., pp. 213–15, for a description of the futile attempt by Shell to resist. Akins points out that "the loss of all oil from Libya alone would have meant the drawing down of more than half of the European oil reserves within a year. It seemed unlikely, indeed inconceivable, that France, Germany, Spain or Italy would have allowed that to happen; especially as the goal would apparently have been only to protect the Anglo-Saxon oil monopoly which they had long sought to break." James E. Akins, "The Oil Crisis: This Time the Wolf Is Here," *Foreign Affairs,* vol. 51 (April 1973), p. 471.
33. Russell and Bohi, *U.S. Energy Policy,* p. 36.
34. At a meeting just before the Tehran negotiation, the OECD members had made it clear that they were in no position to withstand an embargo. They urged the companies to accept OPEC's demands and, according to Akins, "felt some satisfaction with the Tehran agreement." "Oil Crisis," p. 474. For a more critical view of OECD behavior, see Adelman, "Is the Oil Shortage Real?" pp. 80–81.

assurance against embargoes in support of any OPEC member's demands; and since its terms were to last through December 1975, it also offered the promise of restoring some stability to oil prices. But in return the companies agreed to increased taxes (the tax rate was raised from 50 to 55 percent), higher posted prices (38 cents a barrel), and yearly upward adjustments to compensate for world inflation. Similar agreements were shortly concluded at Tripoli (which settled prices for Mediterranean oil) and Lagos (African crudes). The fate of these agreements should give pause to those who propose a long-term agreement in which OPEC guarantees supplies in return for a stable real price.

The members of OPEC also moved to increase formal participation in oil-producing affiliates. Radical countries, like Libya, Iraq, and Algeria, tended to nationalize outright, whereas conservative regimes, like Iran, Saudi Arabia, and other Gulf states, operated with "participation agreements" to increase host-country equity. As a result, in 1971 and 1972 the ownership of a large proportion of the world's oil reserves changed hands.[35]

Moreover, when the U.S. dollar depreciated in late 1971 and 1973, OPEC responded by raising posted prices (which were denominated in dollars), by some 8.49 percent effective January 1972 and 11.9 percent in June 1973. In June 1973 OPEC and the oil companies agreed to an automatic adjustment of dollar postings referenced to an index based on major currencies.

The ability of OPEC to dictate new terms whenever it saw fit had become apparent by mid-1973. And the OPEC actions after the October war in the Middle East abandoned even the pretense of negotiation. That OPEC could gain control of the global oil market during 1971 and 1972, when the growth in oil consumption had been lowered by slow economic growth, was a forewarning of what would happen if a really tight market developed.

THE FIRST PRICE SHOCK. In 1973 such conditions were created by the synchronized global expansion. In the United States, demand for refined oil products increased by 7.4 percent in 1972 and 5.7 percent in 1973.[36] At the same time, domestic oil production was level in 1972, and in 1973 it declined by about 2 percent.[37] The U.S. government was forced

35. Lenczowski, *Middle East Oil,* pp. 9–12.
36. U.S. Department of Energy, Energy Information Administration, *1980 Annual Report to Congress,* vol. 1 (Government Printing Office, 1980).
37. American Petroleum Institute, *Basic Petroleum Data Book* (Washington, D.C.: API, 1979).

GRAINS AND PETROLEUM   115

to abandon its oil import quota system in 1973, when the pressure for imports became irresistible. From 1971 to 1973 U.S. imports rose from 3.9 million to 6.3 million barrels a day (mmbd).

The politically motivated cutbacks in production by the Arab oil producers as a result of the October war created an ideal situation for large price increases. But an increase in oil prices had been imminent even before the war began. On September 15–16, at a meeting in Vienna, the OPEC members had agreed to renegotiate revisions of the Tehran, Tripoli, and Lagos agreements on prices. When talks with companies had not reached agreement, on October 16 (ten days after the outbreak of the war) six Gulf countries decided in Kuwait to raise the posted price from $3.01 to $5.12 a barrel. (It was at this same meeting that the Arab nations had decided to cut monthly production levels by a minimum of 5 percent from September levels.) Meanwhile, the prospects of production cutbacks had induced a huge scramble for inventories, and individual OPEC members began raising their prices by auctions and unilateral boosts to posted prices. Auctions in Nigeria and Iran in November brought prices of about $17 a barrel. On December 22 the six Gulf nations raised the posted price of benchmark crude to $11.65 a barrel.[38] The price of petroleum had quadrupled in three months. And oil prices were now being set by the OPEC cartel.

The major oil companies did, however, retain an important, if somewhat diminished, role in the international oil distribution system after 1973.[39] They received more oil than they could refine and market from direct equity in production operations and "buy-backs" of oil produced on behalf of host countries, and they sold this surplus to so-called third-party customers.[40] The major companies also continued the sharing arrangements that facilitated the matching of different quality crudes and the evening out of shortfalls and bottlenecks. Since they acted to distribute the global shortage in 1974 evenly by redirecting consignments, they virtually nullified the attempts of the Arab members of OPEC to embargo the United States and the Netherlands.[41]

38. This account rests heavily on Lenczowski, *Middle East Oil*, especially pp. 12–28.

39. Mohnfeld estimates that the volume of crude oil available to the major oil companies (outside the OECD) on the basis of long-term contracts in 1973 was 25.0 mmbd, which constituted about 90 percent of the crude oil traded internationally. By 1978 they received 16.9 mmbd (or about a 50 percent share). Jochen H. Mohnfeld, "Changing Patterns of Trade," *Petroleum Economist*, vol. 47 (August 1980), pp. 329–32.

40. Mohnfeld, in ibid., estimates the volume of third-party sales by the majors at between 6 and 7 mmbd in 1973 and 3.7 mmbd in 1978.

41. For a review of oil company behavior during the 1973–74 embargo, see Wyant, *The United States, OPEC and Multinational Oil*, pp. 155–61.

Table 5-5. *World Growth of Supply, Demand, and Reserves of Crude Oil, Selected Periods, 1955–79*
Average annual percent change

Item	1955–68	1968–73	1973–79
Production			
World	7.07	7.35	2.23
United States	2.23	0.24	−1.53
Centrally planned economies	10.75	7.60	7.03
Western Europe	5.98	−0.26	35.70
Other	9.22	9.92	0.19
Consumption[a]			
World	7.54[b]	7.20	3.20[c]
United States	3.55	5.08	2.09[c]
Centrally planned economies	8.51[b]	8.64	6.71[c]
Western Europe	12.53	7.45	0.15[c]
Other	9.21[c]	8.74	3.05[c]
Reserves[d]			
World	7.31	9.77	−0.69
United States	0.46	2.93	−5.35
Centrally planned economies	9.77	20.15	−8.33
Western Europe	5.03	35.80	13.70
Other	8.20	8.51	−0.86

Source: American Petroleum Institute, *Basic Petroleum Data Book* (Washington, D.C.: API, 1979), sec. 2, table 1; sec. 4, table 2; sec. 7, table 2.
a. Estimated demand for refined petroleum products.
b. Data available only for 1959–68.
c. Data available only for 1972–78.
d. Estimated proved world reserves of crude oil as of January 1.

Although the short-run demand for oil was considerably less responsive to price increases than many experts had expected, oil-consumption growth declined significantly from 1973 through 1978 (see table 5-5).[42] But the substantial reduction in the rate of expansion of production in the largest oil-producing countries that also occurred allowed nominal oil prices to remain stable. (At the end of 1978, the average official price was $12.93.) With the exception of 1977, when production was 31.8 mmbd, OPEC production remained below the 1973 level of 31.3 mmbd until 1979. Almost all the growth of noncommunist oil production from 1973 to 1979 stemmed from non-OPEC producers, the United Kingdom

42. Although OECD real gross national product grew by 17 percent from 1973 to 1979, OECD energy use was up only 7 percent over the same period. But because indigenous production of energy in the OECD rose only 5 percent, dependence on foreign oil in 1979 was still at about 1973 levels. *OECD Economic Outlook*, no. 27 (July 1980), p. 119. The decline in domestic oil production in the lower forty-eight states of America, coupled with growing consumption, raised U.S. imports from 6.26 mmbd in 1973 to 8.81 mmbd in 1977. *Monthly Energy Review* (September 1980), p. 30.

(up 1.6 mmbd) and Mexico (up 1.1 mmbd) making the largest contributions.

Saudi Arabian production decisions were the most important. In 1974 the Saudis imposed an annual production goal of 8.5 million barrels a day—a rate some 1.5 million barrels a day lower than its capacity at the time. But other OPEC members also contributed to changes in OPEC supplies. As Danielson has noted, "Each member country of OPEC except Algeria has produced at a level substantially below capacity during at least one year since 1973, and most have produced far below capacity every year (between 1973 and 1978). . . .OPEC shut-in capacity averaged a high of 28 percent in 1975 and a low of 17 percent in 1977."[43] Saudi production ran at about target level in 1974; but faced with the decline in global oil demand resulting from the 1974–75 recession, the Saudis severely cut back their production to only 6.9 mmbd in 1976. On the other hand, they acted to prevent prices from rising when in 1977 they raised production above target levels (Saudi production in 1977 was 9.2 mmbd). In 1977 the Saudis, together with the United Arab Emirates, resisted the proposals of other OPEC members for a 10 percent increase in prices in the first half of the year and an additional 5 percent increase in the second half. Until a compromise price increase totaling 10 percent was reached in June 1977, a two-tier system functioned, with the Saudi and UAE prices some 5 percent below those of the rest of OPEC.

THE SECOND PRICE SHOCK. The second oil price surge of the decade began toward the end of 1978. Political turmoil led to the reduction of Iranian output from 5.8 mmbd in August 1978 to 0.5 mmbd in January 1979. Overall OPEC production declined, though Saudi Arabia and other OPEC members raised their production levels—Saudi Arabian production reached a post-embargo peak rate of 10.1 mmbd in December 1978.[44] The disruption of Iranian supplies also altered the pattern of trade, since it forced the major oil companies to reduce their third-party sales.[45]

When the new Iranian government resumed production in March 1979, it set a production target of 4 mmbd—some 2 mmbd less than prerevolution levels. It canceled the agreement with the Iranian consortium and contracted relatively small amounts with a large number of

43. Albert L. Danielson, "The Theory and Measurement of OPEC Stability," *Southern Economic Journal*, vol. 47 (July 1980), p. 55.
44. Walter J. Mead, "An Economic Analysis of Crude Oil Price Behavior in the 1970's," *Journal of Energy and Development*, vol. 5 (Spring 1979), p. 225.
45. Mohnfeld, in "Changing Patterns of Trade," estimates that third-party sales declined from 3.7 mmbd in the third quarter of 1978 to about 1.5 mmbd by the end of 1979.

customers, thereby reducing sales to the major companies to only 0.9 mmbd (some 2.2 mmbd less than they had received previously).[46] The upward pressure on prices continued for several reasons: the prospect of a permanently lower global production path; the increased demand for inventories because of expectations of further price increases; anticipations of further production interruptions; the reduced supply of inventories because of depletion during the cutback; and the effects of further structural changes in the international distribution system.

There was an atmosphere of crisis as the uncertainty associated with the disruption of traditional trading relationships led consumers to scramble for supplies. Companies that were deprived of oil formerly purchased from the majors turned either directly to producer governments or to the Rotterdam spot market to replenish their supplies. As the Rotterdam price rose above existing contract prices, producer governments took advantage of the rush for stocks by reducing volumes and raising prices of oil sold under long-term contracts and increasing their sales in the spot market.

Both the patterns and the conditions of trade became increasingly fragmented. Bilateral sales between consumer and producer governments doubled in two years. The volume of OPEC government sales to consumer governments or companies sponsored by them rose from about 3.8 mmbd in 1978 to between 6.8 and 7.8 mmbd in 1980.[47] In addition, the conditions of sale became more complicated. Whereas price variations had previously been due largely to quality and transportation differentials, they increasingly reflected the varied outcomes of bilateral negotiations. Although some oil was still sold at official prices, about 30 percent of OPEC sales involved some type of premium.[48] Contracts also included a variety of restrictions, such as provisions for the use of producer-country ships at uneconomic rates, prohibitions on shipments through the Suez canal and on sales to Israel or South Africa, and requirements that oil be used only in the home market of the purchaser.

 46. Ibid.
 47. Ibid.
 48. As Neff points out, the premium took many forms. "In early 1980, for example, Kuwait simply charged a $5.50 per barrel premium on quantities in excess of a basic volume for each purchaser; Iran required that purchasers of crude also buy fuel oil; Mexico required that buyers take heavy as well as light crude; and Algeria collected a $3 per barrel fee to finance exploration." See Thomas L. Neff, "The Changing World Oil Market," in David A. Deese and Joseph S. Nye, eds., *Energy and Security,* A Report of Harvard's Energy and Security Research Project (Ballinger, 1981), p. 30.

Table 5-6. *Contract and Spot Market Prices for Crude Oil, 1977–80*
Dollars per barrel

Quarter	Rotterdam spot market price	Contract price, Saudi Arabian light
1977:1	13.25	12.09
1977:2	12.51	12.09
1977:3	12.47	12.70
1977:4	12.76	12.70
1978:1	12.89	12.70
1978:2	12.72	12.70
1978:3	11.83	12.70
1978:4	14.45	12.70
1979:1	18.13	13.34
1979:2	21.12	14.54
1979:3	23.57	18.00
1979:4	28.27	22.00
1980:1	28.13	26.00
1980:2	27.72	28.00
1980:3	27.63	29.33
1980:4	33.95	31.33

Source: Rotterdam spot market price, f.o.b., 1 percent sulfur, from U.S. Central Intelligence Agency, National Foreign Assessment Center, *International Energy Statistical Review*, various issues (available from National Technical Information Service, Springfield, Va.); price of Saudi Arabian light crude oil, f.o.b. Ras Tanura, from *International Financial Statistics*, vol. 34 (February 1981), and previous issues.

Since the market fragmentation reduced the flexibility of crude oil production and distribution, refiners, marketing companies, and consumers had to hold larger levels of inventories at later stages of the production process. Thus for both transactions and precautionary reasons, crude oil inventories held in almost every important industrial country rose during 1979 and 1980.[49]

Before 1979 the international spot market had been primarily devoted to small volumes of marginal sales of petroleum products. But in 1979 it became an important channel for crude oil, accounting for an estimated 10 to 20 percent of all crude sales.[50] As shown in table 5-6, the spot market

49. For example, the following were the oil stocks in four industrial countries (millions of barrels, end of December for the United States and Japan, and end of June for West Germany and the United Kingdom):

Year	United States	Japan	West Germany	United Kingdom
1978	1,277	411	214	151
1979	1,340	461	243	149
1980	1,403	495	304	171

U.S. Central Intelligence Agency, National Foreign Assessment Center, *International Energy Statistical Review* (May 26, 1981), p. 18, and previous issues (available from National Technical Information Service, Springfield, Va.).

50. Jochen H. Mohnfeld, "Structural Changes in World Crude Oil Trade," *Intereconomics*, vol. 7 (January–February 1980), p. 6.

Figure 5-7. *World Crude Oil Production, 1973–79*

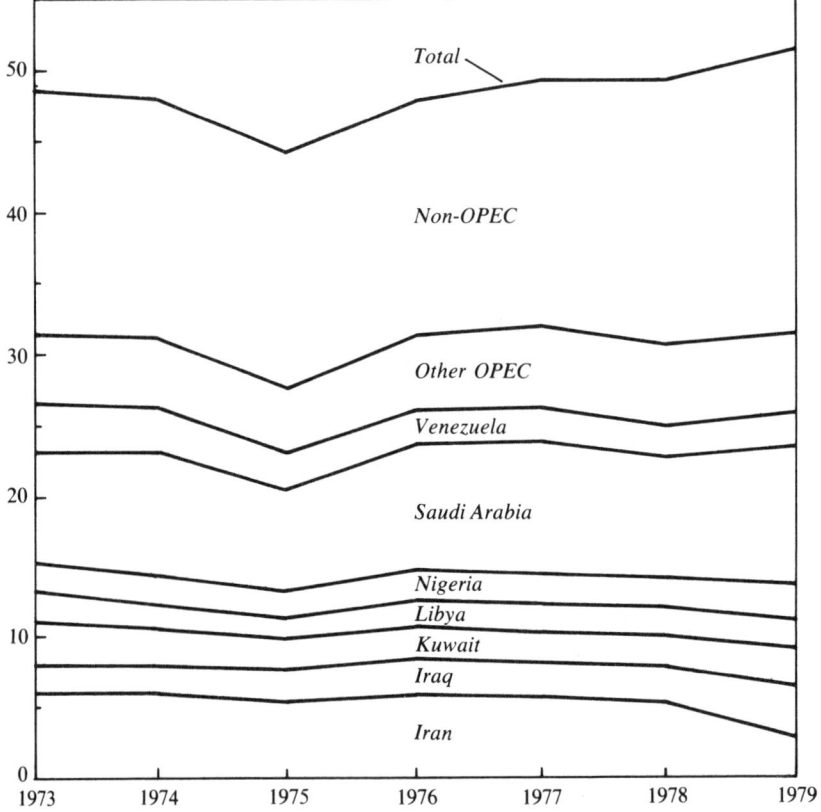

Sources: *International Statistical Review*, April 23, 1980, and previous issues.

price also foreshadowed movements in official contract prices in 1979 and 1980. The spot market price rose sharply throughout 1979, while the large adjustments in contract prices were delayed until late 1979 and 1980.

It is somewhat surprising to look at the global production data during the two oil crises in the 1970s (figure 5-7). The actual volume of oil sold in 1974 and in 1979 was nearly equal to the volume sold in 1973 and in 1978, respectively. Although the failure of supply to grow with demand will clearly exert upward pressure on prices, the size of the scarcity experienced was essentially the result of panic buying by consumers. Programs that removed the need for such buying might have kept the price increases lower.

How Are Petroleum Prices Set?

To formulate an effective policy to counter the inflationary consequences of oil price increases, one should understand how oil prices are set. The absence of a consensus about what determines oil prices has increased the difficulties of making predictions and policies regarding the international oil market. In this section we briefly review several theoretical models that might be applied to oil price behavior and then consider how well such models fit the facts.

Theoretical Foundations

The theory of price determination for a storable depletable natural resource like oil requires incorporating intertemporal considerations normally absent from the more conventional supply and demand framework.

For efficient use, the price of oil should reflect not only current production costs but also the fact that each drop of oil consumed brings the day closer when more expensive energy substitutes will have to be used. In competitive markets the component of the current price of an exhaustible resource in excess of production costs is referred to as an intertemporal rent. Just as the rent on more fertile land will rise as the margin of cultivation is extended, so the price of oil should rise as the market moves to more expensive energy sources.

But at what rate should the price of oil rise? For owners of oil to be able to choose indifferently between selling their oil today and waiting for the higher prices that will be available tomorrow, when more expensive energy sources have to be used, they should expect similar returns from exchanging oil for another asset and from keeping it in the ground. In the simplest case, when production costs are zero, this condition will be met for competitive producers when oil prices are expected to rise at the rate of interest.[51] Thus, as shown in figure 5-8, in a competitive market with a finite endowment of oil, and an alternative, or backstop, technology available at a price P_n, prices will rise toward P_n

---

51. For an analysis of the case in which production costs are considered, see David Levhari and Nissan Leviatan, "Notes on Hotelling's Economics of Exhaustible Resources," *Canadian Journal of Economics*, vol. 10 (May 1977), pp. 177–92.

Figure 5-8. *Price Paths in a Market for a Depletable Natural Resource*

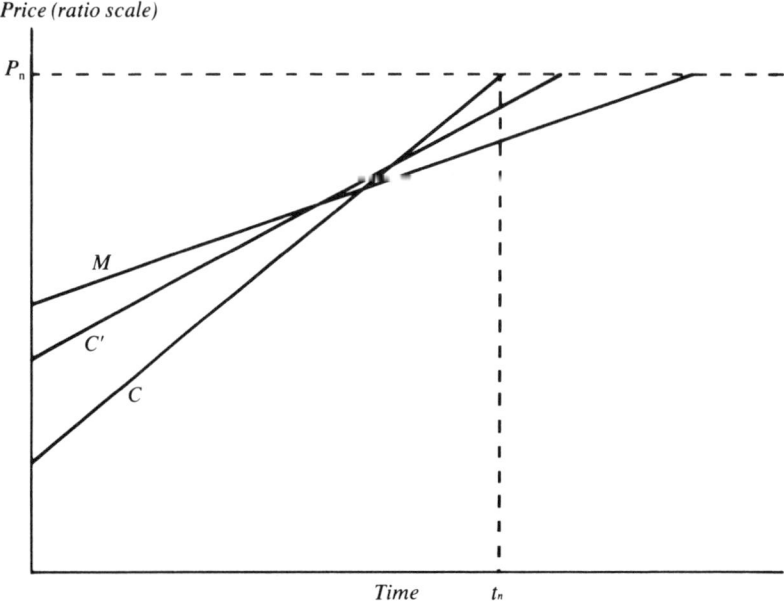

at the rate of interest (given by the slope of line C) until the last drop of oil is exploited. At that time, the backstop becomes the source of energy and its price is P_n (at time t_n). According to this model, the price will rise if (a) the costs of the backstop are increased, (b) demand increases, or (c) the rate of interest falls.

A monopolist, on the other hand, takes into account the effects of sales on the price. To maximize the value of oil holdings, a monopolistic seller would want to be sure that the marginal benefits from sales in each period were the same. Again if marginal production costs are ignored, the profit-maximizing price path for a monopolist is one in which marginal revenue increases at the rate of interest.[52] In general, when demand is highly sensitive to price (elastic), the price path set by a monopolist will be higher but rise more slowly than the path determined by a competitive

---

52. This result is shown in Harold Hotelling, "The Economics of Exhaustible Resources," *Journal of Political Economy*, vol. 39 (April 1931), pp. 137–75. See also William D. Nordhaus, *The Efficient Use of Energy Resources* (Yale University Press, 1979), especially pp. 14–21.

market (compare paths *C* and *M* in figure 5-8).[53] Thus, as has been pointed out, the monopolist is the conservationist's friend.[54]

Another model—the so-called dominant extractor model—comes closer to reality by acknowledging that the market structure might fall somewhere between pure monopoly and competition. Stephen Salant has worked out the solution for the case in which a monopolist or cartel is the core of a market that also has a competitive fringe.[55] Whereas the competitive fringe ignores the effects of its actions on the price, the monopolistic core maximizes its profits along an excess-demand curve equal to the difference between the market demand and competitive supply schedules. Along the equilibrium path the price earned by competitive firms and the marginal revenue of the core group must both rise at the rate of interest. The price path will have two distinct phases: in the first, while competitive producers have stocks, the price increases at the rate of interest. In the second, prices will probably rise more slowly as production is confined to the core group.[56]

Two qualifying points should be mentioned. First, the preceding analysis would not be relevant if abundance of the energy stock made depletion so distant that the intertemporal rents in the current price were negligible. In such cases, of which coal is an example, the intertemporal aspects of the pricing problem would be irrelevant (for short-term analysis) and the normal flow models of microeconomic theory would accurately describe price behavior.[57]

Second, all these models portray long-run behavior. They assume implicitly that short-run considerations, such as temporary shifts in demand and levels of inventories and production capacity, can be ignored.[58]

---

53. Stiglitz shows that where extraction costs are zero and there is a constant elasticity of demand, the proportionality between marginal revenue and prices implies identical price and extraction behavior by monopolists and competitive firms. Joseph E. Stiglitz, "Monopoly and the Rate of Extraction of Exhaustible Resources," *American Economic Review*, vol. 66 (September 1976), pp. 655–61.

54. Robert M. Solow, "The Economics of Resources or the Resources of Economics," *American Economic Review*, vol. 64 (May 1974, *Papers and Proceedings, 1973*), pp. 1–14.

55. Stephen W. Salant, "Staving Off the Backstop: Dynamic Limit-Pricing with a Kinked Demand Curve," *Advances in the Economics of Energy and Resources*, vol. 2 (JAI Press, 1979), pp. 187–204.

56. This assumes an elastic demand curve.

57. For the argument that intertemporal considerations are not relevant in current oil-pricing decisions by producers, see M. A. Adelman, "Constraints on the World Oil Monopoly Price," *Resources and Energy*, vol. 1 (September 1978), pp. 3–19.

58. These theoretical issues of pricing are discussed in more detail in appendix D.

Theory and Practice

Do any of these theories explain the behavior of oil prices in the 1970s? Some analysts have suggested that although OPEC has influenced the timing of price movements, higher oil prices have simply been a response to higher inflation rates. But the dramatic change in the trend of real oil prices in the 1970s refutes this conjecture. Others question whether OPEC has been instrumental in raising prices and argue that the oil price hikes resulted from a tight global market.[59] According to the competitive model, a permanent and previously unanticipated outward shift in the demand curve or an inward shift in the supply curve would induce an upward shift in the price path. But this view is probably more useful for explaining some of the short-run price fluctuations than for explaining price movements over the decade as a whole. The ratios of global aggregate reserves to production in the early 1970s do not indicate an oil shortage. From 1955 to 1968, for example, world reserves grew at an annual average rate of 7.3 percent, a rate that was remarkably like that of global production (7.1 percent) and consumption (7.5 percent). From 1968 to 1973, reserves grew even more rapidly than production—increasing at an average rate of 9.8 percent a year.[60] And Nordhaus, using a model similar to the competitive paradigm described above, concluded that the implied competitive price of oil in the early 1970s was considerably lower than the price that existed *before* the 1973 increase.[61] This competitive market explanation also ignores the fact that oil prices increased substantially in the early 1970s, when the global market was not actually tight or expected to become tight.[62]

A third explanation for oil price behavior focuses on the change in oil ownership in the early 1970s and the likely effects of such a change on the rate at which oil fields were depleted. If companies felt their control

---

59. For example, "The record shows, we believe, that [OPEC] has been a price follower more than a price leader," and "in retrospect it is clear that in 1973–74 as in 1979–80 supplies were never reduced below the level of normal demand. In both periods a surge of panicky buying . . . created an extra demand." William M. Brown and Herman Kahn, "Why OPEC Is Vulnerable," *Fortune* (July 14, 1980), pp. 66–69.

60. Free-world reserve growth from 1955 to 1968 and 1968 to 1973 was 7.1 and 8.4 percent respectively. American Petroleum Institute, *Basic Petroleum Data Book*, sec. 2, table 1.

61. William D. Nordhaus, "The Allocation of Energy Resources," *BPEA, 3:1973*, pp. 529–76.

62. "By mid-1972, excess producing capacity, a rarity in world oil (i.e. outside North America), was almost universal." Adelman, "Is the Oil Shortage Real?" p. 72.

over the oil fields was tenuous, they would apply a considerable discount to expected profits far into the future. Governments, on the other hand, do not face the risk of expropriation and are likely to value future income streams more highly. Thus, in terms of the model outlined above, the effects of such a change in ownership are equivalent to a one-time change in the rate of interest—from path C to C_1 of figure 5-8, for example— again a development that might account for the dramatic rise in oil prices in the early 1970s.[63] Proponents of this "property rights" view point out that their explanation anticipates a jump in the price path in both competitive and monopolistic markets. Some go so far as to suggest that the oil market remains competitive.[64]

The most common explanation for the oil price increases, however, is that the oil market changed from an oligopolistic market of oil companies to an organized cartel. In terms of the model outlined above, the consequences of a change from a competitive to a monopolistic market structure would be a one-time jump to a higher price path (from path C to M of figure 5-8). The perception that the oil market has undergone cartelization leads some analysts to draw on conventional cartel theory, which stresses the tensions associated with apportioning the supply restrictions that are needed to keep prices high, and to argue that when OPEC faces this test, the cartel will break down.[65]

But a change in market structure or in property rights should induce just a one-time shift in the oil price path. Although such a shift seems to have occurred in 1973–74, these theories have to be supplemented in accounting for the rise—of similar magnitude—experienced in 1979 and 1980.[66]

In fact neither the competitive-pricing model nor the theory of the cartel that acts like a classical monopolist seems to fit OPEC. Competitive producers should increase supply when prices rise and reduce supplies when they fall. In figure 5-9 we chart the real price of oil against oil supply and industrial production (which proxies for normal demand).

---

63. Of course a more disaggregated view of the nation might recognize the interest particular political leaders could have in protecting themselves, if they were displaced from power, by having money in the bank. This argument leads to an increase rather than a decline in the rate of production.

64. Walter J. Mead, "An Economic Analysis," pp. 212–28.

65. Osborne, however, argues that there are strategies to make a cartel viable. D. K. Osborne, "Cartel Problems," *American Economic Review*, vol. 66 (December 1976), pp. 835–45.

66. This leads some to view the 1979–80 price increase as a temporary deviation from the long-run path. See, for example, Mead, "An Economic Analysis," p. 227.

Figure 5-9. *Growth in Free-World Production and Price of Crude Oil, 1970–79*

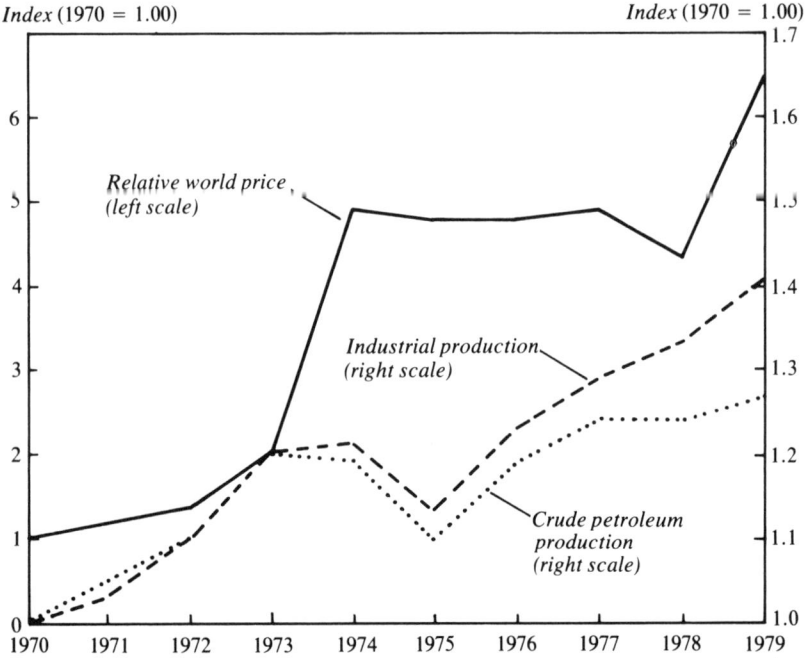

Sources: World price is for Saudi Arabian light crude oil, f.o.b. Ras Tanura, from *International Financial Statistics*, vol. 33 (December 1980), and previous issues, deflated by the UN manufactured goods export price index, from United Nations, *Monthly Bulletin of Statistics*, vol. 34 (July 1980), and previous issues. For 1972–79 the index is based on fourth-quarter prices. Crude oil production is from American Petroleum Institute, *Basic Petroleum Data Book*, sec. 4, table 2. Industrial production is the UN industrial production index for market economies.

Oil supply followed demand in 1975 and declined, even though real prices were near those of 1974. Supply then increased despite flat real prices in 1976 and 1977. This fits more closely the pattern of supply being adjusted to demand in order to influence prices than of movement along the supply curve of a competitive market. And since for the most part supply shifts during the period 1973–78 were the result of deliberate decisions—and not, as in agricultural markets, acts of God—the data suggest that suppliers set prices rather than responded to them.

But OPEC's pricing decisions do not seem to have been those of a pure profit-maximizing monopolist either. There is increasing evidence that the demand for oil at prices in the range at which they were kept from 1974–78 remained highly inelastic. A cartel or monopolist would

Table 5-7. *OPEC Crude Oil Production and Supply Coordination: Deviations from Trend, 1974–78 and 1974–79*

Country or group of countries	Average percent deviation from mean		Coefficient of correlation with the rest of OPEC	
	1974–78	1974–79	1974–78	1974–79
OPEC	3.9	3.6	...	...
Iran	4.8	18.2	0.41	−0.65
Iraq	7.1	12.9	−0.08	−0.05
Kuwait	6.2	8.3	0.03	0.14
Libya	14.0	13.4	0.53	0.57
Nigeria	7.2	7.4	0.73	0.71
Saudi Arabia	6.4	7.2	0.91	0.66
Venezuela	8.8	7.4	−0.09	−0.10
Other	6.6	6.3	0.49	0.53

Source: *International Energy Statistical Review* (April 23, 1980), p. 2, and previous issues.

not set a price that corresponded to an inelastic portion of the long-run demand curve.[67]

The failure of OPEC to choose the profit-maximizing price could be attributed to miscalculation, because of uncertainty about the long-run demand elasticity at prices not previously reached. It could also be conjectured that although revenues might be raised with a higher price, the cartel might have difficulties in prorationing very low output levels among its members. On the other hand, OPEC's choice of price might have been intentional. A core producer with a competitive fringe will tend to set prices lower than a complete monopolist.

For a core producer group with a competitive fringe, the point at which marginal revenue becomes negative might correspond to an inelastic point on the market demand curve. The core group must reckon that higher prices will not only cut off demand but may also raise supply in the competitive fringe.

Which countries belong to the core? The production data do not support the notion that Saudi Arabia has performed the task of balancing the market alone. Though quantitatively the Saudis have accounted for an important share of the fluctuations in OPEC supplies, their share in fluctuations has been similar to their share in production. As table 5-7 indicates, absolute deviations of Saudi production from average were 7

---

67. After surveying a number of studies, Nordhaus concludes, "A good guess would be that long-run final [energy] price elasticities are in the −0.7 to −1.1 range, implying that long-run crude [oil] price elasticities are from −0.2 to −0.5." William D. Nordhaus, "Oil and Economic Performance in Industrial Countries," *BPEA, 2:1980*, p. 346.

percent over the 1974–79 period, an amount similar to that of other cartel members. If the Saudi supply behavior were dominated by a concern to keep prices on a specific path, while other OPEC members ignored such considerations, one would expect a fairly low correlation between fluctuations in the Saudi supply and the supply of other OPEC members. In fact, however, Saudi supply movements seem to have been coordinated with other OPEC members (from 1974–78, for example, the correlation coefficient is 0.91).

Thus if the Saudis exercise a disproportionate amount of influence over the market, it might be due more to their power to threaten substantial changes in market conditions than to their having actually done so. It appears that the majority of OPEC members have acted in a fairly cohesive way.

Cartel Strategy

Cartel members have to make two kinds of decisions: first, what the price will be, and second, how the quantity associated with that price will be divided between suppliers.

The motivations behind price-setting decisions are likely to be far more complex than short-run profit maximization.[68] High prices encourage substitution and conservation decisions that may not be reversible. They also encourage research and development directed toward lowering the costs of other energy sources. The gains from higher current profits must be weighed against possible future losses. And usually those with larger stocks will be inclined to weight future prices more heavily and prefer somewhat lower prices today—a fact that may explain Saudi preferences for lower prices.

There are also of course other facts that have to be weighed by OPEC members. At the margin, the benefits from domestic economic development, foreign investment, and keeping oil in the ground must be equalized. The macroeconomic and redistributive consequences of oil price changes make the price of oil an important political variable because of the short-run costs associated with disrupting the world economy.

68. See, for example, General Accounting Office, *Critical Factors Affecting Saudi Arabia's Oil Decisions,* Report to the Congress by the Comptroller General of the United States (GAO, 1978).

OPEC may well be muddling through rather than following a grand design.[69] Much uncertainty surrounds many of the relevant parameters in the oil market. What is the appropriate price for alternative technologies? How much oil is there in the ground? What is the demand elasticity? Behavior predicted in models that assume perfect foresight and profit maximization may not provide the correct answers.[70]

Since OPEC is uncertain about the appropriate trajectory for the contract price, it may use the spot price to determine what that price should be. A number of analysts have noted the tendency for OPEC's contract prices to follow the price in the Rotterdam spot market when the spot price rises above the contract prices. On the other hand, OPEC seems to resist downward adjustments of its contract prices when the Rotterdam price falls below contract prices.[71]

OPEC has apparently not developed a formalized set of rules for allocating market shares, monitoring production, disciplining cheaters, and allocating side payments. Shares could plausibly be allocated according to need, as shown by per captia income, the cost of production, production capacity, or reserves. But the empirical studies do not seem to have found a single conclusive explanatory criterion.[72]

All in all, the picture of an awkward but effective cartel emerges. Two factors seem to be critical in facilitating cartel cooperation: first, the clear understanding of the benefits of cooperative action, and second, the

69. See, for example, M. A. Adelman, "The Clumsy Cartel," *Energy Journal,* vol. 1 (January 1980), pp. 43–53.

70. For a survey of the empirical attempts to estimate the optimal OPEC price path, see Shawkat Hammoudeh, "The Future Oil Price Behavior of OPEC and Saudi Arabia: A Survey of Optimization Models," *Energy Economics,* vol. 1 (July 1979), pp. 156–66. He concludes: "There is a consensus that current prices are higher than OPEC's long-run interest would dictate." Many of the experts who disavow such optimization models would disagree with that consensus.

71. Nordhaus formally models this ratchet-type process in "Oil and Economic Performance in Industrial Countries."

72. For a discussion of the revenue needs of OPEC members as a constraint on output reduction, see Theodore H. Moran, *Oil Prices and the Future of OPEC: The Political Economy of Tension and Stability in the Organization of Petroleum Exporting Countries,* RFF Research Paper R-8 (Washington, D.C.: Resources for the Future, 1978). Wyant, *The United States,* found that in 1974 and 1975 there was a direct relation between excess capacity and per capita income. But Mead, "Economic Analysis," found that between 1974 and 1977 low-absorber countries (those with high incomes and small populations) actually increased their market shares, as did countries with the largest levels of production. Danielson, "Theory and Measurement of OPEC Stability," found that during 1977 and 1978 the countries with the largest reserve levels were those that restricted supplies by the largest proportions.

widespread belief that keeping oil in the ground is a sound investment.[73] And because revenues from oil have been so large and events have conspired to create two major oil crunches, OPEC has been able to achieve spectacular success with a rather informal decisionmaking approach.

Even if, over the long haul, optimizing models successfully chart the price path, these models implictly assume that cartel leaders or competitive producers will have the capacity to maintain prices close to the optimal trajectory and the willingness to use that capacity to stabilize prices in the event of an unforeseen increase in excess demand. During the 1950s and 1960s the multinational oil companies had enough capacity and incentive to perform the price-smoothing function. Although they might have been able to boost their profits in the short run by raising prices during a temporary shortage, such an action might have had considerable costs. First, it would have antagonized producer host countries whose earnings were tied to the *volume* of oil produced in the form of specific royalty fees. Second, large profits could have provoked host countries into taking actions that might not easily have been reversed when the shortage was over. Third, if the multinational oil companies (which were largely United States–owned) were seen to be "profiteering" in consumer countries, governments might have intervened or promoted their own independent companies. And fourth, a volatile price would have upset the operation of an oligopolistic market in which price competition could prove detrimental to long-run profit maximization.

But during the 1970s there was little excess production capacity on hand in the non-OPEC oil market. Since OPEC members can explicitly collude with one another, they do not have to be as concerned about the problems of coordination associated with a volatile price. Political forces push the OPEC members toward raising prices in the face of a shortage. Sovereign countries need not worry that high profits will lead to expropriation, and it is hard for political leaders to justify selling the national patrimony at prices that are lower than the market will bear. Rational producers in such a market may not deem it profitable to incur a permanent reserve of capacity to offset an increase in excess demand

---

73. For a description of the conservationist tendencies of a non-OPEC country, see U.S. Library of Congress, Congressional Research Service, *Mexico's Oil and Gas Policy: An Analysis,* prepared for the Senate Committee on Foreign Relations and the Joint Economic Committee, 95 Cong. 2 sess. (GPO, 1979).

perceived as temporary—particularly when such an increase adds vastly to their short-run profits. When any of a number of transitory disturbances jolts the market, the price path followed by the oil market may stray far from an equilibrium trajectory, because of the weakness of the equilibrating forces and because of the lags in adjustment to unanticipated changes.

Consumer behavior, influenced by these market conditions, enhanced price volatility in the 1970s. During the 1960s consumers could depend on the oil companies to offset any shortages from alternative sources. But during the 1970s the prospect of a shortfall induced hoarding, since consumers sought to shield themselves from disruption.

It is therefore possible that exogenous political factors, such as the October war and events in Iran and Iraq, created inventory demands that sent spot prices soaring. OPEC discovered that demand was considerably less elastic than it, or anyone else, had thought and that higher prices could lead to increased revenues. It is also possible that, particularly in 1979–80, the price that cleared the market reflected the transitory demand for stockbuilding and was considerably higher than OPEC's optimal price, given permanent demands for use.

In sum, therefore, while the several models of oil market behavior can suggest the qualitative implications of such factors as market structure, ownership, alternative technologies, and aggregate demand and supply conditions, the small historic sample of price behavior makes it difficult to formulate an empirical model in which one could have much confidence. And even if the correct model could be determined, it would not allow the accurate prediction of short-run movements in the oil market, since the equilibrating forces bringing that market back to its long-run price path work slowly and poorly.

CHAPTER SIX

The Policy Choices: Some General Considerations

THE DESCRIPTION of the inflation process in chapter 1 introduces several complexities into the design of anti-inflation policy. When inflation is caused by factors other than excess aggregate demand, fiscal and monetary policies alone are not adequate to solve the problem. An effective anti-inflation policy must address two basic issues: (1) how to break the momentum of an inflation inherited from the past, as reflected in a repetitive cycle of domestic wage and price increases, and (2) how to respond to new disturbances, both domestic and foreign. While the causes of the inertia and the evaluation of policies to control it are not the subject of this study, the implication of commodity price changes for anti-inflation policy can be appraised only within the context of an economy that has an industrial sector characterized by relatively fixed price markets that impart a degree of inertia to the inflation process.

Inflation can be reduced by a sustained application of fiscal and monetary restraint, but the costs in unemployment and lost incomes will be high. How high remains a matter of some controversy among economists. To a large extent the controversy reflects differing value judgments about the relative costs of inflation and unemployment. There exist, however, important differences in interpretations of how industrial markets operate and what magnitude of unemployment is required.

Most studies of inflation have assumed that markets are relatively competitive (that is, prices are largely a reflection of the market clearing of demand and supply), and therefore that the fundamental cause of inflation is excess demand. According to many of the studies, however, long-term wage and price expectations delay the adjustment to a more restrictive policy. Thus the conflict between inflation and unemployment is temporary, not permanent. Some economists hold, in addition, that the conflict is extended by the perception of the participants that government policy will ultimately give way under the political pressure of increasing unemployment, leading businessmen and workers to discount any short-term shift of policy toward restraint. Thus a more credible or firmly held government policy would shorten the lags and reduce the costs.

But other studies emphasize that elements of bilateral monopoly are prominent in price and wage determination, and they delay or even prevent the adjustment to supply and demand. They see key economic agents as stubbornly resisting even determined monetary and fiscal policies of nonaccommodation.[1]

Fluctuating commodity prices raise special problems precisely because other prices cannot be expected to change immediately to offset them. If all markets displayed the flexible-price behavior of the competitive model, fiscal and monetary policies would be an adequate basis for controlling inflation. Alternatively, if all prices and wages reflected the outcome of a bilateral monopoly or fixed-price model, various forms of incomes policies might be the most effective means of control. But since the actual economy is a mixture of market structures, either of these policies will be frustrated when used alone.

The sharp changes in primary commodity prices during the 1970s have focused attention on two important issues of anti-inflation policy.

First, at the aggregate level, should the monetary authorities seek to accommodate the inflation pressures of an exogenous price shock by expanding the money supply to finance the higher price level; or should they hold firm to their previous monetary targets and force an offsetting reduction in other prices at the cost of a lower level of real output? The same issue arises for fiscal policy, since it is an alternative means of regulating total demand. And if a price shock originates abroad, both fiscal and monetary policy must address the related problem of whether or not to offset the drain of purchasing power into increased import

---

1. All these viewpoints have a voluminous literature. Two statements of the contrasts as they apply to policy are William Fellner, *Toward a Reconstruction on Macroeconomics: Problems of Theory and Practice* (Washington, D.C. American Enterprise Institute for Public Policy Research, 1976); and Arthur M. Okun, *Prices and Quantities: A Macroeconomic Analysis* (Brookings Institution, 1981). Okun seems to accept the argument that the system has a unique long-term equilibrium as defined by the competitive market analysis. He argues that the importance of the adjustment rigidities, however, leads to a situation in which the short-run disequilibrium dominates the formulation of optimal policies.

demand: that is, a rise in import prices is equivalent to an excise tax in its depressive effect on domestic demand.[2]

Second, are there any microeconomic policies that could avoid or dampen the inflation effects of commodity market disturbances?

These two issues are examined in the rest of this chapter. In the first section we review the arguments for and against accommodation. Next we examine the arguments for and against government intervention in commodity markets to stabilize prices. And finally we discuss the relative merits of different kinds of stabilization schemes, like buffer stocks, taxes, and subsidies, and we examine some important issues relating to the operation of such programs. (The following chapter is directed specifically to the markets for grains and petroleum, where the merits of contingency planning for supply disruptions seem greatest.)

Demand-Management Policy and Inflation Shocks

In the years immediately before 1973, discussions of inflation and macroeconomic policy focused on the effort to define a rate of resource use (usually expressed in terms of the unemployment rate) that would be consistent with stable or nonaccelerating inflation. This issue took the form of a debate: could fiscal and monetary policies reduce unemployment at the cost of a finite increase in inflation, or would any unemployment rate below a "natural rate" lead to an ever-accelerating rate of inflation and any rate above lead to continuous deceleration? The commodity price shocks of 1973, on the other hand, reminded economists that inflation can increase even if unemployment is at or above any so-called natural rate—that is, one consistent with a stable long-run inflation rate. The question for fiscal and monetary policies is whether to accom-

---

2. If the price shock is accompanied by a redistribution of income to groups with a low marginal propensity to spend (such as the members of OPEC), the price shock will induce a decline in real output similar to that induced by an excise tax. Thus a policy devoted to maintaining the previous path of real output may actually require a shift to a more expansionary fiscal policy or a shift in monetary policy more than proportionate to the impact of the price shock on the average price level. This fiscal effect of shocks that originate abroad concerned many economists in 1974. See, for example, George L. Perry, "The United States," in Edward R. Fried and Charles L. Schultze, eds., *Higher Oil Prices and the World Economy: The Adjustment Problem* (Brookings Institution, 1975), pp. 71–104.

Alternative Views of the Policy Choices

In an economy where not all prices and wages are fully flexible, the crucial question for policy is how domestic wages respond to the initial price disturbance. This issue can be illustrated by specifying an initial planned path for future inflation, physical output, and unemployment. The simplest case is that in which there is no feedback effect of high prices on wage rates, and real wages are allowed to decline. If the economy is held to the planned path of output (by an increase in the money supply, for example), a pure price shock will temporarily raise the inflation rate and permanently increase the price level, as shown by the solid lines in figure 6-1.[4] If, however, wages and other prices respond to the price increase, the situation becomes more complex. When the feedback of nominal wages is positive but less than proportionate to the rise in the price level (cost-of-living escalation clauses in labor contracts are one example of such a response), the impact on the inflation rate is drawn out in time and there is a multiple effect on the price level (as shown by the dotted lines). The process dampens, and the inflation rate returns to its initial path with no loss of output. But if the feedback effect on nominal wage rates is unity (a full resistance to wage reductions), there will be a *protracted* increase in the inflation rate and an unending rise in the price level (as shown by the dashed lines) as long as output and unemployment adhere to the prior path. A somewhat intermediate result would occur if expectations of future inflation had a unitary effect on

---

3. An extensive literature on this issue has developed in recent years. Edward M. Gramlich, "Macro-Policy Responses to Price Shocks," *Brookings Papers on Economic Activity, 1:1979*, pp. 125–66 (hereafter *BPEA*), and the discussion that follows offer a general review. The paper also includes an extensive citation of previous studies. A recent analysis that uses the rational expectations framework is Alan S. Blinder, "Monetary Accommodation of Supply Shocks under Rational Expectations," NBER Working Paper 465 (Cambridge: National Bureau of Economic Research, March 1980).

4. Most disturbances to the price level have a direct effect on real income, much as an excise tax drains off purchasing power. Others may imply a change in aggregate supply, such as an adverse weather change. We have excluded this aspect of the issue by referring to a pure price shock in which policy is assumed to have compensated for any real income effects. In a simple sense, the baseline for policy is one in which unemployment is maintained on its previously preferred path.

Figure 6-1. *The Impact of Price Shocks on the Inflation Rate and Price Level*

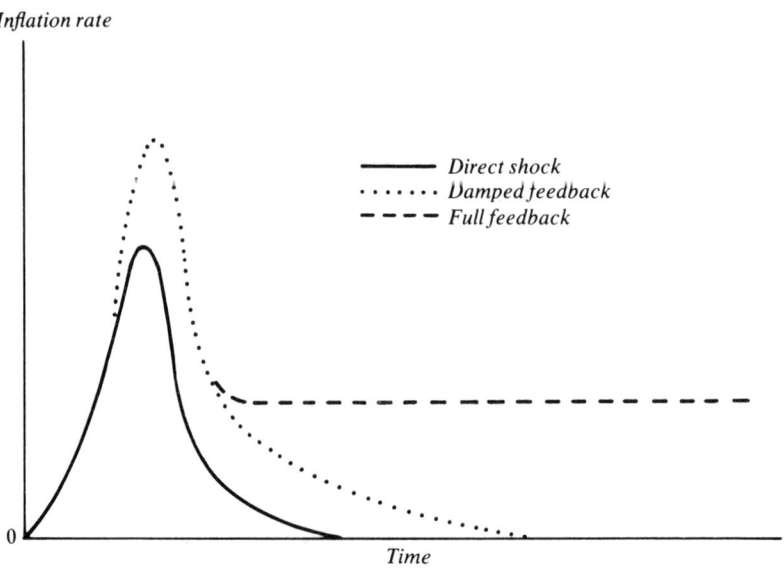

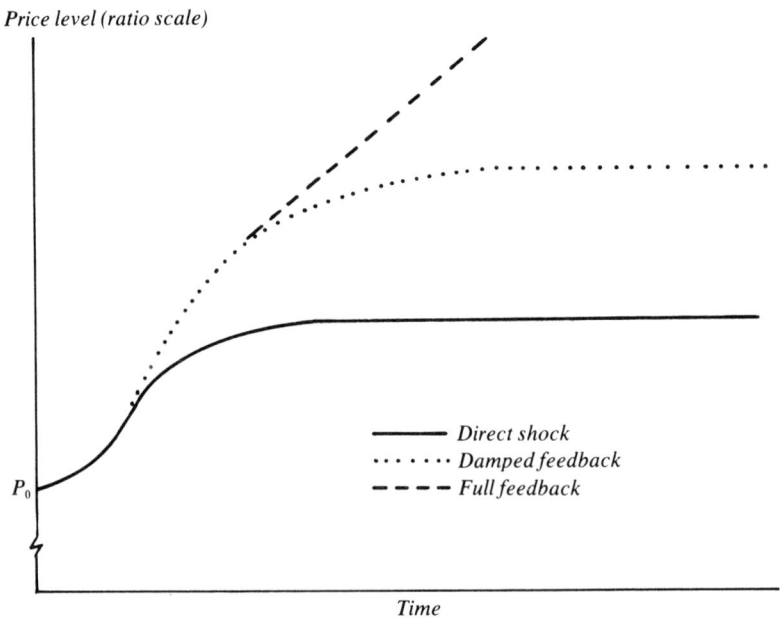

wage rates but if the revision of expectations were less than one-for-one with respect to the initial shock—that is, if to some extent its transitory nature were perceived. There would be a sustained increase in the inflation rate but along a path below the initial surge.[5]

The strongest case for accommodation (adjusting policy to maintain an unchanging path of real output) exists when there is no feedback effect of the higher prices on wage inflation. The policy choice is between a *temporary* surge of inflation and a *temporary* rise in unemployment.[6] A reduced supply of beef, for example, implies a need for beef prices to rise relative to prices for other goods. If the change has to occur within an unchanged average price level (nonaccommodation), the reduction in other prices and wage rates will require some loss of output and employment until the adjustment is complete. Yet the same restructuring of relative prices could occur if other prices remain constant and the average price level rises to accommodate the increase in beef prices. Thus an accommodative monetary policy could allow for a change in relative prices while avoiding the unemployment costs. Such a decision must involve political as well as economic factors, since it depends on a society's valuation of the relative costs of inflation and unemployment.[7]

5. In empirical work this range of alternative views about the feedback effect is formulated in terms of a specification of a proportionate markup of prices over wages; a relationship between wage-rate changes, the unemployment rate, expectations of other wage-rate changes (a relative wage linkage), and expectations of future price changes (a real wage linkage): $w = a(1/u) + b_1 w_1^e + b_2 p^e$; and an adaptive formulation of expectations as a moving average of past actual changes. The first version, discussed above, assumes $b_2 = 0$; the second is consistent with $b_2 > 0$ and $b_1 + b_2 < 1$; and the third implies $b_1 + b_2 = 1$. The final, more intermediate case, also implies $b_1 + b_2 = 1$, but it allows for a wider range of processes that generate expectations. There is no agreement at the empirical level on which of these formulations is most representative of reality, though few would accept the first version of no feedback. If the initial price shock reflects an effort to get a higher real price, full indexing of wages implies an accelerating future path of inflation, as no one will accept a decline in his real income.

6. We have ignored one possible case in which all prices and wage rates are sufficiently flexible for the full adjustment of relative prices to occur before a change in policy can affect the economy. In that case price shocks would create no problem for anti-inflation policy. Such a situation does not seem plausible for modern industrial economies. Some economists have also argued against any accommodation whatsoever, on the grounds that it erodes private sector perceptions of the government's commitment to price stability in the future.

7. It is often overlooked by the proponents of accommodation that their advice should be symmetric with respect to deflationary price shocks. Too often an inflationary shock leads to calls for accommodation, whereas a deflationary shock is seen as an opportunity to increase output and employment, not as a signal to contract monetary growth. In retrospect it does appear that the 1975–76 decline of farm prices did generate just such overoptimism about the inflation outlook.

A more complex decision must be made when there is a feedback effect of prices on wage rates, because accommodation of the direct effects on the price level does not end the matter. If one chooses to accommodate the direct effects because the unemployment costs are high, logically one should accommodate the secondary effects. Indeed it begins to sound as though one never resists inflation, because the costs are high. As long as the process is self-dampening, however, a consideration of the secondary repercussions simply magnifies the inflation costs without changing the magnitude of the unemployment costs, and makes the arguments against accommodation stronger than in the first instance. Such a partial feedback effect on wage rates is incorporated in most empirical studies of the policy options.[8]

The costs of accommodation policy are greatest when wages reflect a full pass-through of past price inflation or of expectations of future price inflation. The formulation of expectations about future inflation is likely to be complex. Yet given an initial pattern of such expectations for future periods, it is reasonable to assume that an unforeseen surge of prices in the current period will raise such expectations, though perhaps by a small amount. Unless some other determinant of wages (such as the unemployment rate or the actual inflation rate) declines below its initially hypothesized path, the rate of wage and price inflation would seem to be higher for all future periods. Therefore, the choice is between a *protracted* increase in the inflation rate along with an ever-rising price level and a *temporary* decline of real output below its prior path. The return of the inflation rate to its previous path, therefore, requires at least a period of temporary higher unemployment if the unemployment rate is the sole means whereby policymakers can influence the future path of prices and wages. The policymakers would in this case be pushed even further toward nonaccommodation.[9]

The Unemployment Costs

The choice of an appropriate policy response to price shocks also cannot be divorced from the broader debate about the effectiveness of

8. This is the version examined by Gramlich in an empirical model that incorporates a specific measure of the relative social costs of inflation and unemployment. He concludes that the optimal policy calls for a high degree of accommodation because the initial reduction in output has only a weak offsetting effect on inflation. See Gramlich, "Macro-Policy Responses," pp. 150–55.

9. Inclusion of the secondary repercussion on wages and other prices does increase the magnitude of the inflation costs, but it does not affect the unemployment costs of

THE POLICY CHOICES 139

aggregate demand management in regulating inflation—that is, the extent to which a given reduction in real output and employment will reduce the rate of wage and price inflation. In empirical studies this debate takes the form of a disagreement over the magnitude of the role of the unemployment rate in wage determination. In a survey of several "Phillips curve" studies of this trade-off, Arthur Okun found that the estimated reduction in U.S. inflation that could be achieved by an extra percentage point of unemployment maintained for a year averaged about 0.3 percentage point.[10] The inflation benefits do increase if the restraint is maintained for a longer period, because of adjustment lags and the reinforcement effects of lower wage inflation on prices and back onto wage rates. But even an optimistic estimate based on historical relationships would imply that in the United States an effort to offset 1 percentage point of inflation would require an increase in unemployment of one million workers for a two-year period. If the degree of responsiveness is as low as the empirical studies indicate, one can argue that nonaccommodation simply makes a bad situation worse. Yet our own empirical results in chapter 3 implied that the United States ranked relatively high among industrial countries in the responsiveness of inflation to changes in output; the weak relationship between inflation and aggregate demand in other countries pushes them even further toward accommodative policies.

International Implications

The policy choice is further complicated by the need to consider international repercussions. In a world of flexible exchange rates a decision by one country to be less accommodative to a price shock than its neighbors leads to an improvement in its competitive position and an appreciation of its currency. The appreciation of the currency reduces import prices—providing an additional mechanism by which a deflationary policy affects the average price level. In fact, it is reasonable to assume that the initial exchange-rate appreciation will overshoot the long-run equilibrium if the domestic restraint is concentrated in the

---

nonaccommodation. An offsetting shock to the price level induced by higher unemployment would be subject to the same magnification.

10. Arthur M. Okun, "Efficient Disinflation Policies," *American Economic Review*, vol. 68 (May 1978, *Papers and Proceedings, 1977*), pp. 348–52. A 1979 study of prices found that demand restraint is unlikely to reduce price inflation within individual industries at any given rate of wage inflation. See Hendrik S. Houthakker, "Growth and Inflation: Analysis by Industry," *BPEA, 1:1979*, pp. 241–56.

monetary area. A rise of the interest rate relative to those of other countries will attract capital and raise the exchange rate. This short-run appreciation to offset the interest-rate differential will be greater than the appreciation in the long term, when the interest-rate differential has returned to a more normal level or the asset adjustment has been completed. Thus the mechanism of offsetting changes in import prices will dampen the effect of the inflationary shock, spreading it out into future periods. But one must remember that such a policy cannot be followed by all countries, since it involves passing the initial costs of adjustment to others. In fact, a competitive bidding-up of interest rates runs the risk of inducing a general recession. Even without a change in interest-rate differentials, however, the perception by investors that one country will be less accommodative might lead to an inflow of capital to that country and a beneficial appreciation of its currency.

Summary

None of the alternative views outlined above of the economic consequences of a price shock would support a policy of either pure accommodation (fixed real-output path) or pure nonaccommodation (adherence to a fixed path for inflation), but they do lead to sharply different conclusions about what the degree of accommodation should be. Because views about the relative costs of inflation and unemployment differ, it is not surprising that the policy advice is conflicting. But certainly the simple prescription of either extreme can be rejected. Such rules simply allocate the costs in an arbitrary way that depends on the economy's reaction to a reduction in nominal demand, since the reduction is split between a lower price level and a lower level of real output. In some markets the reduction will result in lower prices; in others it will be largely absorbed in lower output and employment. Research can contribute to an understanding of the issue by clarifying the nature of the feedback effects and the dimensions of the unemployment-inflation trade-off. But the issue will always remain a heavily normative one.

The most important conclusion that emerges from the studies is that no macroeconomic policy can completely avoid the domestic costs of an external price shock. Accommodative monetary policies increase price variability; nonaccommodative policies increase output variability. Both are distasteful and costly, and both could prove counterproductive in the long run. A superior policy would avoid having to apply either

THE POLICY CHOICES 141

measure. Aggregate demand restraint as a response to a commodity price increase is a particularly inefficient policy. First, it depresses sectors of the economy—for example, housing and capital goods—that might not be the source of the excess demand. Second, besides the obvious costs in forgone output, it foments social tensions by falling most heavily on the poor and minorities, who are usually the last hired and first fired. Third, a high variability in output undermines capital formation—since it adds to the risks of such activity—thereby increasing the probability of future capacity shortages and sharp price changes in basic material markets. These problems for macroeconomic policy emphasize the potential attractiveness of microeconomic policies to mitigate the source of the disturbances directly.

Rationale for Government Intervention

In a market subject to shifts in demand and supply, consumers and producers as a group will gain from price stabilization. The allocation of those gains between the two sides of the market and the size of the net gain, however, are heavily dependent on the nature of the basic demand and supply functions, the source of the disturbances and other assumptions about risk, the formation of expectations, and the degree of the stabilization.[11]

Private markets in storable commodities themselves embody strong mechanisms to provide the optimal degree of price stabilization over time. At the simplest level this will be reflected in the adjustment of inventories. Expectations of a future price increase create the opportunity for profit through the purchase of the commodity in the current period and its sale in the future period. Such intertemporal transactions are profitable as long as the difference between the expected future price

---

11. In the simplest case of linear demand-supply functions subject to additive shifts, a stabilization of supply shifts will increase producers' surplus more than it reduces consumers' surplus; the opposite is true for a stabilization of price changes that originate from demand shifts. Introducing further complications into the analysis changes the distribution and size of the benefits. In addition, using the concept of consumer-producer surplus in the analysis limits the assessment to the private benefits of the participants, with no consideration of externalities or the effect on other markets. A recent survey of the theoretical work is provided by Stephen J. Turnovsky, "The Distribution of Welfare Gains from Price Stabilization: A Survey of Some Theoretical Issues," in F. Gerard Adams and Sonia A. Klein, eds., *Stabilizing World Commodity Markets: Analysis, Practice, and Policy* (Lexington Books, 1978), pp. 119–48.

and the current spot market price exceeds the carrying costs (interest plus storage costs minus the convenience yield) by an amount sufficient to compensate for the risks. By shifting supplies between the current and the future period, such activities serve to narrow the range of price fluctuations. At the same time they complicate the explanation of the current price, which will reflect expectations of future demand and supply conditions as well as current conditions.

Futures markets are another way to reduce private risks of unforeseen future price changes. On the one hand, the farmer hedges against unforeseen changes in the future price of his grain by selling a futures contract. Subsequent declines in the spot market price of grain will be offset by a profit on that contract. On the other hand, the speculator provides insurance to hedgers—through the assumption of the risk of price fluctuations. His is an exposed position not offset by a position in the spot market. In practice, of course, the volume of contracts in futures market is not limited to covering exposed positions in the spot market. Arbitrage (purchase in today's market for future delivery) does place a ceiling on the futures price equal to the spot price plus carrying costs, but there is no corresponding floor, because today's shortage cannot be met by tomorrow's supply.

The opportunity for storage and the existence of futures contracts therefore provide a mechanism by which the private market can absorb all available information about current and expected future market conditions to allocate a commodity over time efficiently. Government regulation of such markets may be needed to prevent the dissemination of false information, the manipulation of the market, and the development of monopolies. Those who argue for a much greater degree of intervention, however, seek to identify more fundamental areas of market failure. The three main reasons for intervention are that private expectations are not optimal, private and social costs differ, and private and social benefits differ.

Information Efficiency

For storage to be optimal, forecasts of future prices should also be optimal; that is, be based on an efficient use of all available information and not err systematically. An optimal ex ante forecast may be wrong ex post. A much debated question is whether or not the explicit or implicit price forecasts of competitive markets are optimal. Those who

THE POLICY CHOICES 143

believe they are point out that when the current price does not reflect all worthwhile information, those who are privy to that information can make a profit. Any contribution made by such participants toward equilibrating the market will be rewarded. By buying when the price is too low, stabilizing speculators raise the price; by selling when it is too high, they lower it. Those with special forecasting skills will dominate the market, while those who err and destabilize the price by buying when it is too high and selling when it is too low will be chastened by their losses.[12] Assuming that an underlying model does explain market behavior, the market forecast should be the same as that of a model that uses all available information. If the market reflects so-called rational expectations about future prices, it will incorporate all worthwhile new information rapidly and market predictions will not be systematically wrong.[13] Proponents of rational expectations believe that the great volatility in many competitive market prices does not result from irrational destabilizing behavior, but from the fact that many unpredictable events influence these prices.

An extensive body of literature has attempted to substantiate the claim that competitive markets process information efficiently without a systematic bias. Poole recounts that "numerous investigators have analyzed an enormous amount of data using many different techniques and no serious departure from the predictions of the (rational expectations) hypothesis has been found."[14]

The view of speculators as skilled specialists who guide the market

---

12. Milton Friedman, "The Case for Flexible Exchange Rates," in *Essays in Positive Economics* (University of Chicago Press, 1953), pp. 157–203. The literature has turned up cases in which destabilizing speculation might be profitable. See, for example, William J. Baumol, "Speculation, Profitability, and Stability," *Review of Economics and Statistics*, vol. 39 (August 1957), pp. 263–71. But Johnson has noted that such counterexamples have implicitly either selected a group of especially clever destabilizing speculators who make money at the expense of other destabilizing speculators—leading to an overall loss—or imputed to destabilizing speculators profits that could not be realized. Harry G. Johnson, "Destabilizing Speculation: A General Equilibrium Approach," *Journal of Political Economy*, vol. 84 (February 1976), pp. 101–08. Johnson himself goes on to describe a case in which a destabilizing speculator might gain.

13. See John F. Muth, "Rational Expectations and the Theory of Price Movements," *Econometrica*, vol. 29 (July 1961), pp. 315–35.

14. See William Poole, "Rational Expectations in the Macro Model," *BPEA, 2:1976*, pp. 463–514, especially pp. 467–71. Poole's statement is most relevant to financial markets. The evidence is less convincing for commodity markets. See Gordon W. Smith, "Commodity Instability and Market Failures: A Survey of Issues," in Adams and Klein, eds., *Stabilizing World Commodity Markets*, pp. 161–91.

toward optimal behavior seems valid when speculative activity is only a small fraction of the market. As mentioned in chapter 2, however, under certain circumstances pure speculative activity can become divorced for a long time from the underlying market forces. The social ramifications of such activity might well compel government intervention.

In most competitive trader-dominated markets, however, a convincing case cannot be made for government participation on the grounds of informational inefficiency. And even if such markets are inefficient, it does not follow that the government knows better, or that if it does, it ought to intervene as a market participant. A better approach might be the speedy and widespread dissemination of the superior government information.[15]

Private versus Social Costs

Even if one accepts the view that the participants efficiently process all available information—that is, expectations are rational—prices in futures markets explain only a small part of the actual variation in spot market prices.[16] The participants therefore have a large uncertainty about future prices.

Keynes was particularly critical of the results of such fluctuations. He felt that the risks associated with stockholding because of price volatility, coupled with the uncertainty about the ultimate "normal price" and the length of time stocks would have to be held, led to insufficient private stockholding.[17] "Nothing," he wrote, "could be more inefficient than the system by which the price is always too high or too low," and he called for government intervention to stabilize the prices of volatile commodities.[18] Keynes reinforced his argument for government price stabilization by pointing to inadequate borrowing facilities that con-

---

15. This point is made by Milton Friedman in his chapter "In Defense of Destabilizing Speculation," in *The Optimum Quantity of Money and Other Essays* (Aldine, 1969), pp. 285–91, especially p. 288.

16. Smith, "Commodity Instability," pp. 171–72.

17. A similar argument is to be found in Hendrik S. Houthakker, *Economic Policy for the Farm Sector* (American Enterprise Institute for Public Policy Research, 1967), pp. 51–60.

18. John M. Keynes, "The Policy of Government Storage of Foodstuffs and Raw Materials," *Economic Journal*, vol. 48 (September 1938), pp. 449–60. Johnson points out, that farmers were wise in not having accumulated stocks during the 1929–33 depression. "If a farmer had stored wheat in 1930 and if the costs of storage were 10 cents a year, he would have been unable to have made a profit at any time until the present. If he had stored

strained producers and speculators from storing for the long run. But this simply pushes the question one step back without answering it. Long-term lending occurs for many reasons. Why are private funds not available for the undertaking of (socially) adequate storage?

Keynes's argument implies that private and social risks are divergent. Arrow and Lind have argued that for many projects the social risk premium will be lower than the private risk premium,[19] since the government can spread the risks associated with any particular investment among many people. But Stein and Smith reject this argument, noting the extensive opportunities that exist for risk diversification in the private sector. They point to conglomerates, portfolio funds, and equity markets as examples.[20] In particular, with the development of large-scale capital markets it is hard to believe that a distinction between private and social costs can be an adequate basis for extensive government involvement. Although government borrowing costs are lower, much of the difference is caused by taxes; and the risk argument could be made for universal government financing of all forms of private activity. In this respect there is nothing special about commodity markets.

Private versus Social Benefits

A strong argument for government intervention, if there is one, must lie in a divergence between private and social benefits.

FEARS OF GOVERNMENT INTERFERENCE. Private stockholders may not store for extreme contingencies, because they do not expect to receive the true scarcity value of their stocks during such periods. The traditional economic analysis of competitive markets implies a constant set of rules and regulations that ensure free trade and the enforcement of contracts and property rights. During extreme situations, however, the rules of the game are often changed, either by the government or by private citizens who take the law into their own hands. It is difficult for governments to resist taking actions that interfere with the market

---

wheat in 1931, he would have realized a substantial gain within two years. . . . But what basis would a farmer have had for knowing that he should have stored in 1931 but not in 1930?" See D. Gale Johnson, "The Nature of the Supply Function for Agricultural Products," *American Economic Review,* vol. 40 (September 1950), p. 553.

19. Kenneth J. Arrow and Robert C. Lind, "Uncertainty and the Evaluation of Public Investment Decisions," *American Economic Review,* vol. 60 (June 1970), pp. 364–78.

20. John Picard Stein and Rodney Topper Smith, *The Economics of United States Grain Stockpiling,* report prepared for the Council on International Economic Policy (Rand, 1977), pp. 23–24.

system during periods of shortage. Popular pressure frequently compels such measures as windfall profit taxes, price controls, rationing, export embargoes, and even confiscation. And often during famines merchants lose the rewards of their foresight when their granaries are raided. Such activities introduce a divergence between expected private and social gains and lead to socially suboptimal storage. Possible recommendations might be that the government improve its maintenance of law and order or that it foreswear the use of export and price controls. But speculators are well aware that governments change and that good intentions might easily be swayed by popular pressure. Thus the existence of an expectation of intervention may compel intervention.

VARIABILITY OF INFLATION. Even a fully anticipated positive inflation rate entails costs, since the erosion in the value of money leads people to hold lower cash balances than they would if the rate were zero. It also increases the frequency with which people must incur the administrative costs of changing prices (printing price tags, menus, and so forth).

The unsteady and unanticipated inflation rate that would result from governmental accommodation of commodity price booms and busts and their secondary effects would be more harmful. When inflation is unanticipated, it distorts the real allocation of resources, since people confuse relative price changes, to which resource allocation should respond, with general changes in the price level, to which it should not. If the future rate of inflation is certain, borrowers and lenders can simply take account of that rate when they negotiate. Savers can do the same when they plan for their retirement, and labor unions and corporations can anticipate the actual buying power of their wage bargains. An uncertain inflation rate, on the other hand, undermines confidence in the true value of any contract denominated in dollars. Savers will be unsure of the value of their assets, borrowers about the burden of their debts. If they are risk-averse, they will require greater rewards for putting up with this uncertainty. As a result, risk premiums will be built into interest rates, wages, and other long-term contracts.[21]

If commodity price fluctuations impose costs on society beyond those of having to pay an increased price, they will not be reflected in the returns to the private market speculator and the degree of stabilization will be less than optimal. As discussed previously, modern economies are characterized by some markets in which shifts in demand and supply induce large price changes and other markets in which changes in

21. These issues are discussed in more detail in Okun, *Prices and Quantities*, pp. 278–96.

quantity are the chief means of adjustment. Any attempt to stabilize the overall price level by inducing a price change in the inflexible sector to offset changes in the sensitive sector might prove far more costly than stabilizing the price in the sensitive sector itself. Indeed, it is the extreme sensitivity of commodity prices to changes in demand and supply that suggests that control over supplies in these markets is likely to be more efficient than control over the aggregate money supply. This does not mean that monetary policy should be abandoned as a weapon against all types of inflation but rather that it should be supplemented in the case of commodity price changes.[22] In fact, macroeconomic policy is of great importance to primary commodity markets, which need a stable environment to function efficiently.

Although indexation would be effective in a world of "pure" inflation in which all nominal magnitudes changed simultaneously by the same proportions, this traditional solution to inflation variability is not the answer to price level changes induced by relative price adjustments. Indeed, it may actually propagate a misallocation of resources and worsen the inflation by delaying real changes that need to take place. For example, if workers have to absorb a reduction in real income because food has become relatively scarce, a cost-of-living allowance will prevent this adjustment if it fully compensates them for any price increase. Hypothetically, in a fully indexed economy any small relative price adjustment could spark an infinite upward or downward movement of the overall price level.

Resource Allocation

Some economists believe that increased price stability provides a positive benefit by promoting improved resource allocation.[23] They

---

22. In "The Economics of United States Grain Stockpiling," Stein and Smith rejected inflation as a rationale for government intervention in primary commodity markets: "While it is true that an increase in the price of grain would initially raise the price of grain-intensive goods such as bread and meat, it is not true that this effect would spill over into higher prices for all goods and services. The increased use of dollars to buy grain-intensive items would leave less money to spend on other items and this would exert a downward pressure on the prices of the latter" (p. 25). But their argument presumes a price flexibility that does not exist in the modern industrial economy. If the monetary authorities maintain constant nominal incomes, downward pressure is exerted on output as well as prices.

23. For further consideration of this argument, see Dale Hathaway, "Grain Stocks and Economic Stability: A Policy Perspective," in David J. Eaton and W. Scott Steele, eds., *Analysis of Grain Reserves—A Proceedings,* U.S. Department of Agriculture, Economic Research Service, report 634 (USDA, 1976), pp. 1–11, especially pp. 2–4.

argue that stabilizing long-run prices will reduce long-run uncertainty and increase the consumption and production of the commodity concerned. They argue that if producers could be assured of stable prices, they would incur lower risks when undertaking long-run investments, and that if people who use primary commodities as inputs in production processes where substitution is limited could be more certain of their costs, their demand for such commodities would increase.[24] Such propositions need to be qualified. They incorporate two questionable assumptions: (a) that stabilizing prices will stabilize revenues for producers or total costs for consumers and (b) that stabilizing prices will stabilize profits—the real motive for undertaking investment.

First, in markets with shifting supplies stable prices can lead to less stable revenue. When there is a crop failure, the higher prices farmers receive may compensate them for their loss of output. Keeping the prices they receive for a small crop constant may therefore destabilize their revenues. Second, as Poole in particular has stressed, revenue stabilization is not equivalent to profit stabilization.[25] In the short run, when a producer's costs are fixed, stabilizing revenues will stabilize profits. Over the long run, however, incomes might actually be more variable if either costs or prices (but not both) are stabilized. In particular, inflation and deflation lead to the expectation that prices and costs will be positively correlated in their long-run movements. Fixing only prices, or only costs, will loosen this stabilization effect. Stabilizing costs, revenues, and the rate of inflation would reduce uncertainty, but stabilizing only one of them would not.[26]

Producers also fear that fluctuating prices might affect the long-run demand for their products. High prices often induce consumers to find substitutes, and when prices recede, they do not return to their original consumption patterns. For example, copper producers have been concerned that a high copper price might induce the fixed-costs outlays required for conversion to aluminum in the automotive market and that

24. Ronald I. McKinnon, "Futures Markets, Buffer Stocks, and Income Stability for Primary Producers," *Journal of Political Economy*, vol. 75 (December 1967), pp. 844–61. McKinnon in particular has advocated government support for long-run futures markets.
25. William Poole, "McKinnon on Futures Markets and Buffer Stocks," *Journal of Political Economy*, vol. 78 (September–October 1970), pp. 1185–94.
26. This argument supports Arrow's point that the absence of some markets for future goods may cause others to fail. For a discussion of the absence of future goods markets, see Kenneth J. Arrow, "Limited Knowledge and Economic Analysis," *American Economic Review*, vol. 64 (March 1974), pp. 1–10, especially pp. 7–10.

this would result in permanently lost demand. The stimulus given to U.S. consumption (and production) of isoglucose, or synthetic sugar, by the 1974 surge in sugar prices is another example.

Noneconomic Reasons for Intervention

Strategic, political, humanitarian, and other social objectives may justify government intervention in primary commodity markets. Some reasons for government stockpiling are, for instance, to reduce vulnerability to war or embargo, to provide aid, to reduce domestic and international political tensions, to feed the poor, and to prevent starvation from famine. Unfortunately, stated and actual reasons for stockpiling have not always corresponded, so that neither goal has been efficiently attained.[27] Although stockpiles clearly do serve important functions, they are often targets of political pressure groups with particular rather than national interests at heart.

The issues of resource allocation and noneconomic objectives of government intervention are central to recent international discussions of North-South relations and a "new international economic order." Primary commodity–producing countries have been concerned about the alleged decline in the terms of trade for these products during the 1950s and 1960s and the damage to their development because of fluctuations in these prices and export revenues. They have pressed for a stabilization of prices at a high level, indexation to the prices of manufactured goods, and greater participation in subsequent stages of processing. These concerns have spawned much research and policy discussion, and they have been the major objective of many proposals for international commodity agreements. But they are not relevant to the subject of this study and its focus on the role of primary commodity markets as an initiating source of inflation.

Conclusion

In this section the arguments for government intervention in primary commodity markets have been reviewed. The competitiveness of many

27. Examples of alterations that were made in U.S. strategic goals in order to support U.S. domestic nonferrous metals producers are provided in Glen H. Snyder, *Stockpiling Strategic Materials: Politics and National Defense* (Chandler, 1966). A detailed discussion of conflicting objects is also found in C. P. Brown, *Primary Commodity Control* (Oxford University Press, 1977), especially chaps. 4 and 5.

of these markets, the evidence of their efficiency in processing information, the possibilities of private risk diversification, and the inefficiency that results from using different interest rates to evaluate social and private projects suggest a laissez-faire approach. The case for intervention rests only on the divergence between social and private benefits.

Given this study's concern with inflation, there are two main arguments for intervention. First, the substantive existing role of government in these markets, its perceived propensity to change the rules of the game, and the lack of credibility of any pledge to swear off intervention in the future lead to a truncation of extremes in the distribution of speculators' expectations of futures prices. In effect, speculators doubt that they will be allowed to reap the monetary benefits of their farsightedness. Second, the cost of realigning relative prices in an economy with many fixed-price markets without inflating the average price level creates a costly variability in the overall inflation rate that is not reflected in the benefits to the speculator.

At the same time, there are a host of noneconomic reasons that might be used to justify an interventionist policy. These are important because of the conflicts that may arise between the economic and noneconomic objectives of a specific stabilization program. A failure to clearly identify and limit the objectives of intervention has been the main reason why commodity-stabilization programs have failed in the past.

Alternative Means of Intervention

Given that, in theory, the degree of price stabilization in private commodity markets will be less than socially optimal, one would still need to determine the means of intervention and its costs before concluding that an expanded public role is desirable. Although the intervention could be done on a purely national basis, the international scope of commodity markets, the problem of free riders, and the obvious political issues arising from the relations between producer and consumer countries have led to a focus on various forms of international agreements.

While much attention has been directed to international commodity

THE POLICY CHOICES

agreements in recent years, they are not a new idea. There are many historical examples of agreements for such commodities as wheat, tin, coffee, and cocoa. And, as was seen in chapter 4, government intervention in commodity markets was an important cause of price fluctuations in the 1970s. Several authors who have attempted to review this history have drawn conclusions like the following:

Previous attempts to stabilize the prices of commodities by purchases and sales from buffer stocks have ended in failure. . . . Proponents of such schemes either ignore the historical record or feel confident that the mistakes of the past can be avoided simply by creating larger buffer stocks in the future.[28]

Yet an equally large number of studies conclude that some policy intervention would be desirable. Most of this apparent conflict, however, comes from a failure to distinguish the differing objectives of past agreements and the differing means of achieving those objectives.

There are three main objectives of commodity market intervention: (1) to reduce price fluctuations; (2) to stabilize income, particularly the earnings of producers; and (3) to maintain a price above a long-run market equilibrium. The international interest in commodity agreements during the 1970s, for example, focused primarily on the second and third objectives. Likewise, most agreements have implicitly reflected a concern with these two objectives. In addition, there are four main mechanisms for intervention: (1) compensatory finance, (2) buffer stocks, (3) controls on supply, and (4) taxes and subsidies.

Compensatory finance does not involve direct intervention in commodity markets and is used only to stabilize income (usually the earnings of exporters). If such a proposal is simply a savings account, it offers little that an exporting country cannot provide for itself. Most proposals, however, normally have an implicit element of transfer, since importing (developed) countries would provide the initial capital financing of the fund and withdrawals would be charged a less-than-market rate of interest. Even without an element of subsidy, such proposals may be attractive to exporters, whose ability to borrow in private markets is limited during the low point of commodity market cycles. Compensatory finance proposals are therefore popular with exporting countries but meet few of the concerns of importers. Because our interest is in price stabilization, we do not consider this form of intervention further.

28. Stephen W. Salant, "The Vulnerability of Price Stabilization Schemes to Speculative Attack," Federal Trade Commission Working Paper 27 (FTC, June 1980), p. 1.

Buffer Stocks

A buffer stock operated by an international agency is an attractive stabilization device.[29] Stocks are managed to moderate the price movements of a storable commodity by selling the commodity when its price threatens to exceed a target price or buying when the price falls below a minimum target. They are an instrument that achieves its objectives rapidly and directly. Provided its resources are adequate, a buffer scheme can be operated to stabilize a world price without full international membership. Indeed, the United States has by itself strongly influenced the international price of tin.[30] Without universal participation, however, the stabilization of the world price confers benefits on free riders, and thereby provides an incentive *not* to join an agreement.

Buffer stocks require considerable capital resources: cash to prevent prices from falling, commodities to prevent them from rising.[31] Technical problems, such as refrigeration and prevention of vermin, make it difficult and costly to store many commodities, and the integrity of the buffer-stock manager must be beyond reproach. Besides being storable, a commodity is suitable for a buffer-stock stabilization plan only if (1) it is relatively homogeneous, so that stabilizing the price of a particular grade, type, or stage of fabrication can strongly affect the overall price, and so that changes in tastes and technology do not affect the price relationship between the types of the commodity; (2) there is an organized international market, so that the buffer stock will have a specific designated price; and (3) there is an integrated international market, so that the price stabilized will pertain to most or all of the international trade in the commodity.

A pure buffer stock is attractive for relative price stabilization, though

---

29. Buffer stocks could also be operated by subsidizing national stockholding programs in association with target prices that trigger buying and selling activity. See Richard W. Fisher and Robert V. Roosa, "An Alternative Common Fund Proposal," *Journal of Commerce* (March 21, 1977), p. 4; (March 22, 1977), p. 4.

30. See Gordon W. Smith and George R. Schink, "The International Tin Agreement: A Reassessment," *Economic Journal,* vol. 86 (December 1976), pp. 715–28.

31. For estimates of buffer stock costs, see Paul W. MacAvoy, "Economic Perspective on the Politics of International Commodity Agreements" (University of Arizona, Institute of Government Research, 1977), pp. 10–11. As far as price stabilization is concerned, the exhaustion of the assets of a buffer stock should not be regarded as a failure, since the degree of stabilization normally will still be greater than without the stock.

in the case of shifting demand it competes with compensatory finance as a way to stabilize income flows. But despite its limited objective, it illustrates many of the problems of commodity agreements.

First, a focus on cyclical stabilization implies an ability to isolate the secular trend. If this were easy, private speculation would contain the fluctuation of prices within a band determined by carrying costs. But since it is difficult, price stabilization might not achieve much success. And the penalties for failure can undermine the program. If the buffer stock operates with a band for price fluctuation, selection of a wide band leaves room for the trend to be determined by market forces, but the result is a limited degree of stabilization. Changing the band too often will also undermine the usefulness of the scheme; changing it too seldom will increase the risk of losing touch with the underlying market forces.

An error in operating the buffer stock might actually lead to more instability in prices than there would otherwise be. For example, if a buffer stock were depleted because of an increase in demand that was erroneously perceived to be temporary, the subsequent need to replenish the stock could lead to an even higher short-run price and to greater price instability than would have occurred without the stock.

This danger suggests the need to have some kind of flexibility in the stabilization objectives. Just as one might prefer a "crawling peg" rather than a fixed exchange rate to prevent the need for sudden large revisions of the exchange rate, so commodity operations might follow rules that take into account both the levels and the rates of change of prices and stocks. Another way to introduce some flexibility into the price band is to center it around a moving average of actual prices. In this way, secular changes in prices would be tracked more quickly and less abruptly.[32]

Second, although a buffer scheme may entail net social gains, the allocation of the benefits between producers and consumers is complex and leads to problems of assigning the capital and operating costs. As discussed earlier, there is a substantial literature indicating that the distribution of the direct benefits between producers and consumers depends on a wide range of factors, such as the form of the demand-supply functions, the source of the disturbances, and the treatment of

---

32. See, for example, Hendrik S. Houthakker, *Economic Policy for the Farm Sector* (American Enterprise Institute for Public Policy Research, 1967). For an application to the analogous problem of exchange rates, see R. M. Goodwin, "Stabilizing the Exchange Rate," *Review of Economics and Statistics,* vol. 46 (May 1964), pp. 160–62.

risk.[33] From our own perspective, which emphasizes the effects on inflation, there is the additional consideration that the more industrialized countries with large fixed-price sectors should pay the major share of the costs, because the external cost of commodity market disruptions is more significant for them.

Third, government stabilization policies should supplement private stabilization activities rather than be substitutes for them. Public price stabilization schemes risk removing the incentives for the private market to accomplish any stabilization whatsoever, as European agricultural policies have removed the incentives for private futures markets. This danger provides the rationale for operating the buffer stock with minimum price intervention bands within which private markets can operate (or for other kinds of arrangements that are triggered only under extreme contingencies). It also implies that the subsidization of incremental private stockholding might be the most economic way to attain the social optimum and that the rules of operation in any public scheme should be clearly conveyed to the private market so that they can be taken into account.

Houthakker and McKinnon argued that society ought not to be indifferent about the distribution of a given level of storage between public and private hands.[34] Private traders enjoy a convenience yield from having stocks of a commodity on hand so that they can meet the specific requirements of any buyer who might come along. Since the government does not engage in ordinary merchandising, its convenience yield is lower; it is therefore more efficient to have stocks in private hands. At the same time, however, it is desirable to supplement private stockholding.

Houthakker's scheme calls for a stabilization agency to stabilize the price of a futures contract for the commodity rather than its spot price.

---

33. It suffices for our purposes to underscore the possible divergence of producer and consumer interests in price stabilization; nevertheless, it is interesting to note that when speculation is destabilizing—that is, when speculators sell low and buy high—consumers and producers may both lose from price stabilization—that is, they have a common interest in an unstable price. Although producers (consumers) gain when the price is high (low), both will gain overall. To arrive at this curious result, one must recognize that when consumers and producers gain, speculators and society as a whole will lose. See Paul A. Samuelson, "The Consumer Does Benefit from Feasible Price Stability," *Quarterly Journal of Economics*, vol. 86 (August 1972), pp. 476–93; and Johnson, "Destabilizing Speculation," pp. 101–08.

34. Houthakker, *Economic Policy for the Farm Sector*, chap. 7; and McKinnon, "Futures Markets, Buffer Stocks, and Income Stability."

The agency should stand ready to buy a specified futures contract whenever it fell to a certain level, and it should sell whenever a certain level was exceeded. Since the futures and the spot prices are interrelated, in that the futures price cannot exceed the spot price by more than the cost of carrying inventories (minus the convenience yield), support of the price in the futures market indirectly supports the spot price, thereby implicitly subsidizing private stockholding.

This is an appealing proposal if one perceives the problem, as Houthakker does, to be one of excessive risk to stockholding. By providing a more stable pattern of price behavior in the futures market, the private stockholder is induced to hold more inventories when current prices are low (hedging his position in the futures market), and to cut into current inventories during a shortage if he is sure of getting future supplies. However, the proposal encounters difficulties when the futures market correctly perceives future conditions. By selling contracts when futures prices are high, the authorities may suppress information to the current spot market that now is a time to conserve and hold for the future. Similarly, if it is known that supplies will be bountiful in the future, society would desire to encourage consumption today.[35]

An alternative approach calls for the subsidization of private carrying costs. Thus government can encourage larger private stocks by contributing to storage costs and facilitating low-interest loans. But although these measures increase stocks, they do not necessarily translate fully into price stabilization unless the government varies the size of the subsidy. At any given time the stockholder must weigh the expected gain of holding his stock against its sale in the current market. A fixed subsidy for carrying costs simply lowers the minimum price in the distribution of expected future prices at which the continued holding of the stock is profitable.

Many of these concerns are reflected in current U.S. policies for grain reserves. The private holding of stocks by farmers is subsidized by government payment of the storage costs. Severe penalties, however, are imposed for sales below a release price, which is expressed as a percentage of the support price. Between the release price and a higher call price the government does not pay storage costs. At the call price the Commodity Credit Corporation loan must be repaid.

35. This problem is mitigated somewhat with a government reserve, because if the government sells in the face of futures prices above the current price, private stockholders will purchase the government stock.

In practice, a pure buffer stock (without production controls) has attracted little support in international negotiations because it does not address the fundamental concern of producing countries: the desire to achieve a higher long-run average price. Because it encourages price stabilization, the buffer stock appeals to consuming countries that are worried about the inflationary effects of periodic cycles. In general, it would also provide the benefits of a more stable income flow to producers, but they perceive the *existence* of a buffer stock, as opposed to its *establishment* (when commodities are being purchased), as frustrating their efforts to achieve a higher average price. Therefore, international negotiations tend to break down in an unending dispute over the price band for intervention and the means of ascertaining the long-run fundamental trend of prices.

Supply Restrictions and Export Controls

Limitations on production have been by far the most common means of intervention. They are directed primarily at maintaining the price above the long-term free-market equilibrium (the third objective mentioned above), but they do confer some benefits of price and income stabilization.

For price stabilization a reserve of idle production resources is inferior to a buffer stock unless carrying costs are high. In the first instance society has lost the products that could be produced, whereas with a buffer stock total long-run production need not be less. If the idle resources could be easily converted to other uses, supply, in the absence of government intervention, would be responsive to price changes and the initial problem of unstable prices in the face of inelastic supply would not exist. In agriculture it is evident that land cannot be brought back into production as quickly as a buffer stock can be released. Thus the primary effect of production controls is to truncate the lower range of potential price fluctuations. Production controls are also an inefficient way to achieve the resource transfer—higher earners to producers—that their proponents desire. Consumption is discouraged and substitutes are encouraged by the artificially high price.

The use of export quotas allows the individual producer countries to choose the means of meeting the quotas (stockholding, production

THE POLICY CHOICES   157

restrictions, or export taxes). Quotas can be applied to storable or perishable commodities and do not require extensive capital outlays. They avoid some of the complexities of stock management and can be implemented at relatively short notice to deal with unanticipated events. On the other hand, they are a clumsy mechanism for adjusting to short-term changes in market conditions. In practice, they have reduced the global efficiency of production by allocating market shares on the basis of historical performance, a practice that frequently penalizes new or rapidly expanding efficient producers.[36]

Any system of supply restriction requires the continuing honesty and compliance of all participants. As in cartel arrangements, there are incentives to cheat: producer benefits are proportional to the total restriction by all suppliers and not that of the individual. Usually the scheme's success will depend on a large producer that is prepared to bear the residual adjustment burden (such as Saudi Arabia allegedly does within the OPEC cartel). The effectiveness of supply measures also depends on their comprehensiveness, since an arrangement can be undermined by the expansion of nonmember exports. But if importing countries agree to police the arrangement and to discriminate against nonmembers, this problem may be controlled. Because consumers do not benefit, however, they are not willing to assist in enforcement. Although supply restrictions may be effective in coping with surpluses, they are not particularly reassuring when it comes to shortages. It is easier to hold supplies off a market than it is to create them in the face of a strike, a crop failure, or a capacity bottleneck.[37]

If a transfer of resources between producers and consumers is desired, a compensatory finance program will be less costly than supply restrictions to society as a whole. Thus, for example, a farm program that uses target prices to determine the amount of payments to farmers costs less than a system of support prices enforced by production restrictions.[38]

36. The International Tin Agreement placed restrictions on export country stockholdings, which forced a supply adjustment to excess supply. See Smith and Schink, "International Tin Agreement," p. 717.

37. A useful discussion of international efforts to restrict supply is provided by David L. McNicol, *Commodity Agreements and Price Stabilization* (Lexington Books, 1978), chap. 4.

38. The social benefits of target prices as opposed to support prices are seldom realized in practice because of the association of payments under target price programs with welfare payments. Similarly, the government prefers to hide the subsidy in higher market prices to consumers rather than to have it appear as an identifiable element in the budget.

Sales Taxes and Subsidies

Sales taxes and subsidies can be used for price stabilization. By introducing a variable wedge between the price paid and the price received, they can stabilize the producer or consumer price (or hold it within a certain range) but not both. In fact, they make the other price less stable. If demand falls or supply rises, the buyer (seller) price can be stabilized by the imposition of a sales tax (subsidy). Conversely, a rise in demand or a fall in supply requires a subsidy (tax) to prevent the buyer (seller) price from rising. Stabilization with taxes or subsidies will usually result in a net social loss—the so-called deadweight loss from taxation. In general, the less elastic the supply and demand functions, the greater the relative advantage of buffer stocks over taxes and subsidies: the required size of the buffer stock is reduced and the deadweight loss from taxation is increased.[39] The tax or subsidy method might be preferred, however, if storage is costly, if the commodity is perishable, or if storage has not been previously undertaken. Taxes and subsidies do not require extensive long-term preparation; but to prevent price increases, buffer stocks must have been accumulated in advance.[40]

Summary

If the objective is price stabilization, for both consumers and producers buffer stocks are normally the most efficient method of intervention in commodity markets. On the other hand, compensatory finance schemes that avoid the loss of output implicit in any proposal to restrict output are the most effective response to income stabilization and a shift of resources to producers. Yet there are no historical examples of a pure buffer stock program. A buffer stock is not responsive to the desires of producing countries for a higher average price nor can it guarantee that the floor price will be maintained during a prolonged recession. The capital costs of a stock sufficient for all contingencies may be prohibitive. Thus, in practice, producers have insisted on combining a buffer stock

39. A high degree of elasticity of demand and supply in response to price changes reduces the problem of extreme price fluctuations in private markets. But if the elasticity reflects a high degree of substitutability with other products, the sympathetic rise or fall of other prices continues to affect inflation and the social arguments for price stabilization.

40. In the next chapter we return to the issue of taxes as a stabilization tool, since taxes are a good way to recapture the wealth that would otherwise be transferred to foreign producers as the result of a market disruption.

THE POLICY CHOICES

with supply restrictions—even though compensatory finance is a less costly alternative to supply restrictions. This linking of a bad method (production controls) with a good one (buffer stocks) is sometimes used as an argument against the good. But this argument ignores the fact that in most markets (for example, U.S. agriculture) governments will impose the production controls in any case to protect producers—creating the risk of asymmetric prices.

The operation of buffer stocks raises some problems that must be set against their benefits: (1) What is the optimal degree of stabilization? (2) How does it avoid interference with the long-run price? (3) How is substitution for private stocks to be minimized? (4) How are the costs to be allocated among producers and consumers? (5) How can the problem of free riders be overcome in trying to achieve widespread participation? And (6) should the stock be publicly or privately held?

Given the difficulties of negotiating reasonable agreements in international markets, it is not surprising that individual countries have often preferred to go their own ways. Yet their reliance on production controls, export and import quotas, and tax and subsidy schemes have been essentially beggar-thy-neighbor measures that have imposed large costs on the world economy. Both consumers and producers have a legitimate interest in greater price stability than can be provided by private markets (though the precise allocation of the benefits is a complex issue). A focus on the gains of lower inflation would point toward a preponderance of the benefits going to industrial countries because of their greater proportion of fixed-price markets (although their gain does not imply an offsetting loss to producers) and therefore that these countries should be prepared to pay a greater share of the costs of operating the stabilization program.

CHAPTER SEVEN

Commodity Stabilization Policies: Some Specific Proposals

THE PROBLEMS confronting a program of commodity price stabilization, as was seen in the previous chapter, are formidable. There is much uncertainty about many technical issues; the conflicts of interest, even within a country, make it difficult to keep the program focused on stabilization alone; and, in the international area, governments differ widely in the objectives they would like such a program to achieve, and they deeply resist any restrictions on their own freedom of domestic action. Yet the costs of past disruptions and the continual threat of a new crisis argue for increased effort.

Every commodity market has unique characteristics that must be considered in designing a workable stabilization program. In this chapter we present specific proposals for two important markets: grains and petroleum. These proposals are intended to exemplify the way in which stabilization plans should work within given institutional constraints. Thus, for instance, our grain market proposal acknowledges the primacy of domestic considerations in national grain programs, the dominant role of the United States in international grain trade, and the interests of U.S. domestic producers and consumers in grain policy.

As was pointed out in chapter 2, the grain and petroleum markets, both because of their size and the magnitude of their price fluctuations, account for the main part of the inflation threat posed by primary commodity markets. These markets are not private, and governments are already deeply involved in them. In fact, the problem of price instability is partly the result of actions taken by governments to isolate their domestic markets and of the threat that they will act in future crises with policies that are essentially "beggar-thy-neighbor."

After examining the policy options for grains and petroleum, we conclude the chapter with a brief discussion of international programs for other commodities.

Grain Price Stabilization

The lessons of the 1972–75 food debacle are clear. The objections of farm-interest groups to large government-held grain stocks, which they felt depressed prices, and the desire to relieve taxpayers of the "burden" of financing such stockholdings had led the United States to relinquish its role as the world granary without designating a replacement. Furthermore, governments in most other developed countries had sealed off their domestic economies from disruptions in the international grain market. They avoided the ramifications of price fluctuations in the world market while continuing to draw on it to meet unforeseen quantity fluctuations in their own domestic markets. As a result, the burden of adjustment to variations in world production and consumption fell heavily on consumers in the United States and certain less-developed countries. American consumers who subsidized producers during the years of agricultural surplus received little in return; they were charged the highest price during the period of shortage.

This asymmetric agricultural policy continues today. The price-support system, theoretically tied to the cost of production, provides a floor to price fluctuations, but there is no comparable ceiling. At the same time, the inability of the United States to convince other countries that it will meet their needs during crises reinforces their emphasis on subsidizing domestic grain production and reduces the long-run demand for U.S. grain exports.

Most of the existing proposals for increasing price stabilization focus on larger grain reserves. The greatest difficulties are encountered in the attempt to arrive at an equitable distribution of the costs and benefits of that stockholding. During the 1970s U.S. policy emphasized the need for a multinational grain agreement like the International Wheat Agreement of the 1950s and 1960s. The contrasting approach emphasizes a series of bilateral agreements.[1]

1. The discussion here refers only to price stabilization. Emergency famine relief and food aid questions are not considered. For discussion of a plan for emergency assistance to less-developed countries, see D. Gale Johnson, "Increased Stability of Grain Supplies in Developing Countries: Optimal Carryover and Insurance," *World Development*, vol. 4 (December 1976), pp. 977–88.

Multilateral Agreements

Under most proposals for an international agreement, individual nations would retain control of reserves, but they would be required both to maintain specific reserve levels and to buy and sell according to internationally set guidelines.[2] Negotiations for a wheat agreement have advanced, but the problems of reconciling consumers' and producers' interests and of determining such issues as the optimal intervention rules, price band widths, and stock levels stand in the way of any agreement. The 1949 International Wheat Agreement, for example, which was not as ambitious as the current reserve proposal, was the result of seven international meetings and three years of intensive deliberation. And even then, two important countries, the Soviet Union and Argentina, refused to join.[3]

Without universal participation, complex policing arrangements, which inevitably interfere with free trade, are needed to prevent free riders from enjoying the benefits of price stabilization without contributing to the costs. Most proposals do provide for excluding nonmember producers or consumers during periods of shortage or glut. Nonetheless, since major trading countries, particularly the Soviet Union, can *induce* such situations simply by entering a normal market on a large scale, continuous monitoring and restrictions on trade would probably be required if any of those nations did not participate.[4]

Even with full participation, an international agreement would encounter serious difficulties.

LOCATION OF RESERVES. It would clearly be less costly if stocks were pooled centrally or regionally rather than held separately. Many import-

---

2. See, for example, Philip H. Trezise, *Rebuilding Grain Reserves: Toward an International System* (Brookings Institution, 1976); and J. Hillman, D. G. Johnson, and R. Gray, "Food Reserves for World Security: A Consultant Study on Alternative Approaches," background document for the Expert Consultation on Cereal Stock Policies Relating to World Food Security, Food and Agriculture Organization of the United Nations, FAO publication ESC/CSP: 75/2, Rome, February 24–28, 1975.

3. See J. W. F. Rowe, *Primary Commodities in International Trade* (Cambridge University Press, 1965), pp. 164–69, for an account of the workings of the previous wheat agreements.

4. The 1976 Soviet cereal shortfall was about 70 million metric tons. The total size of stocks advocated for a reserve range between 15 to 20 million tons (Alexander H. Sarris and Lance Taylor, "Cereal Stocks, Food Aid and Food Security for the Poor," *World Development*, vol. 4 [December 1976], pp. 967–76), and 64 million tons (Trezise, *Rebuilding Grain Reserves*, p. 18).

ing countries rely on international trade for their residual requirements over and above domestic production. Since imports are not perfectly correlated among individual countries, a unified plan would require less stocks than independent national storage. If each country insisted on physical control of its own stocks, unnecessary expenses might be incurred in shipping grain that would later have to be sold in world markets.

It is widely believed, however, that internationally controlled stocks are not feasible at this time. If countries do not trust one another, the value of the entire scheme is diminished. But by the same argument, the absence of international control over stored supplies makes it folly for any country to rely on the nationally held stocks of others as sources of supply. A country fearful of a future shortage is not likely to sell to a country experiencing a current shortage. Thus the trade liberalization that is supposed to be generated by increased security of foreign supplies will not be forthcoming.

NATIONAL AUTONOMY. A credible plan for international grains must recognize the primacy of domestic interests. As Johnson has frequently emphasized, national policies that prevent domestic adjustments of consumption and production in response to world supply conditions help to create price instability in international markets.[5] A plan to stabilize the international wheat price is not compatible with a high degree of national autonomy, since it will inevitably lead to disagreements about domestic agricultural practices.

The international price of wheat is a trader's price and does not guide most production and consumption decisions. The relevant consumer and producer prices are determined by domestic policies. Production in the United States, for example, is heavily influenced by domestic price supports and acreage controls, and consumption in Europe, Japan, the Soviet Union, and China takes place at government-determined prices. Since these prices affect the levels of international demand and supply, it is impossible to plan on stabilizing the international wheat price through buffer stock interventions without coordinating domestic agricultural and food policies. When excess supplies depress the world market price, attention must turn to producer-country price supports and other interventions that are seen as the causes of the glut; when there are shortages, the failure of consuming nations to pass on higher prices to their consumers will be the source of friction. Inevitably,

5. See Johnson, "Increased Stability of Grain Supplies," p. 980.

domestic policies will become the bone of contention, with conflicting international and domestic pressures undermining the agreement.

THE EFFECT OF BREAKDOWN. It is always possible that the level of stocks held will prove inadequate and the agreement will be inoperative. No arrangement can guarantee full coverage for every contingency, and most are designed to ensure against events likely to occur 90 to 95 percent of the time. As reserves are run down and the probability of depletion increases, pressure mounts to undermine the agreement. When depletion of reserves makes higher prices imminent, the prospect of selling one's reserves at low prices and of having to repurchase at higher prices is not attractive. Countries will hoard supplies rather than sell them in the international market. This in turn will increase the pressure on the agreement. Conversely, a state of glut provides incentives to dispose of supplies before the collapse of the price floor.

Given widespread knowledge of the reserve situation, the prospect of successful speculation sets in motion a powerful force for the breakdown of the agreement. Perhaps even more damaging than the breakdown itself will be its detrimental effect on future cooperative efforts. Those who have adhered most diligently to their part of the agreement will be the most adversely affected. Without special arrangements, U.S. consumers, who have not hitherto been protected against higher prices, will be among that group.

Bilateral Agreements

An effective plan to stabilize international grain prices must not have the flaws of the reserve scheme noted above. An optimal solution must satisfy several economic and political prerequisites. To attain its assigned objectives, a plan must be credible as well as dependable in both the short and the long run. It should also be compatible with diverse, self-interested domestic food policies and not be affected by the failure of one or more major grain-trading countries to join. Furthermore, it must be so structured as to take full advantage of the main feature of the international grain trade, namely, the dominance of a few countries in providing world export supplies. The plan should involve sharing and minimizing the costs of grain reserves and, most important, should enhance the food security of those nations that choose to participate.

To accomplish these objectives, a less comprehensive approach than the international reserve scheme might be adopted. Countries seeking

COMMODITY STABILIZATION POLICIES 165

to guarantee their ability to stabilize their domestic grain prices by having adequate supplies available at all times at reasonable prices could become part of a priority grain market. Such arrangements could be negotiated on a bilateral basis between the United States—and/or other large exporters—and particular importing countries. Alternatively, an international agency could serve as an intermediary, like an insurance broker, matching commitments and options to buy and sell. The scheme could be operated in various ways.[6] For countries that are almost self-sufficient, the option to buy a certain quantity of supplies at a specific price might be the best approach. Countries would pay an annual premium to the exporter. For countries that have larger and more steady requirements, the conventional reciprocal arrangement under which the importer guarantees to buy a minimum quantity at a floor price in return for the exporter's promise to supply up to a maximum quantity at a ceiling price might be a better method. The United States and other exporting nations would then determine the best way to provide for the fulfillment of their commitments. Government stocks, a subsidy to private holdings, and intervention in futures markets could all be considered.

During periods of normal prices, the world would trade in a single market. During shortage and surplus periods, there would be two markets (or possibly more if different insurance programs have been worked out). At such times, exporters would satisfy their preferred customers first and then sell their remaining supplies in the residual market. Such an arrangement would largely accomplish the twin objectives of ensuring adequate supplies and sharing the costs of stockholding. It would also enjoy the efficiencies derived from pooling and centralizing stocks.

U.S. consumers would be included in the priority market. Under previous arrangements U.S. consumers have borne the major share of adjustment to scarcities; under this arrangement more of the burden of adjustment would be borne by the residual market. Such a plan is not inherently restrictionist; long-term contracts and commitments are, after all, an accepted feature of the market system. Importing countries could assure supplies by choosing a program that combined any and all of the available choices—domestic stockpiling, purchases in the residual market, and purchases on contract in the priority market. Such programs could then be easily merged with each nation's domestic food programs.

6. Bilateral agreements have been concluded by the United States with the Soviet Union, Japan, and China, but the plan envisioned here would be more detailed and binding.

Countries that like risks can take their chances in the residual market. But their failure to participate would not undermine the effectiveness of the plan for those that did. Importing countries would have complete freedom to dispose of their quotas wherever they chose to.[7] Those people who had bought calls (options to buy) could realize capital gains for their foresight.

A specific stabilization program emphasizing bilateral agreements has been proposed by Groenewegen and Cochrane.[8] Their suggested means of segmenting the market is a variable export levy that limits the fluctuation of domestic prices to a band defined by the current loan price (based on variable cost of production) and an upper ceiling limit (perhaps 150 percent of the loan rate). Other countries would then be offered the opportunity to sign an agreement to receive a minimum prespecified volume of grain at the domestic (pretax) price.[9] The authors go on to propose that countries signing such agreements should be required to hold reserves and manage them under the rules used in the United States. As discussed in the previous section, such specific constraints on other countries' policies are a source of conflict but are not critical to the basic plan. Less-developed countries might be treated in a separate category. They could be offered membership either in a famine reserve or in an internationally administered crop-failure insurance plan;[10] or they might be offered membership in the international arrangement at subsidized rates.

Since the bilateral agreements internalize the costs and benefits of price stabilization, they provide incentives for a net addition to world reserves rather than simply pass the burden to nonparticipating nations. The export nation can compute with certainty the range of export variation for which it has a contractual obligation.

Developing specific rules for an optimal stockpiling policy involves many complex technical issues. In recent years several studies have addressed both the theoretical and empirical questions.[11] Although the

7. An insurance plan contingent on domestic crop failure might entail a commitment to confine use to domestic consumption.

8. J. R. Groenewegen and W. W. Cochrane, "A Proposal to Further Increase the Stability of the American Grain Sector," *American Journal of Agricultural Economics*, vol. 62 (November 1980), pp. 806–11.

9. The authors argue that an export levy is not unconstitutional when used in conjunction with a domestic price stabilization program.

10. See Johnson, "Increased Stability of Grain Supplies."

11. A fairly complete bibliography of these studies is provided by James P. Houck and Mary E. Ryan, *Economic Research on International Grain Reserves: The State of*

results of individual studies vary widely, a typical conclusion is that a reserve (public and private but excluding working stocks) averaging about 10 percent of world production would be sufficient to hold prices within a band 20 percent above and below the long-run price.[12] If the stock levels of 17 percent in 1972–73 are accepted as representing minimum working stocks, this would imply a world reserve ratio averaging 25 to 30 percent. This compares to the average of 29 percent maintained in the 1960s and 26 percent in 1976–77, the peak market year for the 1970s.

Many studies that specify an optimal stock argue for a much smaller level of reserves, one close to the present level; but it is also true that those studies usually ignore the external or social benefits of price stabilization and focus on the direct benefits to consumers and producers. A consideration of the external results of inflation, the main theme of this book, would sharply increase those estimates of the optimal stock.

The only commodity agreement that withstood a postwar commodity boom was the International Wheat Agreement of 1949. Under this agreement countries were allocated quotas, and exporters promised to supply particular amounts at maximum prices during times of shortage in return for an obligation on the part of importers to buy at minimum prices in times of plenty. C. D. Hadbury noted the considerable success of the agreement during the Korean War. He looked not only at the price of wheat contracted under the agreement but also at a weighted average of prices sold in the world as a whole.[13] The average year-to-year fluctuation in this price from 1949 to 1953 was 2.7 percent. Whereas before the agreement the price of wheat had usually fluctuated more widely than the price index of foodstuffs or the index of general commodity prices, in the 1950–51 commodity boom the weighted price of wheat rose by only 8 percent, though the food index rose by 27 percent and the general index by nearly 70 percent.

Although it is often argued that the prices in a residual market will be less stable than in the absence of the stabilization program, Hadbury found that the price of wheat outside the agreement was relatively more stable. He offers this explanation: "The 1950–51 commodity boom was

Knowledge (University of Minnesota Agricultural Experiment Station, 1979). A recent detailed study is Bruce L. Gardner, *Optimal Stockpiling in Grain* (Lexington Books, 1979).

12. Gardner, *Optimal Stockpiling*, pp. 93–110; and Houck and Ryan, *Economic Research*, p. 31.

13. C. D. Hadbury, "An Experiment in Commodity Control: The International Wheat Agreement, 1949–53," *Oxford Economic Papers*, vol. 6 (February 1954), pp. 82–96.

predominantly a speculative occasion caused by panic-stricken governmental stockpiling following the outbreak of the war in Korea and the fear of short supplies. . . . It seems eminently reasonable to suppose that the existence of guaranteed sales under the wheat agreement . . . was sufficient to allay these fears as far as wheat was concerned."[14]

Summary

At present the United States claims to be the supplier-of-last-resort to the world market. But without enough grain reserves to meet extreme contingencies, the promise that the United States would not invoke export controls in the future is not credible. Such fears reinforce efforts of other countries to insulate their domestic economies from the world grain market. These reactions limit the average level of U.S. grain exports, with substantial costs to U.S. farmers, and increase the variance of price fluctuation to which U.S. consumers are exposed.

Multinational agreements encounter serious problems that imply that they will be inherently unstable. A program based on bilateral agreements avoids many of these difficulties. By reducing the uncertainty of potential variations in exports and reducing the benefits to free riders, it helps to provide an adequate grain reserve to meet contractual obligations and domestic needs.

Such a program could be relied on to do what it promised. Its credibility would rest on explicit contractual obligations and prior payments. The contracts would have the force of international law and, if need be, international arbitration. And because these commitments are limited, complete fulfillment could be guaranteed, and the United States, as a long-term participant in the market, would have every incentive to honor them. Ironically, a bilateral arrangement would probably be *more* effective than a multinational one in inducing trade liberalization, because of its greater reliability. Unlike any ambitious commodity agreement that induces speculative runs when it breaks down and engenders bitterness and mistrust, a partial agreement that is effective can actually have a calming effect on the market by minimizing the need for preclusive purchasing.

We conclude that an international agreement on grain reserves is unlikely. Yet the United States appears unwilling to act alone on a reserve program because of the fear that its own consumers and

---

14. Hadbury, "Experiment in Commodity Control," p. 90.

COMMODITY STABILIZATION POLICIES   169

producers would bear an unfair share of the costs. A series of bilateral agreements would reduce the problem of free riders and enable the United States to operate a centralized national reserve program. The external benefits suggest that such a reserve should be much larger than that supplied by the private market or current government policies. Because the United States is both a consumer and a producer of grains, a unilateral reserve program would avoid some of the conflicts intrinsic to international commodity agreements, where the interests of producers and consumers diverge.

Energy Policy

Energy policy must deal with two important problems: the high cost of energy that results from *dependency* on the output of a few producers with substantial market power, and the *vulnerability* of the economy to supply disruptions. Complicating the policy debate over both these issues is an equally important concern: the equity or distributional implications of the policy actions. Essentially, policies to deal with dependency must focus on increasing and diversifying the sources of supply and improving the efficiency of energy use. These measures are necessary but do not deal with the second issue, vulnerability. It is unfortunate that the debate in the United States over energy policy has focused so exclusively on the issue of dependency on imports, without considering measures to reduce the damage of supply disruptions. As was seen in chapter 5, the 1973 oil crisis caught the industrial nations unprepared, even though, retrospectively, it seems in part to have been the logical result of developments in the previous decade. All the industrial nations paid heavily for that lack of preparedness. Even so, the second crisis of 1979 found them little better prepared.[15]

The initial preoccupation with dependency might have been justified because most of the policy efforts—reduction of imports and develop-

15. The poor performance of the United States with regard to its strategic stockpile is an example. In early 1981 the reserve contained only 121 million barrels—equivalent to about twenty days of imports. U.S. policies have also discouraged private measures to reduce vulnerability: secure domestic supplies have been relatively penalized by price controls and insecure imports have been subsidized by an allocation system in which importers did not pay the marginal cost of their purchases. Furthermore, the allocation of shortages among oil companies during crises has weakened private incentives to plan for such contingencies. In general, centralized efforts at allocation during the crises have contributed to the problem rather than improved it.

ment of alternative supplies—also contributed to reducing vulnerability. It is clear, however, that the United States will remain dependent on oil imports for many years to come, that its principal allies cannot hope to become independent, and that the changes in oil-market structure are not a passing arrangement. At the same time, it is apparent that consuming nations cannot count on the continued political stability of oil-exporting nations. The policies to respond to oil disruptions are also less developed than the mechanisms to deal with disruptions in other markets, such as those for agricultural products and financial bonds. In fact, much of the energy legislation of the 1970s seemed to ignore the issue of vulnerability and may often have worsened the problem. After the 1979 price surge and the outbreak of the Iran and Iraq war, this situation began to change.[16]

The External Costs of Disruption

There are substantial social costs associated with volatile movements in oil supplies. Of course, private decisionmakers will consider the possibilities of disruptions in making their inventory, production, and consumption decisions.[17] To the extent that the costs of a disruption are incorporated in private costs, such events raise no special policy issues. Producers, for example, will choose production processes that reduce their costs during periods of disruption at the cost of less-efficient production in normal times. Government intervention cannot improve on this outcome. But private decisionmakers will fail to take all the effects of disruption into account. The following are some of the major economic effects that we discussed earlier:

Inflation. A sudden surge in oil prices drives up the cost of *all energy*

---

16. A recent publication addresses some of the policy alternatives and explores experience in other countries. See David A. Deese and Joseph S. Nye, eds., *Energy and Security,* A Report of Harvard's Energy and Security Research Project (Ballinger, 1981). A conference on policies during supply disruptions was organized at Wye Plantation, Maryland, under the sponsorship of the Energy Committee of the Aspen Institute for Humanistic Studies on May 9–10, 1980; a second conference was sponsored by the American Enterprise Institute for Public Policy Research in Washington in September 1980; and a third conference was held at Yale University in November 1980. We have benefited from access to the papers and discussions of those conferences.

17. For an analysis of private market behavior in response to anticipated embargoes, see George S. Tolly and John D. Willman, "The Foreign Dependence Question," *Journal of Political Economy,* vol. 85 (April 1977), pp. 323–47.

COMMODITY STABILIZATION POLICIES   171

consumption, raising the price level both directly and indirectly as wages respond to increases in the cost of living.

Unemployment. Besides inducing an inflationary surge, such prices are likely to impart a severe contractionary impulse to the global economy for four reasons. (1) The redistribution of income associated with high oil prices withdraws purchasing power from consumers and transfers it to oil producers that have high short-run marginal propensities to save. (2) The common refusal of monetary authorities to offset the decline in real money balances caused by the higher price level raises real interest rates and reduces investment. (3) The shift in consumer demand from energy-intensive sectors has severe contractionary effects on employment in these sectors—effects that other sectors cannot absorb fast enough. (4) Some countries, usually developing ones, may be forced to "adjust" rapidly by contracting their economies because of an inability to finance their balance-of-payment deficits. This adds to the contractionary pressure on the world economy.

An uncertain environment. Depending on the macroeconomic policy response, oil-market disruptions increase either the variability of inflation or the variability of output. The deepest global recession of the postwar period, in 1974, can be partly attributed to the sudden rise in oil prices. The increased likelihood that such an event will be repeated has been factored into investment decisions. The higher risk of recessions builds a risk premium into real interest rates that discourages investment capital, thereby adversely affecting productivity and real income in the long run.[18]

In addition, private markets will not reflect the very considerable

18. An additional decline in the terms of trade (the ratio of export to import prices) is mentioned by Nordhaus as a further cost of an increase in oil prices. According to this view, higher oil costs induce balance-of-payment deficits, which in turn lead to currency devaluation and declines in the terms of trade. See William D. Nordhaus, "The Energy Crisis and Macroeconomic Policy," *Energy Journal,* vol. 1 (January 1980), pp. 11–19. Should OPEC nations choose to invest heavily in a particular country, however, its balance of payments could actually improve. In fact, higher oil prices seem to have strengthened the U.S. dollar in the short run. For a discussion of the relation between oil prices and the dollar, see Paul Krugman, "Oil and the Dollar," NBER Working Paper 554 (Cambridge: National Bureau of Economic Research, September 1980).

The link between changes in exchange rates and changes in the terms of trade may also be somewhat tenuous. In practice, devaluations in the currencies of developed countries induce declines in their terms of trade in the short run. But in theory, since devaluation lowers (raises) both export and import prices in terms of foreign (domestic) currency, the terms of trade could change in either direction or not at all. See, for example, Charles P. Kindleberger and Peter H. Lindert, *International Economics* (Irwin, 1978), pp. 292–93.

domestic social problems associated with violent shifts in the availability and price of a vital commodity, and the implications for U.S. foreign policy of continued vulnerability to oil-market disruption are enormous. Finally, as discussed in the previous chapter, private stockholders believe that governments will not let them reap the full rewards of their foresight if there is a disruption.

The Permanent Effect of Short-Run Disruptions

As discussed in chapter 5, OPEC, from one point of view, is a clumsy cartel in which producers are highly uncertain about which price path will maximize their long-run profits.[19] The weakness of the equilibrating forces that keep the oil market on a particular long-run track suggests that prices could respond asymmetrically to upward and downward movements in excess demand. Increases in spot market prices (reflecting excess demand) could lead to an upward revision of producers' contract prices, while declines in spot prices could intensify efforts to restrict supply.[20] A major objective of policy during periods of disruption should therefore be to prevent a competitive upward bidding of world spot market prices.

Strategies to Deal with Market Disruptions

The essential elements of an effective policy for oil market disruptions fall into two categories: (1) agreement among nations about the allocation of a production shortfall, to minimize the impact on the world market and to minimize the disincentives to individual action raised by the free-rider problem, and (2) domestic policies within the consuming nations to limit the impact on production and inflation of the adjustment to the new import level. Oil market policies could be implemented along multilateral, bilateral, or unilateral lines (though these need not be mutually exclusive). Multilateral coordination could be achieved by international

---

19. See M. A. Adelman, "The Clumsy Cartel," *Energy Journal*, vol. 1 (January 1980), pp. 43–53.

20. Empirical support for the view that this is the practice is found in a paper by Phillip K. Verleger, Jr., "The Relationship Between Spot and Contract Crude Oil Prices" (Yale University, October 1980). Specifically, this notion is formalized in the model of oil market pricing in William D. Nordhaus, "Oil and Economic Performance in Industrial Countries," *Brookings Papers on Economic Activity, 2:1980*, pp. 366–68 (hereafter *BPEA*).

agreement either among both consuming and producing countries or simply among consuming countries.

A COMMODITY AGREEMENT FOR OIL? One commonly advocated cooperative solution is a long-term commodity agreement between producers and consumers. An example of such a proposal is contained in the report of the Independent Commission on International Development Issues (known as the Brandt Commission).[21] The report calls for an agreement on energy to include production assurances, special arrangements for supplies for developing countries, demand restraint commitments, indexed price increases at levels that give incentives for production, guarantees of the accessibility and value of financial assets, large investments in additional production of energy in the developing countries, and increased funding and distribution of the results of energy research.

The barriers to achieving such an agreement seem insurmountable. Since the short-run demand for oil is extremely price-inelastic and is nonlinear, producers gain from the instability of supplies. A disruption would raise producers' revenues by far more than an equivalent glut would lower them. A credible agreement would require a buffer stock or excess capacity to keep prices stable if a supply shortfall occurs. Although consumers could be enlisted in price maintenance during periods of glut, it is hard to imagine producers and consumers cooperating in the joint management of a buffer stock when their interests are so divergent. Given the sorry record of commodity agreements during crises, consumers could scarcely be expected to depend on the goodwill of producers to utilize their excess capacity during a disruption. Even if they wished to, producers could not make an effective agreement to prevent such risks of major price increases as accidents, war, or sabotage.

Proponents of such an agreement have to explain why it would not be subject to the failure of other commodity agreements during periods of scarcity, and also why it would have a better chance of stability than the Tehran agreements concluded in 1971, which contained similar provisions that were broken almost as soon as the ink had dried.

Bilateral arrangements between particular producing and consuming

21. *North-South: A Programme for Survival,* Report of the Independent Commission on International Development Issues under the Chairmanship of Willy Brandt (MIT Press, 1980), pp. 160–71. Many of the policies advocated in the commission's proposal have considerable merit of their own even if not part of an international agreement (for example, financial and technical assistance for energy conservation and production in non-OPEC developing [and developed] nations).

countries have become increasingly common. Although countries will inevitably attempt to secure supplies in this way, such competition does not reduce the vulnerability of consumers in the aggregate. Because the seller cannot honor the agreement if the disruption is in his own production, the buyer is forced to scramble in other markets for substitute supplies. But the market fragmentation hinders access to other supplies. Moreover, since oil has been a seller's market, producers have had little reason to agree to bilateral terms that are much worse than those they can get in the open market.

It is a sharply different situation from that of grains, where the dominant producer, the United States, is also a consumer with a great interest in market stability. In that case bilateral contracts would be supported by inventories. The contracts for grain exports are envisioned solely as a way to reduce the free-rider problem.

CONSUMER NATION COOPERATION. Some of the problems of conflicting long-run interests are avoided when agreements are limited to consuming nations. Also, consumer nations need to cooperate in the event of short-run disruptions.

The International Energy Agency, an association of developed countries (most of which are net oil importers), has negotiated an oil-sharing system to be used in case of major disruptions. This agreement can be considered the first step toward an effective international policy undertaken by developed oil-importing countries. The agreement allows any country experiencing a supply shortfall exceeding 7 percent of consumption to call on the other countries to cut back their imports. The methods by which the import shortfall is absorbed domestically is a matter for each country to decide. It can rely on running down its own stocks, allowing market prices to rise, or directly curtailing consumption. A second part of the agreement calls for the maintenance of minimum stock levels equal to ninety days of net imports.[22]

Although this arrangement represents an advance in that it provides a way to deal with major supply disruptions, the agreement does not deal

22. Note that the orientation in these plans is always around such quantities as the ratio of imports to consumption quotas rather than to prices. In the oil market relatively small fluctuations in quantities can result in substantial changes in prices, and therefore small errors in setting such quantities could result in substantial changes in prices. See Martin V. Weitzman, "Prices Versus Quantities," *Review of Economic Studies,* vol. 41 (October 1974), pp. 477–91, for the relative merits of price and quantity controls. Specifying the condition for activating the restraint program as a percentage of oil consumption while specifying the reserve requirement as a percentage of imports represented a compromise between nations with differing dependency on oil imports in total energy requirements.

with "smaller" disruptions (such as those of 1973–74 and 1979–80), whose costs may be extremely high.[23] The oil crises of the 1970s were not marked by big declines in supply but rather by panicky inventory hoarding in response to expected shortfalls.[24] Such sudden surges in demand can be highly disruptive yet not trigger the arrangement. One step has been taken toward dealing with a tight market situation: in May 1980 an agreement was made among OECD countries that in the event of market tightness the national ministers will meet and will consider the imposition of politically binding ceilings on oil imports.[25] Still, in practice, the member nations have been willing to go to great lengths to avoid putting this agreement into effect, because they fear that their own internal policies are inadequate to deal with the adjustment to a government-imposed reduction in imports. Politically, it has been preferable to direct the public's anger toward OPEC rather than put the member governments into a no-win situation. If the participating countries do not take positive steps to repress demand, and, instead, simply monitor the allocation of the shortfall, they will have done little to prevent the full upsurge of world market prices that would otherwise occur. In 1979, for example, they essentially stood aside and let the spot market price spiral up, which in turn forced up contract prices.

Despite the problems of achieving cooperation, international agreements like the International Energy Agency seem to be a prerequisite for developing effective policy responses to a market disruption. Actions by

23. In 1974 OPEC production was similar to that in 1973, so that there was no shortfall as defined by the agreement. In 1979–80 the agreement was in effect but was not activated.

24. In his analysis of the U.S. petroleum crisis in 1979, for example, Verleger found that total supplies of crude available to U.S. refiners were actually higher than in the previous year. He argues that the large increase in desired inventories at all stages of the distribution process, from refiners to (and including) consumers, was the source of the shortage. See Philip K. Verleger, Jr., "The U.S. Petroleum Crisis of 1979," *BPEA, 2:1979*, pp. 463–76.

25. The communiqué issued after the May 1980 meeting contains the following statement: "If at any time tight conditions appear imminent, Ministers will meet at short notice. If Ministers decide that tight oil market conditions exist, IEA countries will take positive, effective short-term action as necessary, in particular, measures to restrain demand in order to prevent the scramble for scarce resources which could otherwise occur. In such cases Ministers will take a decision on the use of individual oil import ceilings." International Energy Agency, *Outlook for the Eighties: Summary of the 1979 Review of Energy Policies and Programmes of IEA Countries* (Paris: Organization for Economic Cooperation and Development, 1980), p. 34. Conspicuous by its absence from the agreement, however, is a firm arrangement on how stocks would be utilized under "tight" conditions. In December 1980 the meeting of oil ministers did take some informal actions to urge the member countries to draw down their own stocks.

individual countries to reduce demand are hindered by fears that the effects of such actions will be dissipated across the overall world market—the free-rider problem.

An effective agreement could avoid the problem of balance-of-payment adjustment associated with sudden surges of oil prices, ensure an equitable distribution of the adjustment burden, and limit the effects of withdrawing purchasing power from the economy. Avoiding sudden increases in the international spot market price of crude oil may also be critical to maintaining a stable level of contract prices.

DOMESTIC POLICY. Reduction of supplies would still cause considerable disruption, however, within each domestic economy. To deal with the shortage, nations would have to allocate available supplies. Without adequate domestic inventories, nations will be forced to bear either the considerable inflationary costs of higher oil prices or the considerable distortions of the suppressed inflation associated with rationing schemes or other allocative devices. There are three main policies that have been suggested to mitigate the impact of the disruption: a permanent import tariff, a tariff during the period of disruption, and a petroleum stockpile. More extreme proposals would involve supplanting the price allocation of the market with direct rationing systems during the period of disruption. Although we examine all these measures in the context of domestic markets, they would be much more effective if they could be undertaken in cooperation with other consuming nations.

Permanent tariff. As mentioned earlier, importing petroleum involves costs to society that are not reflected in the price paid by the individual purchases. These costs can be represented by a premium in excess of the world market price. As such, they could be internalized and reflected in the behavior of private purchasers by enacting a tariff on imports equal to the value of the premium.[26] It is argued that by reducing domestic consumption and increasing domestic production, a tariff would reduce vulnerability to an external disruption by lowering the share of imports in consumption. In addition, if supply in the rest of the market remained unchanged (a questionable assumption), the resulting reduction in demand would lower the world market price and shift the cost of the tariff back to producers rather than forward into the price paid by consumers.

26. Nordhaus, "Energy Crisis and Macroeconomic Policy," has attempted to estimate the magnitude of the premium that results from the macroeconomic costs and placed it at $13 to $46 a barrel.

A tariff is an effective policy if the primary external costs of a world price increase have been a transfer of wealth from the consuming nations to producers. It provides a way to recapture that wealth and redistribute it to domestic consumers through a reduction in other taxes. If producers, either as a cartel or acting alone, establish output at the optimal level in terms of their economic return, a tariff can successfully recover much of the loss of wealth. If, on the other hand, producers' decisions are partly political, the impact of the tariff on world market prices is less predictable.

Since it is unlikely that all the tariff would be fully shifted backward onto producers, a tariff would involve a substantial domestic price increase at its enactment in return for a somewhat reduced vulnerability to an import disruption in the future. It would raise the difficult but not insurmountable problem of managing a large transfer of tax income.[27] But also in an uncontrolled market the price of domestic petroleum output and that of substitutes would rise by an amount equal to the tariff on imports. Thus it would cause a redistribution of wealth within the private sector of the economy substantially larger than the revenues collected with the tariff. If consumption patterns were changed as a result of this redistribution, there would be important economic consequences even without taking account of the social repercussions.

The inflation effect is determined by the share of oil (and its substitutes) in total demand rather than by the value of imports. The tariff would reduce vulnerability to the inflationary effects of a given oil price increase only if it lowered the share of expenditure on oil and oil substitutes in total expenditure. Finally, much of the risk of disruption is associated not so much with import dependency as with the excessive concentration of world production in a few countries. An import tariff does not broaden the base of alternative foreign sources.

An import tariff would be more effective in reducing vulnerability if it were used in conjunction with other measures. One argument against petroleum stockpiles is the upward pressure that is placed on world demand and prices during periods of accumulation. Although the percentage rise in price may be small, the multiplication of the price change over all purchases in the market can result in a sizable transfer of resources to producers. The enactment of a tariff during periods of accumulation is one way that has been suggested to supply the addition to stocks out of current consumption rather than add to the pressure on

27. In the United States each dollar of tariff per barrel would result in $2 billion to $3 billion of tax receipts.

world prices. A general tax on the consumption of oil, however, would raise revenues for the stockpile more effectively.

Disruption tariff. The enactment of a tariff during the period of disruption would restore balance to the world market by reducing demand, potentially clearing the market at a domestic price to consumers no higher than would result from the supply disruption itself. But this requires the assumption that the supply available to the domestic market is completely unresponsive to price fluctuations. More reasonably, by reducing the price to sellers, and thus the volume offered to the domestic market, the tax would actually magnify the price increase to consumers. The price to domestic producers would rise with the tariff and thus encourage domestic supply as a partial offset. Such a tariff would be effective in recapturing the foreign wealth transfers in the form of tax revenues of consuming countries. But the domestic transfer of wealth from consumers to producers would remain. The tariff would exacerbate the inflation problem if the foreign supply responded at all to prices during the disruption, but would be passed backward to producers if the available supply were fixed.

A disruption tariff has been suggested as an alternative to a government stockpile, since budgetary and other problems surround the latter.[28] It is argued that the tariff would strengthen private incentives to hold stocks because of the increased potential for inventory profits during the disruption, when the price differences between domestic and foreign supplies would be magnified. The correct comparison, however, should be between the current purchase price and the expected price during disruption. The expected domestic price is changed by a disruption tariff only if supply is responsive to short-term price changes. That is, the expectation of a disruption tariff stimulates stockpiling only when it is relatively ineffective in recapturing the wealth transferred abroad. It stimulates stockpiling if it increases the domestic price change, thereby exacerbating the problem to which this study is addressed. In addition, the chief limitations on adequate private stockholdings are fears of government intervention to limit profit taking and the external costs associated with the disruption. There is probably no credible action that would convince holders that the government would not intervene, and the external costs of inflation and domestic wealth transfers cannot be internalized by enacting a tax.

28. See, for example, Philip K. Verleger, Jr., "Let the Market Fill the U.S. Petroleum Reserve," *Wall Street Journal,* April 28, 1981.

In short, a disruption tariff and a permanent tariff are both attractive policy options if the major macroeconomic cost of a disruption is considered the transfer of wealth to foreign producers and one assumes that foreign producers won't retaliate. But these tariff proposals fail to deal with the costs that are reflected in domestic inflation and the churning that would take place within the economy as a large amount of income is suddenly redistributed.

Petroleum reserve. The problems associated with tariffs suggest the use of *stocks* to mitigate the effects of supply disruptions in the short run. The release of reserves avoids the harmful effects of the price or nonprice allocation measures. If the shock should prove permanent, reserves help to cushion the disruptive effects of adjustment—they buy extra time for deciding on appropriate long-term measures. If the shock is temporary, reserves may offset it completely. The rebuilding of the stocks would increase the pressure on prices in future periods. Stockpiles may also serve to deter embargoes and threats of embargoes.

The United States, as the largest purchaser in the market, has faced severe constraints on its ability to build up its strategic petroleum reserves. These difficulties are particularly acute during a period of tight supplies in which OPEC members are being urged to maintain production rates that they say exceed their own long-run objectives. While appearing sympathetic to the need for oil supplies to sustain economic growth, the Saudis in particular have fiercely resisted the notion that they should pull oil out of the ground so that the United States might put it back. Smaller countries have a clear advantage in being able to stockpile inconspicuously.

Nonetheless, a policy of renouncing reserves in an effort to induce the Saudis to increase production is shortsighted and is bound to fail. The oil-producing countries probably object to reserve policies because those reserves would reduce their leverage on U.S. foreign policy—the threat of disruption can be as damaging as the action itself. Nor is it reasonable to assume that past U.S. cooperation will prevent oil-producing countries from acting in their own interest in the future. Finally, it is increasingly clear that a disruption is most likely to result from unforeseen events (such as the Iran-Iraq war) rather than from a conscious decision by a major producer.

From a domestic perspective the main issues involve the size and operating rules for a reserve and the method of financing.

1. Costs. Creation of a petroleum reserve is an expensive undertak-

Table 7-1. Macroeconomic Indicators during a Full Year of Oil Supply Interruption in the United States, 1984

Daily shortfall (millions of barrels a day)	Percent of projected imports	GNP loss		Increase in projected inflation rate (percentage points)	Increase in projected unemployment rate (percentage points)	Minimum reserve required to offset interruption (millions of barrels)
		Billions of dollars	Percent of projected GNP			
1	10.5	66	1.6	3	0.5	365
2	21.1	146	3.6	7	1.1	730
3	31.6	226	5.5	15	1.8	1,095
4	42.1	306	7.5	25	2.2	1,460
5	52.6	387	9.4	31	2.8	1,825

Source: Congressional Budget Office, *An Evaluation of the Strategic Petroleum Reserve*, report prepared for the Subcommittee on Energy and Power of the House Committee on Interstate and Foreign Commerce, 96 Cong. 2 sess. (GPO, 1980), p. 6.

COMMODITY STABILIZATION POLICIES   181

ing. Annual borrowing costs would amount to 10 to 15 percent of the purchase price, and physical storage requires initial development costs of about $5 to $10 a barrel, with a small additional change for annual maintenance. But the high borrowing costs simply reflect the general inflation and should be set against the appreciation in the price of the oil and the capital gain that would be realized upon its sale. It would be more correct to use a real rate of interest of 2 to 4 percent annually, and the costs of purchase and storage should be amortized over time. If the strategic petroleum stockpiles were built up to 1 billion barrels, the total start-up costs would amount to about $40 billion to $50 billion ($35 billion to $40 billion purchase price plus $10 billion for storage facilities), ignoring any effect of the purchases on world market prices. A more meaningful measurement, however, would be the net annualized costs, which would total about $1.5 billion to $2.0 billion.

2. *Optimal size.* Specification of the optimal size of the reserve requires some assessment of the probability and severity of a supply disruption. Since 1973 there have been three disruptions, and there were three significant disruptions between World War II and 1973. The chance of a future disruption in any given year might be set at about 1 in 10. The United States consumes about one-third of free-world oil supplies, which might be a rough measure of its share of any production shortfall. In addition, it was evident during 1979–80 that individual supply disruptions do lead to some offset in supplies from other sources. If, for example, the Saudi supply of 9 million barrels a day (mmbd) should be interdicted, the U.S. shortfall would be about 2 mmbd. Finally, as the economic consequences of supply disruptions make clear (see table 7-1), a reserve of one billion barrels is rather easily justified.[29]

An important question concerns the relative role of private and public holdings. At low levels private stockholders enjoy a convenience yield that the government does not, so that, other things being equal, stocks should be privately held. Such accumulation might also be less visible and have a less disruptive effect on relations with oil-producing nations. And a drawdown might be more efficient if pursued on a decentralized basis rather than according to a rigid governmental release process. Private storage is likely to be cheaper, with more intensive use of existing

29. A more sophisticated analysis by the Department of Energy suggests that a reserve as large as 2 to 4 billion barrels could be justified on a cost-benefit basis. See Department of Energy, Office of Oil Policy and Evaluation, "An Analysis of Acquisition and Drawdown Strategies for the Strategic Petroleum Reserve," Draft Working Paper, December 17, 1979.

facilities, and would widen the storage options. At the same time, however, public stocks may be a more effective deterrent and may be easier to use for policy purposes.

The rules for operating such stocks are crucial in determining the extent to which public holdings simply substitute for those that are privately held. Since private stocks are likely to be dominated by considerations of convenience yield, the adoption of some kind of price band, so that high price levels or rates of change are required before sales from the public stock can occur, would seem to minimize the substitution effect. To avoid panic, it is vital that emergency stocks be speedily activated. Nondiscretionary triggers might be one way to avoid the natural delays associated with public policy decisions.

Many aspects of public stockpile policy are extremely difficult to model realistically. It is difficult to be precise about the probability of future disruptions. Stockpiling is best viewed as a dynamic process in which the government is buying during slack periods and selling into a tight market. Thus it moderates the price increase during the disruption, at the cost of higher average prices during periods of acquisition. At any given time, the government must assess its impact on the current market, and producer reactions to purchases on sales, against the uncertainties of future market conditions.[30] Furthermore, one lesson of the previous disruptions was that, in the face of a supply shift, demand will also change sharply as purchasers, fearing future shortages, move to hoard.

3. Financing. The main stumbling block to the development of a U.S. strategic petroleum reserve has been its budget costs during the period of acquisition. With a fill rate of 250,000 barrels a day, scheduled for 1982, the costs would run almost $7 billion annually. Concern with this issue has generated many proposals aimed at moving the costs outside the budget. These proposals include: (a) raising private capital by issuing certificates whose return is tied to the price of oil, (b) creating off-budget debt issues, and (c) mandating private refiners to hold reserves.

Yet there are some economic concepts that should guide such a decision. First, such purchases do consume resources. That is, if funds are spent on a reserve, outlays must be reduced for some other activity—in the form of lower private consumption, lower investment, or a cutback in other government programs. If the funds are raised in the capital

---

30. Department of Energy, "Analysis of Acquisition and Drawdown Strategies," is a very useful modeling of these issues.

markets, private activities financed by debt (primarily capital formation) will bear most of the burden as interest rates rise to squeeze out other uses of the credit. If they are financed by higher taxation, the impact will fall mainly on consumption. Second, private investors are now perfectly free to speculate on future oil prices, and the issuance of financial bonds whose return is tied to the price of oil will add to the funds for stockholding only if such actions are combined with other measures to convince investors that the government will stand aside and let prices rise in a future crisis. Third, even if investors can be convinced that government will not intervene and will allow prices to rise without limit, the amount of stockholding will not reflect the external costs over and above the direct value of oil to users in the event of a disruption. Fourth, the benefits of a reserve will occur to those who are active in the economy in future years and not just the current period. Therefore, they should pay part of the costs.

These considerations suggest that the annualized costs of the reserves (interest plus maintenance costs) should be paid by a continuing tax on oil consumption in future years, just as in the financing of any public capital outlay such as a school building. Insofar as many of the risks are associated with oil imports, there should be a disproportionate levy on oil imports. This objective could be achieved by requiring oil refiners to hold private reserves, but because individual firms will differ in their ability to undertake this new activity, they should be offered the option of meeting such responsibilities through shares in a common facility. Finally, because of its special responsibility to regulate the overall balance of demand and resource utilization, the federal government will have to decide whether to reduce other uses of oil through higher credit charges in the capital markets (debt finance) or lower consumption (higher taxes and lower government expenditures for other programs). Given the current concern about high interest rates and inadequate capital formation, we would expect it to decide on a large tax increase during the periods of acquisition.[31]

Rationing programs. Despite the evident usefulness of a petroleum reserve as the primary response to disruptions, the failure to build such a reserve in the past eliminates this as an option in the near future. In fact, given the historical inability of U.S. policy to plan and act on

31. Details of some alternative programs are analyzed in Congressional Budget Office, *Financing Options for the Strategic Petroleum Reserve* (Government Printing Office, 1981).

contingencies, the specter of immediate budget costs is likely to result in continued postponement. Yet the known extreme sensitivity of prices to small supply changes suggests that the government will not be willing to rely on the market alone for the adjustment to future disruptions. Discussions of the chief alternatives to a stockpile have focused on the choice between an excise tax with a rebate and a rationing program with salable coupons.[32]

Those who argue for the excise tax–rebate system believe that it most closely approximates the market in allocating supplies efficiently. They believe that rationing requires a massive bureaucracy to process exceptions and raises the risk of counterfeiting and that coupons have few inherent advantages over cash in distributing the benefits during a supply shortfall.

The proponents of rationing with salable coupons, on the other hand, believe that the tax-rebate system will cause huge cash-flow problems as the government tries to redistribute the revenues as quickly as they are collected; that it would be inequitable in failing to pay the rebate to those most disadvantaged by the higher price; and that it would exacerbate inflation by increasing the consumer price index and thereby adding to the rise of wages and incomes that are indexed to the CPI. They also view a rationing program as having a known impact on quantities, whereas the tax-rebate program would need to be experimented with to obtain the desired adjustment of demand.

In fact, the economic differences between the two plans are limited; their advocates differ primarily on equity or distributional issues. Those who support the tax-rebate scheme envision some simple system for rebating the funds. Yet any system used to rebate the tax could be used to hand out the coupons, and any distribution system for coupons could be the system for distributing the rebate. Implicitly, to advocate a tax-rebate scheme is to advocate a simple straightforward treatment of the equity issues that are addressed more directly in the coupon proposal. The coupon proposal is likely to encounter a longer delay before it is implemented, because of its direct focus on the distributional issue. Yet the distorting effect of a large tax on the consumer price index and its

---

32. It is generally agreed that a system of salable coupons is superior to rationing without a transfer system. The issues surrounding excise taxes and rationing are discussed in Walter S. Salant, "Rationing and Price as Methods of Restricting Demand for Specific Products," in Michael J. Boskin, ed., *Economics and Human Welfare: Essays in Honor of Tibor Scitovsky* (Academic Press, 1979), pp. 147–62.

effect on the relative structure of wage rates and incomes are serious issues.[33]

Despite the problems of rationing and excise taxes, most advocates of either program will agree that it is preferable to the allocation system that existed between 1973 and 1981. Furthermore, neither of the two programs can operate effectively with such an allocation system.

Under the 1973–81 allocation plan each refiner was required to allocate to the retail outlets it served an equal percentage of base-period volumes. The base period was periodically updated. But since no allocation program can fully reflect the distribution of current demand, supplies were not evenly allocated across markets. In addition, some users (for example, agriculture) were given unlimited access. Finally, individual states were provided with a "state set-aside" of 5 percent that they could allocate as they wished. All these measures tended to exaggerate the required cutback in individual markets.

As a result of this system, the burden of adjusting to the 1979 oil shortage was unevenly distributed. Demand had changed significantly since the base period. And fears of shortages changed driving patterns. When families did not leave the cities on weekends because they feared not finding open service stations, they intensified the supply-demand imbalance. So shortages grew worse in some areas while surpluses developed in others. The outcome was that lines became the method of rationing gasoline—inherently an inequitable one. Even though these peculiarities of the allocative system are now known, it is important to remember that they would exist under rationing or an excise system that reintroduced an allocative program on the supply side. The tax and resalable-coupon systems are market-type methods of scaling back demand, but to be fully effective they have to be combined with a method of allowing supply to adjust to geographic variations in demand.

Summary

A realistic look at the actors in the oil market indicates that a policy based simply on the presumption of goodwill between producers and consumers is bound to fail. Although there are many kinds of disruption,

33. Social security payments, for example, are currently indexed to the consumer price index. Would those recipients get a rebate? There are also major differences in the degree of wage indexing among workers in various industries. Yet if a means cannot be found to get the rebate back to the public quickly, the social and economic disruptions would be severe.

the two oil crises of the 1970s suggest that the short-run problem largely stems from the hoarding of consumers in the face of uncertainty about supplies. Even though consuming nations cannot prevent supply disruptions, they can certainly restrain hoarding by releasing stocks under their control into the market. In essence, the problem is more closely related to mass psychology than to the conventional objective manipulation of economic markets. The widespread *perception* that there are adequate supplies will vastly improve the chances that any given supply actually suffices. The real danger stems from market panic.

Since the market for oil is global, a coalition of consumers that ensured adequate inventories in all its member nations stands a better chance of successfully riding through a crisis than do individual countries taking independent actions. A basic policy to meet the threat of future oil market disruptions requires a combination of a petroleum reserve, a permanent tariff on oil imports and domestic consumption to finance the reserve, and a special tariff on oil during the disruption. The latter two measures are particularly effective in recapturing wealth that would otherwise accrue to producers, but only the reserve is responsive to the problems raised by sharp domestic price increases. Schemes that directly allocate scarce supplies domestically, however, are likely to induce hoarding by those who believe they will not receive adequate supplies. Excise taxes and coupon rationing are additional mechanisms that encounter serious administrative and distributional problems. For this reason, they should be adopted only as a last resort.

Other Commodities

The markets for grains and energy products dominate the concern about the effect of commodity price fluctuations on inflation in the industrialized countries. Despite the extreme price fluctuations that occurred in other commodity markets during the 1970s, their impact on the average price level was small because the value of their use is small as a share of total GNP.[34] In the United States the consumption of these other raw materials is less than 4 percent of GNP (see table 3-4). For agricultural products other than grains, the inflation threat is further reduced because prices for individual products do not move up and down together. Prices are dominated by the vagaries of weather conditions as they affect production, since the demand for such items as coffee and

34. This is evident in tables 3-4, 3-5, and 3-6.

cocoa tends to be relatively insensitive to cyclical income fluctuations. Metal prices, on the other hand, tend to have a common cyclical pattern as demand moves up and down with world industrial production.

Still, the importance of these other commodities to the economics of less-developed countries has made them a focal point of international discussions. The sharp rise in the prices of many of them in the early 1970s also stimulated speculation that these resources were being consumed at an unsustainable rate. It became popular to hypothesize the formation of producer cartels in commodities other than oil and to project a future shift of market power from consumers to producers as the industrial countries became engaged in a struggle over raw material supplies.

Although the rhetoric has cooled in the intervening years, these events—particularly the international negotiations with less-developed countries—have forced the industrial countries to reexamine these markets and to develop a policy perspective on where their main interests lie. One conclusion that has emerged from the review to date is that no single policy is feasible, since circumstances and potential problems vary so much from commodity to commodity. The potential increase in inflation also tends to be but one of many issues that must be considered.

One can, however, dismiss the fear that the future will see numerous cartels spring up in markets other than the oil market. An effective cartel requires a group of producers with homogeneous interests, strict limitations on the entry of new producers, and the absence of potential substitutes on both the demand and supply side of the market. These conditions do not exist for most primary commodities, and there has been no trend in that direction.

Nonfuel Minerals

World reserves of nonfuel minerals are adequate to meet demands in the future without a large rise in relative prices. This is the conclusion of many recent studies of the resource base.[35] As Fischman stated, "The

---

35. See, for example, John E. Tilton, *The Future of Nonfuel Minerals* (Brookings Institution, 1977); Raymond F. Mikesell, *New Patterns of World Mineral Development* (British-North American Committee, 1979); Leonard L. Fischman, project director, *World Mineral Trends and U.S. Supply Problems,* RFF Research Paper R-20 (Washington, D.C.: Resources for the Future, 1980); and Marion Radetzski, "Will the Long-Run Global Supply of Industrial Minerals Be Adequate? A Case Study of Iron, Aluminum, and Copper," in Christopher Bliss and M. Boserup, eds., *Economic Growth and Resources,* vol. 3: *Natural Resources* (London: MacMillan, 1980), pp. 85–104.

principal conclusion is that the United States faces only one type of 'major mineral supply problem': an undue vulnerability, for some minerals, to contingencies that might seriously disrupt supplies or cause a sharp upward movement of prices, with serious economic impacts."[36] In several metals there is a high degree of dependency on a few producers. But it is because they are the lowest cost source of supply. Other sources are available or substitutes for the minerals exist. The threat is one of short-run disruption rather than long-run availability. Instead of resource exhaustion the main concerns have been (1) the development of mining and refining capacity on a timely basis and (2) the threat of sudden disruptions of the market.

The first concern arose from the sharp shift in the ownership of nonfuel minerals from international mining companies to national governments. In 1970, 43 percent of copper-producing capacity in the Western economies was owned in whole or in part by national governments, as against 2.5 percent in the early 1960s.[37] Similar changes are evident for other metals such as bauxite and iron ore.

This shift in the pattern of ownership raises fears that adequate funds to finance the expansion of capacity will no longer be found. In the past, such financing consisted mostly of the internal funds of large private firms with headquarters in the industrialized countries. Today, given the financial constraints on less-developed countries, these funds must come from fixed-interest loans, with the private firms being relegated to the role of managers of the project in its exploration and development stages. Given the long lead times involved, fixed-interest loans can generate cash-flow pressures that make such projects unattractive. Yet private firms, fearful of future expropriation, may be unwilling to commit their own funds on the same basis as in the past.[38]

The slowing of the expansion of refining capacity during the 1970s for the major metals, reported in table 4-1, would seem to support this argument. For the four principal nonferrous metals (aluminum, copper, lead, and zinc), the growth of capacity slowed from 5 percent annually between 1955 and 1970 to only 2.2 percent annually in the last half of the 1970s. On the other hand, there is no discernible evidence that utilization rates on existing capacity were higher, on average, in the 1970s. From this perspective it would seem equally plausible to argue that the slowing

36. Fischman, *World Mineral Trends,* p. 3.
37. Ronald L. Prain, *Copper: The Anatomy of an Industry* (London: Mining Journal Books, 1975), pp. 22–23.
38. Marion Radetzski, "Changing Structure in the Financing of the Minerals Industry in LDC's," *Development and Change,* vol. 11 (January 1980), pp. 1–15.

of capacity growth simply reflects a slower overall rate of world economic expansion and thus a lower demand for metals.

Furthermore, much of the previous conflict between the companies and the host governments reflected the inequities arising from the old colonial system. Institutional arrangements have evolved to accommodate the changing ownership structure. Mikesell cites several recent agreements between private firms and host governments in which the differences have been resolved.[39]

Governments of both developed and developing countries have also recognized the potential funding problem. Several developed countries have instituted investment insurance programs, like the Overseas Private Investment Insurance Corporation in the United States, to reduce the risks of expropriation for private firms. Other governments have participated in joint financing ventures or negotiated treaties in the belief that their inclusion will reduce the threat of a breach of contract. Also, proposals have been made for establishing international resource banks under the auspices of the United Nations, and the World Bank has moved toward more financial involvement. To have the World Bank evaluate and participate in such projects is viewed as one means of reassuring private investment.[40] In summary, Radetzski notes that the developing countries have maintained or even increased their share of the mineral activity in the Western world despite the unwillingness of multinational firms to undertake traditional forms of investment.[41]

Holding reserve stocks is another way to respond to sharp variations in the demand or supply of basic metals, since most can be stored at relatively low cost. In fact, the sale of U.S. government reserves was an important moderating influence on prices in the 1972–74 expansion. As a result of the reassessment of U.S. defense requirements during the 1960s, much of the strategic reserve was declared surplus, and the government waited for the markets to strengthen to dispose of its holdings.[42] These surplus stocks are now largely eliminated, and there

39. Mikesell, *New Patterns of World Mineral Development*, pp. 48–60.
40. These trends are discussed more fully in ibid., pp. 61–76.
41. Marion Radetzski, "Has Political Risk Scared Mineral Investments Away from the Deposits in Developing Countries?" seminar paper 169 (Stockholm: Institute for International Economic Studies, February 1980).
42. The sale of government stocks as a percent of U.S. consumption in the 1972–74 period was as follows: manganese, 27.7 percent; chromium, 21.3 percent; cobalt, 45.3 percent; aluminum, 7.7 percent; copper, 2.7 percent; tin, 20.7 percent; zinc, 13.7 percent; and lead, 11.3 percent. The data are from U.S. Department of the Interior, Bureau of Mines, *Minerals and Materials* (December 1979). Because most of these metals are traded in international markets, the percentages of domestic consumption overstate the impact of the sales on market prices.

has not been an offsetting rise in reported private holdings of inventory stocks. Legal restrictions also prevent the use of the remaining government stocks for economic stabilization. Thus an important moderating force on metal prices that existed before 1975 is now gone.

As was discussed in chapter 6, there are major barriers to establishing effective internationally managed buffer stocks that do not simply substitute for private stocks. The United States does not have the dominant position in these markets that would allow it to proceed with the development of a bilateral program like the one proposed for grains. Yet if one country acts in isolation, the effects are spread over a world market and result in the free-rider problem. Thus the efforts to establish larger stocks have required international negotiation, with all the conflicts over financing and operating rules that plagued such programs in the past. Although establishing larger buffer stocks, within the constraints discussed in chapter 6, would be desirable, the progress in international negotiations is likely to be limited.

As noted in the empirical analysis of chapter 4, however, the variations of metal prices usually result from changes in demand rather than supply. They simply reflect the costs of instability of demand-management policies in the industrial countries, and they reinforce the argument for more international coordination of economic policies to stabilize the growth of world production. In fact, stabilizing aggregate economic conditions would do much to reduce the uncertainties of investment planning on the supply side.

Nonmetal Commodities

Once we move outside the markets for grains, energy, and the major metals, the remaining primary commodities are very heterogeneous. For the most part they consist of markets for agricultural products in which price fluctuations reflect shifts in supply rather than demand. Typically the income elasticities of demand are low, and supply is sensitive to the weather and is characterized by annual or multiyear crop cycles. This situation of random supply disturbances most closely meets the criteria for the effective operation of a buffer stock. Moreover, because the commodity price fluctuations will tend to be uncorrelated with one another, an opportunity exists to economize on capital requirements by pooling the operation of individual commodity stabilization programs.[43]

43. Jere R. Behrman, "International Commodity Agreements: An Evaluation of the UNCTAD Integrated Commodity Program," in William R. Cline, ed., *Policy Alternatives*

COMMODITY STABILIZATION POLICIES 191

A common fund for the financing of international buffer stocks was an important focus of the resolution on an "Integrated Program for Commodities," adopted at the meetings of the United Nations Conference on Trade and Development in Nairobi, Kenya, in 1976.[44] The program focused on ten core commodities, of which only two are metals.[45] Since that time, negotiations have been largely completed for buffer stock programs for sugar, rubber, and tin.

The most detailed empirical analysis of the integrated program is that of Jere Behrman, who used a set of econometric models to simulate the operation of the buffer stocks over the period 1963–72.[46] He concluded that although the financing requirements for the ten core commodities would be substantially larger than the $6 billion estimate of UNCTAD (in excess of $10 billion), both producers and consumers would make significant gains. Producer countries would gain by a shift of resources from the consuming nations and the latter would gain from a reduction of inflationary pressures. Thus from the consuming nations' perspective, the inflation issue, or an assured supply at stable prices, is central to the evaluation of the potential benefits. Behrman also found that a common fund would make a modest contribution to reducing the total financing requirements. The principal danger in the proposed program lies in the resolution's reference to raising the export earnings of the producing countries. It is clear that the producers see the common fund as a way to promote a greater common interest across commodities and thus strengthen their bargaining power.[47] They are not interested only in stabilizing prices; they also seek to raise the average level through restrictions on production or sustained additions to the buffer stock.

Efforts to use commodity agreements to go beyond the common interest of stabilizing prices to one of influencing the secular price trend have historically led to the breakdown of these agreements. Behrman found a rapid increase in the costs of operating a buffer stock when

---

for a New International Economic Order: An Economic Analysis (Praeger for the Overseas Development Council, 1979), p. 102.

44. "Integrated Program for Commodities," Resolution of the United Nations Conference on Tariffs and Trade, TD/RES/93 (IV), Nairobi, May 30, 1976.

45. The group comprised cocoa, coffee, tea, sugar, cotton, jute, rubber, sisal, copper, and tin.

46. Behrman, "International Commodity Agreements." Behrman's models, however, do not incorporate private-sector reactions to public stockpile programs.

47. It is not clear, in fact, how a common fund would achieve this. Integration involves a larger number of producing countries, with an increased potential for conflicting objectives, while the number of consuming countries stays roughly the same.

emphasis in its operation shifted toward raising the secular price trend. Under such a policy the inflation gains to consuming nations are rapidly lost; yet without their cooperation efforts to enforce production restrictions, as an alternative to continuous stockpile purchases, rapidly collapse.

We conclude that, under ideal circumstances, increased international cooperation in the operation of buffer stocks would be desirable. But besides the technical difficulties discussed in chapter 4, the conflict between producers and consumers over efforts to alter the secular price trend are likely to overload such agreements and lead to their breakdown. In most respects, these international conflicts resemble the conflicts within the developed countries over domestic agricultural policy.

Concluding Remarks

The preceding review of primary commodity markets and stabilization policy is pessimistic. There are no easy answers. The events we focused on occurred largely in the early 1970s. Yet the industrial nations have not shown an ability to learn from their mistakes. The lack of significant progress has been conspicuous. The ability to coordinate national economic policies on an international basis has not improved. The United States' attempt to arrange such a "convoy" approach to economic recovery in the mid-1970s simply became a major source of friction between the United States and its allies. The 1979–80 oil crisis was nearly as disruptive as that of 1973–74.

Global inventories for many important commodities remain below historical levels, but little progress has been made toward implementing viable programs that ensure adequate stocks. The talks for an international wheat agreement ended in failure. No attempt was even made to establish international buffer stocks for feed grains. In the United States the holdings of most of the important nonferrous metals in the strategic stockpile remain far below their goal levels, even though the excess capacity and low prices in the mid-1970s afforded an ideal opportunity to rebuild stocks. There has been no official acknowledgment that these holdings performed a vital economic function in the past, a function that might better be served by a program explicitly designed to encourage inventory holdings for economic stabilization purposes.

It remains likely that materials shortages will again involve a scramble for supplies and a great speculative outburst. The Tokyo round of the GATT (general agreement on tariffs and trade) negotiations failed to make headway toward establishing rules on export controls, so that importers will again be forced to fend for themselves. At the same time, both speculators and hedgers have dramatically increased their trading in commodity futures. The poor performance of stocks and financial assets in an economic environment filled with uncertainty about inflation rates, exchange rates, and business-cycle developments has channeled investment away from capital formation and research and development and toward such activities as real estate and gold. Besides increasing the likelihood of a short-run speculative bubble, such activities are detrimental to the long-run growth in raw material supply and processing capacity.

It is clear that the United States and the rest of the world remain extremely vulnerable to disturbances in commodity markets; and it is imperative that they develop more effective national (and international) materials policies to prevent a repetition of the events of the early 1970s. Stabilizing commodity prices will not cure current inflation—which is largely a problem of the momentum of wage and price increases that built up in response to past shocks. But reducing the vulnerability of the economy to commodity disruptions is necessary both for the successful operation of a program to reduce inflation and for the prevention of inflationary outbursts in the future.

APPENDIX A

Calculation of the Impact of Raw Material Price Increases on Inflation

THE CALCULATION of the impact of raw material price increases on final demand prices involves two basic steps: (1) the measurement of the value of raw material components for a base year and (2) the construction of a composite price index by combining these weights with domestic price indexes for individual components of final demand. The methods of computation varied slightly for individual countries because of differences in availability of data. But the primary sources were input-output tables for individual countries and wholesale price indexes.

Raw Material Requirements

The definition of primary commodities includes raw or slightly processed goods in four major categories: agricultural materials, forest products, fisheries, and minerals. For a single country, it would be most desirable to measure domestic consumption as production plus imports minus exports. But the calculation is complicated by difficulties in measuring the raw material component of exports and imports of semifinished and finished manufactures. The heavy concentration on finished goods in exports for the three countries studied required the adoption of a definition of demand as domestic value added plus imports. Since primary commodities were a substantial share of imports, only a relatively small proportion of imports needed to have their raw material component estimated. These raw materials were assumed to have the same value as those in the importing country, since it was not practical to trace them back to the producing country. This adjustment for the

APPENDIX A   195

crude component of other imports was largest for Germany, at 14 percent of all raw materials. The sources of information for individual countries are listed below.

United States

A detailed breakdown of U.S. raw material requirements in 1967 prices is available in a Commerce Department study that included estimates of the raw material component of all imports.[1] Because raw material requirements, measured in physical units, change very slowly, data for 1967 should remain representative of later years. The resulting value estimates of raw materials were divided by the sum of gross national product and imports for 1967. Estimates of raw material requirements for the consumption component of final demand were obtained from the 1967 input-output table for the United States.[2]

Japan

The breakdown of raw material requirements in 1970 was drawn from the input-output table for that year.[3] Twelve sectors of raw material production were identified, and imports of similar products were allocated directly to these industries. The data were adjusted to include the crude component of refined petroleum products. For other imports the crude material component was assumed to equal the ratio of directly identified raw materials to final demand (gross domestic product plus imports) minus these processed good imports. This crude component of other imports was distributed proportionately among the twelve raw material sectors.

West Germany

The West German input-output table has little disaggregation of raw material production, since that production tends to be included with the

1. Vivian Eberle Spencer, *Raw Materials in the United States Economy: 1909–1969*, Bureau of the Census and Department of the Interior, Bureau of Mines, Bureau of the Census Working Paper 35 (Government Printing Office, 1972).
2. "The Input-Output Structure of the U.S. Economy: 1967," *Survey of Current Business*, vol. 54 (February 1974), pp. 24–56.
3. Bank of Japan, Statistics Department, *Economic Statistics Annual, 1975* (Tokyo: Bank of Japan, 1976), pp. 316–22.

processing industries.[4] It was therefore necessary to supplement the data with information on domestic production and imports of specific commodities.[5] The adjustment for the raw material component of other imports was identical to that for Japan.

Price Indexes

Individual price indexes that corresponded to the individual categories of primary materials were available for Japan and West Germany.[6] But for the United States the wholesale price index data of the Department of Labor was supplemented by special tabulations from other agencies in order to reflect average transaction prices rather than spot market prices. The price for coal is a unit value index, f.o.b. mine; the petroleum price is an average cost for refiners; and the price of natural gas is the average wellhead price.[7] Because a price index for timber is not available, it is measured by an average of the producer price indexes for lumber and wood pulp.

A composite price index was constructed for each country by using the raw material weights for the base year. Percentage changes in this index are shown in the top part of tables 3-4, 3-5, and 3-6. The contribution to the inflation of final demand prices is calculated as

$$\frac{P_t - P_{t-1}}{P^*_{-1}} (100),$$

where P_t equals the raw material index in period t, and P^* is the price index for final demand, with the base year equal to 100. The final demand price index is the national income accounts deflator for gross national product plus imports.

---

4. European Economic Community Statistical Office, "Input-Output Table: Germany, 1970" (Paris: EEC, November 1974).

5. Department of the Interior, Bureau of Mines, *Minerals Yearbook,* vol. 3: *Area Reports: International, 1971* (GPO, 1973), pp. 317–46; and United Nations, *Yearbook of International Trade Statistics, 1972–1973,* UN Doc. ST/STAT/SER. G/22, pp. 303–11.

6. Bank of Japan, Statistics Department, *Price Indexes Annual, 1979* (Tokyo: Bank of Japan, 1980); and Federal Republic of Germany Statistisches Bundesamt, *Statistisches Jarhbuch für die Bundesrepublik Deutschland, 1979* (Stuttgart: W. Kohlhammer, 1980).

7. Department of the Interior, Bureau of Mines, *Minerals and Materials* (March 1977); and *Monthly Energy Review* (March 1980).

APPENDIX B

Sources of the Data Used in the Statistical Analysis of Chapter 4

BECAUSE of frequent revisions in the historical data, many of the series were obtained directly from the specific agency, but we have provided published sources for the most recent years.

Prices

Price indexes for specific commodities were obtained from the Statistical Office of the United Nations. Data for recent years are published in the United Nations, *Monthly Bulletin of Statistics,* table 59. The methods of construction are described in United Nations, *Methods Used in Compiling the United Nations Price Indexes for Basic Commodities in International Trade,* ST/STAT/SER.M/29/Rev. 2. Relative prices are computed by dividing the commodity price index by the unit value price index for manufactured goods exports. The manufactured goods price index for recent years is published in special table D of the *Monthly Bulletin of Statistics.*

Production, Inventories, and Capacity

Production data for the main commodity groups (food, nonfood, fuels, and so on) were obtained from the Food and Agricultural Organization of the United Nations. Recent data are published in *FAO Monthly Bulletin of Statistics.* Data on production and inventory stocks of individual agricultural products were obtained from the U.S. Department of Agriculture Foreign Agricultural Service and are published in the *Foreign Agriculture Circular* series. Data on world fish production are from the FAO.

Metals production data are published in Metallgesellschaft Aktiengesellschaft, *Metal Statistics, 1968–1978* (Frankfurt am Main: Metallgesellschaft AG, 1979, and previous issues). Information on inventory stock was obtained from Metal Market, *Metal Statistics, 1979: The Purchasing Guide of the Metals Industry* (Fairchild Publications, 1979); and American Bureau of Metal Statistics, *Nonferrous Metals Data, 1979* (New York: ABMS, 1980). The series on capacity in the metals refining industries are from Leonard L. Fishman and others, *Major Mineral Supply Problems,* a study prepared by Resources for the Future for the Nonfuel Minerals Policy, Executive Office of the President (Washington, D.C.: RFF, 1979), chap. 7, available from National Technical Information Service, Springfield, Va.

APPENDIX C

Statistical Tables for Chapter 5

Table C-1. *U.S. Supply and Demand Balance for Grains: Deviations from Trend, 1961–62 through 1979–80*
Millions of metric tons

Marketing year	Supply production[a]	Demand			Reserves	
		Domestic consumption[b]	U.S. net exports[c]	Total	Change	Initial level[d]
1961–62	−4.7	8.7	2.1	10.8	−15.5	61.2
1962–63	−10.9	2.1	−3.2	1.1	−12.0	45.7
1963–64	−3.3	−3.2	5.2	2.0	−5.3	33.7
1964–65	−22.2	−12.4	2.8	−9.6	−12.6	28.4
1965–66	−4.5	3.6	11.8	15.4	−19.9	15.8
1966–67	−9.2	−1.0	2.2	1.2	−10.4	−4.1
1967–68	9.0	−4.1	1.8	−2.3	11.3	−14.5
1968–69	−2.4	0.5	−10.3	−9.8	7.4	−3.2
1969–70	−4.5	4.2	−8.0	−3.8	−0.7	4.2
1970–71	−28.2	−2.1	−5.7	−7.8	−20.3	3.6
1971–72	16.6	5.1	−5.3	−0.2	16.8	−16.7
1972–73	1.0	6.3	22.1	28.4	−27.4	0.1
1973–74	5.6	0.0	24.5	24.5	−18.9	−27.3
1974–75	−35.9	−41.9	11.9	−30.0	−5.9	−46.2
1975–76	1.0	−33.5	28.6	−4.9	5.9	−52.2
1976–77	3.8	−40.3	21.4	−18.9	22.7	−46.3
1977–78	3.9	−36.6	29.9	−6.7	10.7	−23.6
1978–79	4.7	−24.7	33.8	9.1	−4.4	−12.9
1979–80	23.3	−27.8	47.6	19.8	3.5	−17.3

Source: *Foreign Agriculture Circular: Grains* (June 13, 1980), p. 22.
   a. Deviation from trend consumption, mean ratio of net exports to trend total disappearance in rest of world and maintenance of normal inventory stock.
   b. Deviation from trend consumption, 1962–72.
   c. Deviation from mean ratio of U.S. net exports to trend total disappearance in rest of world, 1962–72.
   d. Deviation from mean ratio of U.S. stocks to trend disappearance in the United States, 1962–80.

Table C-2. Rest-of-World Supply and Demand Balance for Grains: Deviations from Trend, 1961–62 through 1979–80
Millions of metric tons

Marketing year	Supply			Demand			Reserves	
	Production[a]	U.S. net exports[b]	Total	Non-USSR consumption[c]	Soviet net imports[d]	Total[c]	Change	Initial level[e]
1961–62	−29.4	2.1	−27.3	−10.7	−4.9	−15.6	−11.7	8.5
1962–63	6.8	−1.0	5.8	1.9	−4.8	−2.9	8.7	−3.2
1963–64	3.3	5.2	8.5	−0.9	8.3	7.4	1.1	5.5
1964–65	3.4	2.8	6.2	11.7	1.6	13.3	−7.1	6.6
1965–66	−5.6	11.8	6.2	4.3	6.9	11.2	−5.0	−0.4
1966–67	8.8	2.2	11.0	1.7	1.3	3.0	8.1	−5.4
1967–68	9.9	1.8	11.7	8.3	−1.3	7.0	4.7	2.7
1968–69	9.9	−10.3	−0.4	−10.5	−3.1	−13.6	13.2	7.4
1969–70	1.9	−8.0	−6.1	−2.8	−3.2	−6.0	−0.1	20.6
1970–71	−17.2	−5.7	−22.9	−2.1	−4.5	−6.6	−16.3	20.5
1971–72	4.6	−5.3	−0.7	−0.6	4.1	3.5	−4.2	4.1
1972–73	−18.0	22.1	4.1	−4.3	23.7	19.4	−15.3	−0.1
1973–74	−13.8	24.5	10.7	1.1	7.9	9.0	1.7	−15.5
1974–75	−27.4	11.9	−15.5	−13.4	2.9	−10.5	−5.0	−13.8
1975–76	−31.1	28.6	−2.5	−28.5	27.9	−0.6	−1.9	−18.8
1976–77	−19.5	21.4	1.9	−25.9	9.9	−16.0	17.9	−20.8
1977–78	−55.2	29.9	−25.3	−34.6	18.8	−15.8	−9.5	−2.9
1978–79[f]	−18.5	33.8	15.3	−10.0	15.0	5.0	10.3	−12.3
1979–80[g]	−47.3	47.6	0.3	−27.8	32.5	4.7	−4.4	−2.0

Sources: U.S. Department of Agriculture, Foreign Agricultural Service, *Foreign Agriculture Circular: Grains*, issues for June 18, 1977 (p. 82), June 13, 1980 (pp. 22, 26), and August 13, 1980 (p. 16). Production, consumption, and reserves data exclude the United States and the Soviet Union.
a. Deviation from trend of total disappearance minus normal U.S. exports plus maintenance of normal inventory stocks.
b. Deviation from mean ratio of net U.S. exports to trend total disappearance, 1962–72.
c. Deviation from trend, 1962–72.
d. Residual.
e. Deviation from mean ratio of stocks (excluding USSR) to trend non-USSR consumption, 1962–80.
f. Preliminary data.
g. Projected.

APPENDIX D

The Incidence of a Sales Tax on a Depletable Natural Resource

ADVOCATES of higher taxes on oil sales have different objectives. For some the motive is simply to slow down the global rate of consumption of a scarce and depletable natural resource. For others the aim is to recapture for consuming countries some of the revenue accruing to the OPEC cartel. But the inelasticity of the demand for oil is sometimes seen as a barrier to achieving either of these objectives. Conservationists complain that higher oil prices do not do much to reduce consumption; the casual application of the conventional flow analysis of tax incidence (under competitive conditions) suggests that the less elastic the demand curve, the greater the proportion of an ad valorem tax that falls on demanders.

But reasoning on the basis of conventional flow analysis can be misleading if applied to a depletable resource like oil. Since part of the return to the production of a depletable commodity in excess of actual production costs is a rent, it can be taxed away without affecting production or consumption decisions. For a variety of market structures (competitive, monopolistic, or a cartel with a competitive fringe) the producer pays an ad valorem tax levied on the sales of a natural resource commodity available in fixed supply—provided that such a tax is less than the royalty implicit in the before-tax price.

Once it is recognized that the royalties earned in resource production are pure rents, the argument that competitive producers pay the tax becomes plausible. But for a monopolist to fully bear the burden of the tax is unusual. Normally, the monopolistic owner responds to a tax by changing supply—owners of land, for example, may keep more of it idle. But since a monopolist (like its competitive counterpart) will always exhaust a depletable stock, the intertemporally neutral ad valorem tax will be fully borne by the monopolist.

The analysis here also applies to an import tariff placed on a depletable natural resource. When the commodity is entirely consumed within the importing country, the full burden of the tariff will be borne by the exporters. And since the domestic price is unchanged, a tariff will have no effect on the domestic consumption of the commodity or the production of substitutes.

The Competitive Case

First we assume that there is a known finite stock of a natural resource that is widely distributed across producers so that competitive conditions obtain,[1] and that the demand curve (known to all participants) and the rate of interest are the same for all producers and consumers. Since this analysis deals with the taxes on the royalties earned by producers (and not with the taxes that drive marginal revenue below marginal production cost), we also assume that the marginal costs of production are zero. Finally, we assume that at some price P_n an infinite supply of a substitute—a backstop technology—is available.[2]

The equilibrium path here will be one in which the price rises at the rate of interest, peaking at P_n when the resource is exhausted. The producers therefore know that eventually the resource will be worth P_n. They compare the current price with the discounted value of P_n, and their behavior ensures that at any time the price must be equal to the discounted value of P_n. If the price is higher they increase their sales, but if it is lower they postpone sales.

Take, for example, the simple case illustrated in figure D-1 in which the demand curve is vertical up to the backstop price. Until P_n is reached, the same amount q is consumed each period. If the stock is Q, this implies it will last for Q/q periods. In figure D-2, the logarithm of the price is measured on the vertical axis and time is charted horizontally. The price path in this market is derived by working backward through time. At time Q/q, the point of exhaustion, the price must be equal to P_n; before that, it should decline by the rate of interest (given by the slope of line A).

---

1. It is also assumed in our examples that the initial stock is sufficiently large (or the time periods sufficiently short) to permit a solution.
2. The results here do not actually require a backstop technology with infinitely available supply. A sufficient condition is that the demand curve intersect the vertical axis at a finite price.

APPENDIX D 203

Thus by backcasting, one can calculate the price at time $t = 0$; that is, $\ln P_o = \ln P_n - R(Q/q)$.

Now consider the effect of imposing an ad valorem tax on the consumption of the commodity. The tax implies that the highest average revenue obtainable by producers will be $(1 - T)P_n$, since at a higher average revenue for producers, consumers switch to the backstop. Exhaustion must again be at time Q/q, because q is consumed in every period. The possibility of intertemporal substitution by producers ensures the equality of the discounted value of the average revenues in every period. Thus the tax lowers average revenue received by producers at time zero to $(1 - T)P_o$. The producers pay all the tax.

Now consider the case in which the demand curve has some slope. Assume the path (before taxes) is that of B in figure D-3. The new average revenue path will be B' (which implies that producers bear all the tax, and the price path for consumers remains B). An average revenue path higher than B' for producers entails a price path higher than B for consumers. Such a path also implies, however, that at every given moment, less of the commodity is consumed. The stock would not be depleted by the time the price facing consumers had risen to the point where they switched to the substitute. The remaining stock would have to be sold for $(1 - T)P_n$ sometime after time n. Such sales would have a lower present discounted value than those yielding $(1 - T)P_n$ at time n. Producers would therefore have an incentive to sell sooner, thereby lowering the price path toward B. Conversely a path below B would result in depletion before time n. This would give producers an incentive to hold back supplies to obtain an average revenue higher than the present discounted value of $(1 - T)p_n$. Thus the path for the price (with taxes) must remain as B, and the average revenue facing producers will be lowered everywhere by the tax (path B').

The Monopolist

For the monopolist facing zero marginal costs the condition for intertemporal equilibrium is that marginal revenue should have the same present discounted value in each period.[3] The monopolist will plan on charging P_n, at time n, for the last sales he makes. P_n will in turn be

3. This result is proved in Harold Hotelling, "The Economics of Exhaustible Resources," *Journal of Political Economy*, vol. 39 (April 1931), pp. 137–75.

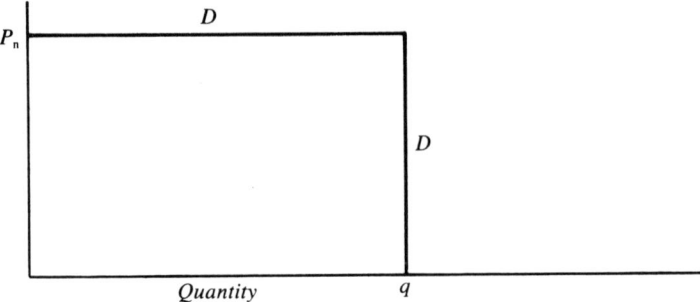

Figure D-1. *Demand Curve: The Special Case*

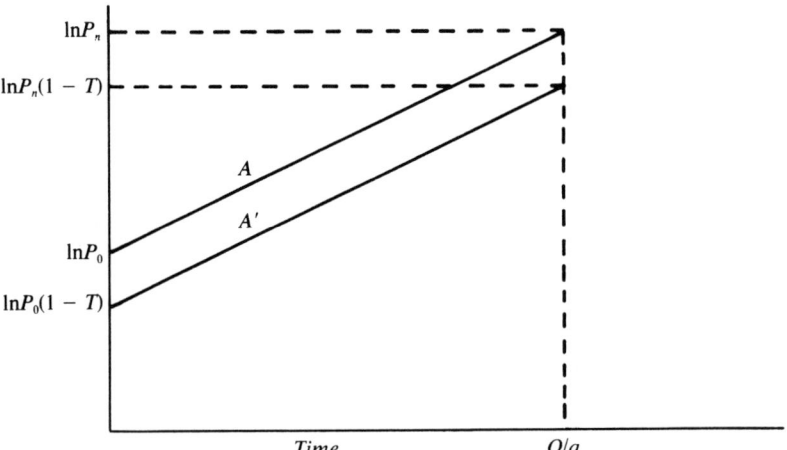

Figure D-2. *Price Paths: The Special Case*

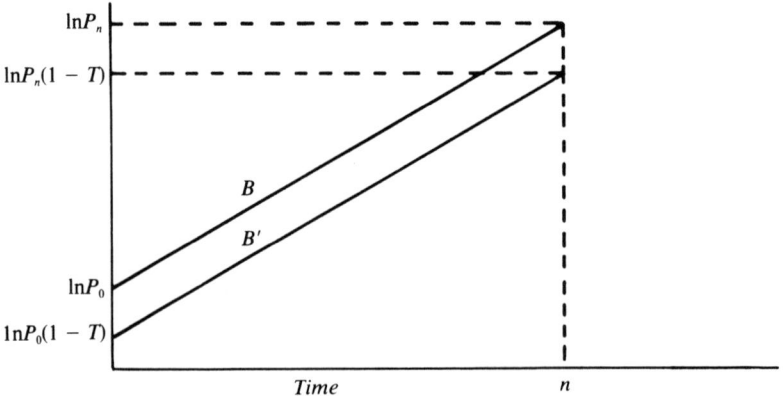

Figure D-3. *Price Paths: The Competitive Case*

associated with a particular marginal revenue MR_n. The monopolist will therefore allocate the rest of his sales across time, so that in each period his marginal revenue matches the discounted MR_n.

The monopolist will not, however, supply a quantity that corresponds to an inelastic point on the demand curve. Thus the solution for the time path of prices depends on whether the curve is elastic or inelastic at the backstop price. A monopolist facing an inelastic demand curve, such as that in figure D-1, would move straight to a price just at P_n and remain there until the stock was exhausted. Although this corner solution implies that the discounted value of earnings declines each year, the solution is a maximum, since the sale of more than q in any year entails a zero total revenue, while the sale of less than q in any year implies postponement for sale at a marginal revenue with a lower discounted value.[4]

If the demand curve is elastic at prices lower than P_n, as illustrated in figure D-4, the solution will usually have two phases, as illustrated in figure D-5. In the first phase the marginal revenue will increase at the rate of interest (line MRM). And since the demand curve normally becomes increasingly elastic at higher prices, the price path (line PM) will rise less rapidly than the marginal revenue path.[5] In the second phase price is at the backstop level. Since the amount produced corresponds to the kink in the demand curve, marginal revenue depends on the direction in which output is changed. For reductions in quantity it equals MR_n, whereas for increases it equals MR^*. The monopolist will be maximizing profits provided that the marginal revenue at the time of exhaustion (MR_n) has a discounted value equal to the marginal revenues along the sloped part of MRM.[6]

Now consider how the monopolist is affected by the imposition of the ad valorem tax, as illustrated in figure D-5. At the point of exhaustion the price to consumers will be P_n. But the producer's average revenue and

4. In this case it is clear that since a tax shifts down the average and marginal revenue curves, the monopolist will bear all of it.

5. As Stiglitz has pointed out, when the demand curve has a constant elasticity, the proportionality between the price and MR curves implies that both the marginal revenue and price paths will have slopes equal to the rate of interest. Joseph E. Stiglitz, "Monopoly and the Rate of Extraction of Exhaustible Resources," *American Economic Review*, vol. 66 (September 1976), pp. 655–61. Since the same termination price obtains in both cases (P_n) and since both price paths increase at the same rate, the rate of extraction by the monopolist is the same as that of the competitive market.

6. For a more extensive treatment, see William D. Nordhaus, *The Efficient Use of Energy Resources* (Yale University Press, 1979), pp. 14–21.

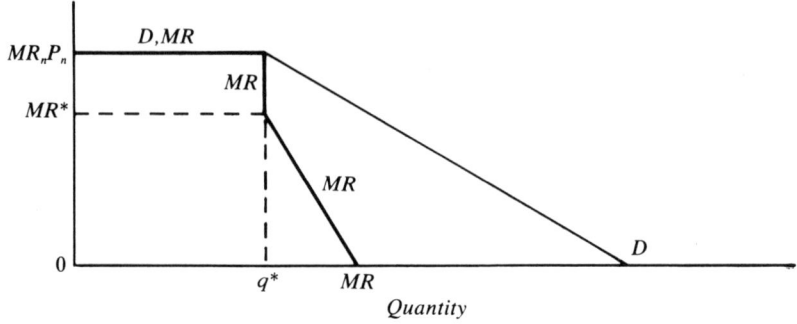

Figure D-4. *Demand Curve: The Monopolist*

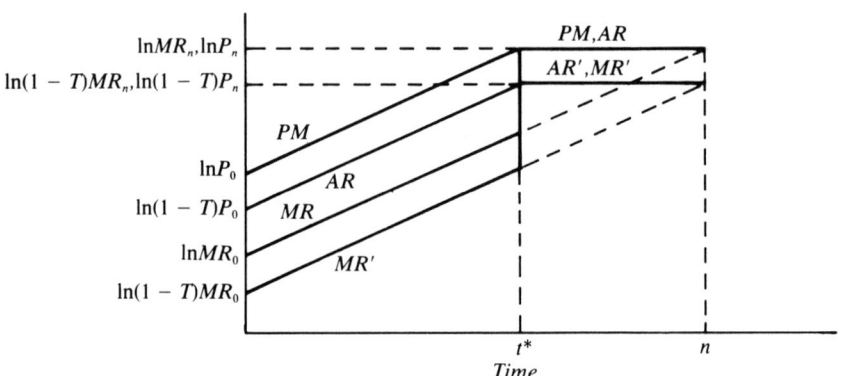

Figure D-5. *Price Paths: The Monopolist*

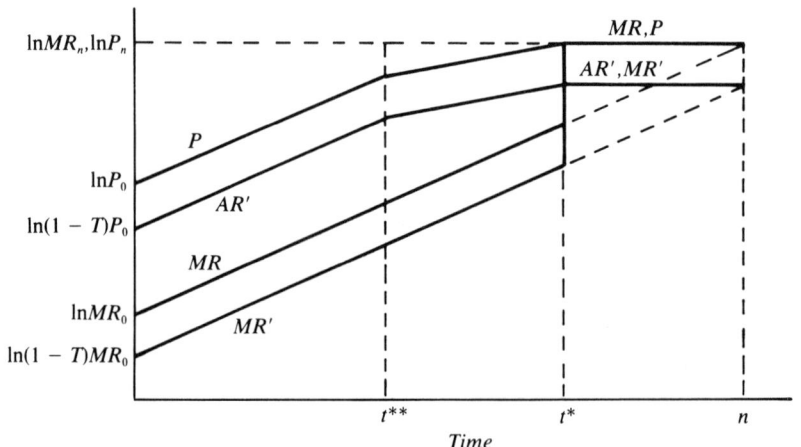

Figure D-6. *Price Paths: The Monopolist with a Competitive Fringe*

marginal revenue at that price will now be lower by the amount of the tax, $(1 - T)P_n$ and $(1 - T)MR_n$, respectively. The new average revenue curve for the monopolist can be derived. The monopolist will choose a path along which the marginal revenue always has the same discounted value. This implies a downward displacement of the average revenue (AR') and marginal revenue (MR') paths by the tax. The proof that this must be the solution follows the argument given for the competitive producers. Assume that the monopolist faces a demand curve with some slope. If the price path facing consumers lay above PM, less would be purchased at every given time. Stocks would remain at time n, when the backstop became economic. These remaining stocks would have to be sold at marginal revenues with lower present discounted values than those obtained at time n. Such a path would not be compatible with profit-maximizing behavior on the part of a monopolist and could not therefore be a solution. Conversely, a more than complete absorption of the tax, and thus a price path to consumers that was everywhere lower than P, would result in the exhaustion of stocks at marginal revenues with lower discounted values than $(1 - T)MR_n$. Thus, like its competitive counterpart, the monopolist would fully absorb the tax.

Once it is recognized that the royalties are a rent, the proposition that the tax is fully borne by competitive producers becomes plausible. But the applicability of the analysis to the case of the monopolist is probably not as widely recognized. In conventional rent theory, the monopolist can always keep some land idle. In the case here, however, as long as the commodity can be sold for a positive price at some later time, it pays to fully exhaust the stock.

The Cartel with a Competitive Fringe

Assume that the market consists of two sets of producers: (1) a cartel that coordinates its production and considers the effects of its actions on the market price, and (2) a group of competitive producers that takes the price as given and ignores the effects of its actions on the price. Salant has derived a solution for equilibrium behavior in such a market, in which each group maximizes its income, taking the behavior of the other group as given.[7] The solution, which is a hybrid of the cases already

7. Stephen W. Salant, "Exhaustible Resources and Industrial Structure: A Nash-Cournot Approach to the World Oil Market," *Journal of Political Economy*, vol. 84 (October 1976), pp. 1079–94.

considered, is divided into two phases: the first lasts until the competitive fringe has depleted its stock; the second is a period of pure monopoly. In both phases the cartel's marginal revenue increases at the rate of interest. In the earlier phase, however, intertemporal production equilibrium for the fringe requires that the price increase at the rate of interest. Thus the typical price path is the one sketched in figure D-6. The price increases at the rate of interest in the first period (until t^{**}), but at less than that in the second. The MR of the cartel, however, grows at the same rate in both periods, and for the period when it has some slope, it has the same present discounted value as at the time of depletion.

Now consider what happens if a tax is placed on sales of the commodity. Start at the point of depletion, time n, which takes place when only the cartel is left as a producer. The tax induces a proportional decline in the cartel's MR curve. Thus during the second phase the cartel will behave like a monopolist, absorb the tax, and produce the same quantities as before. The quantity to be sold in the first phase and the price to consumers at time t^{**} are the same with and without the tax. In the earlier phase the cartel's marginal revenue must equal the discounted present value of the marginal revenue in the later phase. Thus again it is lower by the tax at each given time. This implies a proportional reduction in the cartel's average revenue curve at each given time. Similarly, facing a terminal average revenue that is lower by the tax, and that occurs at the same time as it would without the tax, the competitive fringe will also absorb the tax. Given some slope to the demand curve, a price path that passed some of the tax on to the consumers would mean that some stocks would be left over at time t^{**}. This would entail sales at prices that would have lower discounted average revenues than those earned earlier, which, in turn, would induce some farsighted producers to sell sooner, driving the path toward the previous level. Conversely, more than complete absorption would result in depletion too early. Again the producers would pay all the tax.

Conclusion

The imposition of an ad valorem tax on the sales of a natural resource leaves the optimal supply path of profit-maximizing producers unaffected. If it is no larger than the royalties earned by producers, the tax has no effect on the depletion rate and serves simply to transfer income

APPENDIX D

from producers to the taxing agency. The absence of myopic behavior plays a key role in the model. Producers realize that any attempt to pass the tax on to the consumers will leave them with stocks on hand when the price facing consumers has risen to the backstop level.

The result does rest upon the use of a proportional tax. Since the price (or marginal revenue) increases at the rate of interest, a proportional tax has a constant present discounted value. A specific tax, on the other hand, affects intertemporal production decisions.[8]

The analysis here can be extended to cover a tariff in an open economy. When all consumption takes place in the importing country, foreign producers pay the tariff, while domestic producers and consumers are unaffected. In this case, a tariff rate that initially appropriated the royalties in the spot price and was subsequently increased at the rate of interest would fully appropriate all foreign producer rents. If foreign consumers were not subject to similar taxes, the powerful results obtained here would not apply. In such a case, demand elasticities and relative consumption shares would affect the pattern of resource use and tariff incidence.[9]

If the assumptions we make here are met in the contemporary oil market, the royalties earned by the OPEC countries can be recaptured by the consuming nations if—and this is crucial—they can all act in concert.

8. Although he fails to consider fully the effects of an ad valorem tax, Hotelling, in "Economics of Exhaustible Resources," discusses the intertemporal distortions on the monopolist's production decisions because of a specific tax. For a more formal treatment of the tax incidence issue, see Joseph E. Stiglitz, Partha Dasgupta, and Geoffrey Heal, "The Taxation of Exhaustible Resources," NBER Working Paper 436 (Cambridge: National Bureau of Economic Research, 1980).

9. In the usual analysis of competitive markets for each tariff, there is an equivalent quota. For the depletable natural resource, the intertemporal substitution effects make equivalence a more complicated issue. In the cases above in which the tariff is fully paid by the producers, any tariff is the equivalent of a single quota.

Index

Adams, F. Gerard, 141n, 143n
Adelman, M. A., 108n, 109n, 113n, 123n, 124n, 129n, 172n
Aggregate demand, 2, 3; commodity prices as indicators of, 62; inflationary effect, 4–5, 6, 38, 42–48; management, 139, 141
Agricultural commodities, 25; cyclical fluctuations, 70; flexible-price market, 5; percent of basic commodity trade, 25; prices, 18, 35–37, 52, 54, 59, 60–61; requirements for, 50. *See also* Grain
Akins, James E., 113n
Algeria, 114, 118n
Aluminum, 71, 72, 75, 77
American Petroleum Institute, 111n, 114n
Animal feed grain, 102–06
Anti-inflation policies, 132; accommodation to inflation pressures, 133–34, 137–38, 140; aggregate demand management, 139, 141; indexation, 147; international implications, 139–40. *See also* Stabilization, commodity prices
Arrow, Kenneth J., 145, 148n
Arzac, Enrique R., 103n, 105
Assets: demand for commodities as, 19, 77–84; flexible-price market for financial, 5; yield comparison for, 84–86
Auction markets, 3–4, 10

Balance of payments, 65; Bretton Woods adjustment mechanism, 67–68; oil prices and, 171, 176
Barnett, Harold J., 28n
Baumol, William J., 143n
Beckerman, W., 81n
Behrman, Jere R., 190n, 191
Bennett, James T., 28n
Bilateral agreements, for grain reserves, 164–68
Blinder, Alan S., 17n, 135n
Bliss, Christopher, 187n
Bohi, Douglas R., 110n, 112n, 113n

Boserup, M., 187n
Boskin, Michael J., 184n
Brandt Commission. *See* Independent Commission on International Development Issues
Brandt, Willy, 173n
Braun, Anne Romanis, 83n
Brazil, 70, 72
Brown, C. P., 24n, 149n
Brown, William M., 124n
Brunner, Karl, 39n, 40n
Buffer stocks, 152–56, 191–92. *See also* Stockpiling
Business cycles, international, 2: primary commodity prices and, 25n, 31, 35–37; synchronized, 64–67

Cartel. *See* Organization of Petroleum Exporting Countries
China, People's Republic of, 73, 80, 163
Cline, William R., 190n
Club of Rome, 81
Coal, 51–52, 55
Cochrane, W. W., 166
Coffee, 70, 72, 186
Collective bargaining, 8, 12–13
Comment, Robert, 82n
Commodities. *See* Primary commodities; Primary commodity prices
Common Agricultural Policy, 59, 60
Compensatory finance, 151
Cooper, Richard N., 39n, 64n
Copper, 71, 72, 75, 77
Cost-of-living adjustment clauses, 12–13
Council on Wage and Price Stability, 14
Customer markets, 3–4

Danielson, Albert L., 117n, 129n
Davis, Harold T., 33n
De Carmoy, Guy, 112n
Deese, David A., 118n, 170n
de Macedo, Jorge Braga, 86n
Demand, primary commodities: as assets,

211

19, 77–84; global fluctuations in, 63–69; income and, 28; model for evaluating, 73–77; price and, 34–35. *See also* Aggregate demand
Depreciation: cost, 82; dollar, 114
Dollar, U.S.: depreciation, 114; devaluation, 92–93
Dornbusch, Rudiger, 34n, 42n, 83n, 86n

Eaton, David J., 147n
Eckstein, Albert, 104
Eckstein, Otto, 14n
Energy: cost, 18, 169; oil price effect on, 170–71; vulnerability of economy to supply, 169–70. *See also* Fuel commodities; Petroleum
European Agricultural Policy, 102
European Community, 20, 54, 59, 101
Exchange rates, 45; and anti-inflation policies, 139–40; and asset demand for primary commodities, 83; changes in, 41; commodity price differences and, 58–60, 61; fixed, 67n; flexible, 19, 139; green, 59
Export quotas, 156–57

Falcon, Walter P., 59n
Feldstein, Martin, 82n
Fellner, William, 39n, 133n
Fiscal policy, 133, 134–35
Fischman, Leonard L., 187–88
Fisher, Richard W., 152n
Fishing, cyclical pattern in yields, 70–71
Food commodities: percent of basic commodity trade, 25; prices, 18, 36–37, 60, 101
Foster, Edward, 82n
Fried, Edward R., 84n, 134n
Friedman, Milton, 11n, 143n, 144n
Fuel commodities: price controls, 51–52, 59; prices, 35, 37, 52, 55, 60–61; requirements for, 50

Gardner, Bruce L., 167n
GATT. *See* General Agreement on Tariffs and Trade
Genberg, Hans, 42n
General Agreement on Tariffs and Trade (GATT), 25n, 193
Goldstein, Morris, 15n
Goodwin, R. M., 153n
Gordon, Robert J., 9n, 11n, 38n, 39n
Government intervention: costs and benefits of, 144–46; in futures markets, 142; in grain market, 88, 94; in international commodity trade, 80, 150–51; by inventory depletion, 70; by protectionist policies, 59. *See also* Anti-inflation policies; Stabilization, commodity prices
Grain: acreage setting for, 72, 94, 99; consumption and prices, 99–104; dollar devaluation and prices, 92–93; income and consumption, 92; production, 89, 91, 93, 163; supply and demand balance, 95, 97, 99, 106; support prices, 59; in world market, 19–20, 89, 93–95, 97, 106, 161
Grain reserves: bilateral agreements for, 164–68; changes in world, 94, 99, 107; excess, 91–92; for less-developed countries, 88; location of international, 162–63; multinational agreements for, 162–64, 168; price stabilization focused on, 161; U.S., 22–23, 99, 155
Gramlich, Edward M., 135n, 138n
Gray, R., 162n
Grennes, Thomas, 93n
Groenewegen, J. R., 166

Haberler, Gottfried, 40n, 107n
Hadbury, C. D., 167–68
Hall, Robert E., 9n
Hammer, Armand, 112n
Hammoudeh, Shawkat, 129n
Harris, Simon, 59n
Hathaway, Dale E., 89n, 106, 147n
Heien, Dale, 14, 104
Hickman, Bert G., 65n
Hillman, J., 162n
Hotelling, Harold, 122n
Houck, James P., 166–67n
Houthakker, Hendrik S., 19, 34n, 77–79, 139n, 144n, 153n, 154–55
Hwa, E. C., 87

Independent Commission on International Development Issues, 173
Industrial production: controls, 2, 62, 156; global fluctuations, 63, 64–67, 69
Inflation: aggregate analysis, 42–48; disaggregated analysis, 48–60; excess demand and, 4–5, 6, 38; oil price impact on, 170–71; primary commodity prices and, 1–2, 7, 14, 17, 40; rates, 38, 64n; reaction of economists to, 38–39; unanticipated, 146; unemployment and, 15, 132–33, 134, 137, 139; varying international effects of, 17–18, 42–48. *See also* Anti-inflation policies
International agreements: on buffer stocks operations, 191–92; on grain market,

93–94, 162–63; on petroleum market, 172–76; on primary commodities, 150–51, 159
International Energy Agency, 174–76
Inventories, primary commodities, 34–35, 70, 192; metals, 71, petroleum, 119; precautionary holdings of, 79–80
Investments, primary commodities as, 19, 82, 84–86
Iran, 107, 117, 131
Iraq, 110, 114, 131
Isard, Peter, 42n

Jacoby, Neil H., 109n
Japan: commodity prices and inflation, 52–54; commodity prices and wages, 57–58; dependence on raw materials imports, 48, 50; energy price impact on, 18; exchange rate effect on, 58–59; grain prices, 102; grain production, 163; industrial production, 65, 67; inflation rate, 38, 45, 47; metals consumption, 83–84; monetary policy, 68–69; primary commodity consumption, 29n; and world agricultural market, 20
Johnson, D. Gale, 89n, 95n, 144–45n, 161n, 162n, 163n, 166n
Johnson, Harry G., 40n, 143n
Johnson, Manuel H., 28n
Johnson, Paul R., 93n
Josling, Tim, 59n
Jurg, Niehans, 34n
Juster, F. Thomas, 82n

Kahn, Herman, 124n
Kaldor, Nicholas, 34n
Keynes, John Maynard, 33, 34, 144–45
Kindlberger, Charles P., 171n
Klein, Sonia A., 141n, 143n
Kouri, Pentti J. K., 86n
Krause, Lawrence B., 40n
Kravis, Irving B., 42n
Krugman, Paul, 42n, 171n
Kuwait, 115, 118n

Labor market, 5–6, 9, 12
Lawrence, Robert Z., 39n, 64n, 68n
Leisure, wages and, 111
Lenczowski, George, 110n, 114n, 115n
Less-developed countries: food costs, 101; grain reserves to, 88; importance of primary commodities to, 187; role in international grain agreement, 166
Levhari, David, 121n
Leviatan, Nissan, 121n
Libya, 112–13, 114

Lindert, Peter H., 171n
Lind, Robert C., 145
Lipsey, Robert E., 42n
Livestock products, 50–51
Lucas, Robert E., Jr., 39n

MacAvoy, Paul W., 152n
McCracken, Paul, 65n
McKinnon, Ronald I., 79n, 148n, 154
Malaysia, 72, 80n
Malthus, Thomas Robert, 63
Manufactured goods, 27, 35
Markets, primary commodities, 1, 3–4; competitive, 123, 125–26, 143; disaggregation, 63; factors influencing price impact on, 41; fixed- versus flexible-price, 5–6, 8, 16–17, 81n; futures, 141–42, 144, 154–55; inflation concentration in, 39; monopoly, 122–23, 125, 126–27; price forecasting for, 142–43; speculation in, 33–34, 143–44
Meadows, Donella H., 81
Mead, Walter J., 117n, 125n, 129n
Meltzer, Allan H., 39n, 40n
Metals, nonferrous: consumption, 83–84; percent of basic commodity trade, 25; prices, 36–37, 187, 190; processing capacity for, 71–72, 188–89
Mexico, 117
Mikdashi, Zuhayr, 110n
Mikesell, Raymond F., 187n, 189n
Minerals, nonfuel, 187–88
Mitchell, Daniel J. B., 8n
Mohnfeld, Jochen H., 115n, 117n, 119n
Monetary policy: accommodative, 2, 5, 16, 21, 133, 134–35, 137, 140; and commodity asset behavior, 77–87; expansionary, 68–69, 77–79; nonaccommodative, 15, 21
Monopoly: bilateral, 8, 10, 13; prices set by, 122–23, 126–27
Moran, Theodore H., 129n
Morse, Chandler, 28n
Muth, John F., 143n

Natural gas, 51–52, 59
Neff, Thomas L., 118n
Nordhaus, William D., 40n, 41n, 45n, 81n, 122n, 124, 127n, 129n, 171n, 172n, 176n
Nye, Joseph S., 118n, 170n

OECD. *See* Organization for Economic Cooperation and Development
Oil companies: agreements with OPEC, 113–14, 115, 173; exemptions from antitrust laws, 113; postwar supremacy,

109–10; and profit maximization, 130; role in global oil distribution, 115; shift in power between producing governments and, 108–14

Okun, Arthur M., 3, 9, 133n, 139, 146n

OPEC. *See* Organization of Petroleum Exporting Countries

Organization for Economic Cooperation and Development (OECD), 1, 37n, 43, 72n, 102n; gross domestic product within, 43; industrial production, 65n; inflation rate within, 38, 44; oil agreement, 175; primary commodities imports, 45

Organization of Petroleum Exporting Countries (OPEC), 80, 107, 172; agreements with oil companies, 113–14, 115, 173; formation, 110; oil production, 116, 117, 175n; political enmity within, 110; pricing decisions, 115, 128–31; and profit maximization, 126–27, 129; rise in power, 109, 111; volume of sales, 118

Osborne, D. K., 125n

Perry, George L., 47n, 57, 134n

Peru, 71, 91

Petroleum: change in ownership price theory, 124–25; competitive pricing theory, 123, 125–26; consumer nations agreements on, 174–76; crisis of *1973*, 107, 114–15, 169; crisis of *1979*, 117–20, 169, 170; domestic allocation strategy, 176; embargoes, 80, 114; and global economy, 171; global production, 120; international agreements on, 172–74; inventories, 119; models of market behavior, 20, 121–28, 172n; monopolist theory of pricing, 122–23, 125; price controls, 51, 59; prices, 18, 51, 54, 60, 107–08, 114–20; rationing, 176, 183–85; reserves, 23, 108, 111, 179–83; spot market prices, 20–21, 118, 119–20, 129, 131, 172; tariffs on imports of, 176–79, 186. *See also* Oil companies; Organization of Petroleum Exporting Countries

Phelps, Edmund S., 11n

Political factors: role in commodity pricing, 72–73; role in petroleum pricing, 131

Poole, William, 143, 148

Popkin, Joel, 40–41n, 45n, 52n

Posthumus, Nicholas W., 33

Prain, Ronald L., 188n

Price controls, 51, 59, 81, 82

Prices. *See* Primary commodity prices

Primary commodities: defined, 1n, 24; grouping of, 25; income and demand for, 28–29; international agreements on, 150–51, 159; international comparison of consumption, 29n, 44n; as investment, 19, 82, 84–86; role in world trade, 25; storage, 141–42, 155. *See also* Demand, primary commodities; Food commodities; Fuel commodities; Inventories, primary commodities; Markets, primary commodities; Primary commodity prices; Supply, primary commodities

Primary commodity prices: aggregate demand growth and, 62; causes of fluctuations in, 62–63, 186–87; cycles in, 9–10, 31, 35–37; demand-supply interaction and, 19, 34–35; inflation and, 1–2, 7, 14, 17, 81–82, 186; market-clearing, 8n; measurement of changes in, 48–49; ratchet effect, 13–14, 16; relative, 27, 35; secular trend in, 27, 28–31; short-run movements, 33–35; spot, 34, 142, 144, 154; technological change and, 28–29, 31; wage response to, 6–7, 11–13, 135, 137. *See also* Stabilization, commodity prices

Production. *See* Industrial production

Profits, 82; maximization, 126–27, 129, 130; stabilization, 148

Radetzski, Marion, 187n, 188n, 189

Reserves; foreign exchange, 68; grain, 88, 91–92, 93, 94, 100, 107, 155; petroleum, 23, 108, 111, 179–83; primary commodity, 29–30, 78–79

Resource allocation, 146–49

Reynolds, Lloyd G., 59n

Risk: commodity market, 144–45; exchange-rate, 83n; portfolio selection to avoid, 85–86

Roosa, Robert V., 152n

Rostow, Walter W., 29n

Rowe, J. W. F., 162n

Russell, Milton, 110n, 112n, 113n

Ryan, Mary E., 166–67n

Sachs, Jeffrey, 13, 47n, 57

Salant, Stephen W., 123, 151n

Salant, Walter S., 40n, 184n

Sales tax, 158

Sampson, Anthony, 109n, 112n

Samuelson, Paul A., 154n

Sanderson, Fred H., 89n, 102n

Sarris, Alexander H., 162n

Saudi Arabia, 112, 114, 117, 127–28

Schink, George R., 152n

Schleicher, Stefan, 65n

INDEX

Schultze, Charles L., 134n
Selden, Richard T., 39n
Sheifer, Victor J., 13n
Shoven, John B., 40n, 41n, 45n
Smith, Gordon W., 143n, 144n, 152n
Smith, Rodney Topper, 145, 147n
Smith, V. Kerry, 28n, 63n
Snyder, Glen H., 149n
Solow, Robert M., 123n
Soviet Union, 72, 73, 80; agricultural policy, 19; grain imports, 95, 97, 99, 105–06; grain production, 95, 163
Spencer, Vivian Eberle, 29n
Stabilization, commodity prices, 10–11, 14, 21–22, 134, 193; benefits, 145–46; buffer stocks for, 152–56, 158–59; compensatory financing for, 151, 158–59; costs, 144–45, 147; export quotas for, 156–57; production controls for, 2, 62, 156; and resource allocation, 147–49; and sales tax, 158; and stockpiling, 149; and subsidies, 158; supply restriction for, 157; and taxation, 158
Stagflation, 4
Standard international trade classification (SITC), 24
Steele, W. Scott, 147n
Stein, John Picard, 145, 147n
Stiglitz, Joseph E., 123n
Stockpiling, 149; basic metals, 189–90; petroleum, 169n, 177, 179, 182, 186; public versus private, 181–82
Sugar agreements, 80–81n
Supply, primary commodities, 19; adequacy of, 62–63; factors disrupting, 62; global fluctuations in, 70–73; model for evaluating, 73–77; price and, 31, 34–35

Tariffs, 41; on petroleum imports, 176–79, 186
Taxation: excise, 185, 186; primary commodity, 82; rebate on petroleum, 184–85; as stabilization tool, 158
Taylor, Lance, 162n
Thursby, Marie, 93n
Tilton, John E., 187n
Timmer, C. Peter, 59n
Tobin, James, 14
Tolly, George S., 170n
Trezise, Philip H., 162n
Turnovsky, Stephen J., 141n

Unemployment, 1; costs, 138–39; inflation and, 15, 132–33, 134, 137, 139; oil price increases and, 171

United Kingdom, 29n, 69, 101, 116
United Nations, 24, 189; indexes of beef and corn prices, 70; industrial production index, 69; manufactured goods production index, 29n, 37n; primary commodity price index, 29n, 41, 42, 45, 50, 51, 60
United Nations Conference on Trade and Development (UNCTAD), 29n, 191
United States: basic metal stocks, 189–90, 192; bilateral grain price agreements, 165, 168–69; commodity holdings, 70; commodity price effect on wages, 56–57; commodity prices and inflation, 50–52; energy policy, 169–70; energy price impact on, 18; grain consumption, 99–101, 103–04; grain exports, 22, 99, 102; grain production, 163; grain reserves, 22–23, 99, 155; industrial production, 65, 67; inflation rate, 38, 47; metals consumption, 83–84; mineral supply problem, 187; monetary policy, 68–69; petroleum imports, 111, 115, 116n; petroleum reserves, 23; primary commodity consumption, 29n; primary commodity price index, 50–51; raw material requirements, 48, 50

Van Duyne, Carl, 77n
Verleger, Phillip K., Jr., 172n, 175n, 178n

Wachter, Michael L., 39n
Wage controls, 81, 82
Wage rates: cyclical sensitivity, 8–9; and inflation, 56–58; link to leisure, 111; response to prices, 6–7, 11–13, 14–15, 135, 137; wage-wage determination of, 11–12, 13
Weitzman, Martin V., 174n
West Germany: commodity price effect on, 57; commodity prices and inflation, 47, 54–56; energy price impact on, 18, 55; exchange rate and commodity prices, 58–59; industrial production, 65n; inflation rate, 38, 47; monetary policy, 68–69; raw material requirements, 48, 50
Wheat: dollar devaluation and price, 92–93; international agreements on, 93–94, 162–67, 192. See also Grain
Wilkinson, Maurice, 103n, 105
Williamson, John, 42n
Willman, John D., 170n
Wood, Geoffrey E., 42n
World Bank, 189
Wyant, Frank R., 112n, 115n, 129n

Zambia, 73, 80